"When you need a picker-upper, this is the book to pick up. Plenty of variety and easy reading help make this book a great read and perfect gift book."

CBA Marketplace

"Make a U-turn to the nearest bookstore for the second volume of *God Allows U-Turns*! Allison Gappa Bottke has once again presented the reader with an inspirational road map for our journey of life. As you travel through the pages of this book, you will laugh, cry, and sigh as you are filled with hope and encouragement!"

SUSAN WALES
Author and Producer

"All of us have made mistakes. From time to time, we all make poor choices. But the joy of the Christian life is God's grace. In this book you will find story after story—including one of mine—that remind us that no matter what path we have chosen, *God Allows U-Turns*!"

MARITA LITTAUER
President, CLASServices, Inc.
Speaker and Author

"Whether you are a speedster who loves living in the fast lane or a shunpiker who avoids the busy highways in life, *More God Allows U-Turns* will cause you to brake and reevaluate how you can find joy along the journey."

LISA COPEN
Director, Rest Ministries, Inc.

"With captivating stories, vivid word pictures, and heart-gripping emotion, you'll laugh and cry as you read this book. Most of all, you'll find healing that gives you the strength to offer hope to others as you live out the life lessons in these powerful personal parables."

CAROL KENT
Speaker, Women of Faith Conferences, and Author

"*More God Allows U-Turns* is more than a compilation of stories. It is a book that offers hope and encouragement to its readers. Most of all, it clearly conveys the much-needed message that no matter what has happened in your past, with God there are always second chances."

AARON D. LEWIS
Author and Pastor

"This book will inspire you to new hope and greater healing in your relationship with God and those you love."

PAUL ESHLEMAN
Director, The JESUS Film Project

ALLISON GAPPA BOTTKE

with CHERYLL HUTCHINGS and ELLEN REGAN

TRUE STORIES OF
HOPE AND HEALING

An Imprint of Barbour Publishing

ISBN 1-58660-301-9

Layout and typesetting by Sharon Dean

Cover Design: Robyn Martins

The author is represented by Alive Communications Inc., 7680 Goddard St., Suite 200, Colorado Springs, Colorado 80920.

The God Allows U-Turns logo is a U.S. registered trademark.

Published by Promise Press, an imprint of Barbour Publishing, Inc., P.O. Box 719, Uhrichsville, Ohio 44683, www.promisepress.com

ecpa Member of the
Evangelical Christian
Publishers Association

Printed in the United States of America.

Through Jesus, therefore, let us continually offer to God a
sacrifice of praise—the fruit of lips that confess his name.
And do not forget to do good and to share with others,
for with such sacrifices God is pleased.
HEBREWS 13:15–16

FOR OUR CONTRIBUTORS AND READERS

This book is dedicated to our brothers and sisters in Christ who sent us stories and to our readers around the world who will come to depend upon this and future volumes of *God Allows U-Turns* to uplift and encourage them in their personal walk of faith.

It is our prayer that God will be pleased with the fruit of sharing offered by the contributors whose true stories appear in this second volume of *God Allows U-Turns.* We were overwhelmed by the thousand plus stories we received, stories that openly praised and confessed how God is at work every day in every life.

May these slice-of-life stories touch your emotions and warm your heart. May they bring you to a better understanding of God's love for us all. God's peace and protection to you always.

ALLISON

FOR MY DEAREST LOVED ONES

Kevin K. Bottke
You are a gift from God and I thank Him daily for you.

Christopher John Smith
You are always in my prayers, my sweet son.

Dolores B. Gappa
Bless you for always encouraging me to reach for the stars.
Your support has made me the person I am today.

God has richly blessed me.
I love you all.

CONTENTS

ACKNOWLEDGMENTS

There are countless people to thank for helping this project grow into what it has become today. I trust each of you will know how important you are and how thankful I am for your ongoing support, encouragement, and love.

The phrase *God Allows U-Turns* pretty much sums up my life. As a former "prodigal daughter," I can now see clearly how many times my heavenly Father was there to rescue me, guide me, and give me the wisdom to turn around in my tracks and retreat from ways destined to bring me to destruction. Today, I cannot imagine my life without God's love, without the knowledge that Jesus Christ died for me. I am a living, breathing example of how a life can be drastically changed. . .with God's help.

When I started writing my personal testimony over a decade ago and titled it *God Allows U-Turns,* I had no idea how the Lord would change my life—how He would work in me to share with others the vital message of salvation and forgiveness through this book series.

The inspiration to turn my personal testimony book into a collection of true short stories came to me in late 1999. As we ushered in the new millennium, God was at work, opening one door after another to make this dream a reality. The book you hold in your hands today is the second volume in a series of short story collections that we pray will encourage and uplift people around the world.

To the thousands of *author/contributors* whose stories made us laugh, cry, and praise the Lord with joyful alleluias: You are gems beyond value. May God continue to shine His light on your lives.

To my dearest husband, *Kevin:* Your patience is a blessing, your humor a breath of fresh air, and your love a cornerstone of my life. Having a best friend like you is way too much fun!

To my son, *Christopher:* I have no greater prayer than to see you come to know the Lord as your Savior. . .to make your own "U-turn" toward God. Peace can be yours, Cristofario.

To these special people in my life who show me daily how God's love is all around us: Dolores Gappa, Cheryll Hutchings, Pastor Ron and Sharol Wik, Lisa Copen, Linda Lagnada, Mandy Bottke, Kermit Bottke, the entire "REALTY EXECUTIVE—CONSIDER IT SOLD" team, my publishing team at Promise Press/Barbour, Chip MacGregor, and my AWASA group of awesome ladies!

Most of all, I give praise and thanks to my *Holy Father*. His unconditional love and the plan He had for me even before I was born helped me leave behind the ways of the world, ways that were leading me down paths of destruction into the waiting arms of Satan himself. The Lord alone turned me around and set my path straight. Thank You, my most holy Lord, for giving me the wisdom to understand not only that *God Allows U-Turns,* but that no matter what I have done I can continue to turn my heart and mind toward You. You will always forgive me; You will always love me; You will always bring me the peace I need. Because it is so very true. . .*God Allows U-Turns!*

INTRODUCTION

Dear Reader:

It is no coincidence that when Jesus walked the earth as a man, He taught mostly by sharing stories. . .or "parables," as they were commonly called. Jesus understood the power of a story—especially true stories as they related to His teachings.

True human-interest stories touch us in ways we can't always explain, affecting all of us differently. Such was the case when I first read *Born Again* by Chuck Colson. Mr. Colson's book spoke to me; it spoke to a nation. His words reached out, and the journey that was his saving grace was made real to me in a deeply personal way. Books have been doing this for centuries, teaching us, guiding us, and healing us. We often gain wisdom from a story that speaks to our heart. That is what *God Allows U-Turns* is all about, speaking to our hearts.

I am not so naive as to believe one book of true short stories will heal a nation. Only God can do that. But He is encouraging His children to step out in faith as never before, to challenge the false values that seem to be taking over our country. The stories in this book are all about faith and how vital it is to be a believer every minute of every day. . .not just for an hour on Sunday or at Christmas and Easter. A revival of believers is stepping forward, ready to be counted—no matter the cost. Believers ready to share their quiet faith, bold faith, wavering faith, fallen faith, and resurrected faith. It was not so long ago that I scoffed at believers such as these.

There was a time in my life when I believed that people who prayed were weak. That believing in God was an old-fashioned tradition reserved for senior citizens and little children. You know, for people who "didn't know any better."

This misguided belief was enforced by the "me decade" of the 1970s, when radical individualism was born. I bought the worldly lie that I could be my own god, that I could do what I wanted when I wanted. During the years I charted my own course, believing only in myself and the adage that I was the "master of my destiny," I never realized the fabric of my life was deteriorating from the inside out. Like acid dripping on silk, a hole was growing in my soul. Aided by New Age philosophies, astrological charts, an occasional tarot card reading, and a secular worldview that "god is within me," I was adrift on a sea of confusion, void of any truthful direction.

Unresolved childhood memories made adult relationships difficult. A lack of formal education left me deeply insecure. An extremely violent early marriage and subsequent divorce left me traumatized. The responsibility of motherhood at sixteen was overwhelming. Finances were always a problem. Additionally, I had bought the lie that a "baby" was really a "choice," never once thinking the decision to have an abortion would painfully haunt me for the rest of my life. I lived with one man after another, believing that serial monogamy was perfectly fine and I had every right to live with a man out of marriage. Topping it all off was a drug addiction I steadfastly justified because I was a high-functioning addict. . .able to hold down a budding career in fund-development and raise a child on my own. Folks thought I had it together. Little did they know my life was anything but "together."

If everything was so great, why did I retreat into drugged euphoria whenever possible? Why did I often drink to excess? Why did I jump from one relationship to another? Why was my son in and out of juvenile detention centers? Why did I move from one job to another at frightening speed? Why did my weight go up and down the scale? Why did I often cry myself to sleep at night wondering what was the point of it all? And why, in desperation, did I try to end my life—a life that many thought was so good? I didn't have the answers, and New Age "wisdom" only left me feeling more and more alone and isolated.

It has been said that God sometimes takes us into troubled waters—not to drown us, but to cleanse us. If that is true, we are a world poised on being washed anew. . .because troubled waters are all around us.

Many folks today live just as I did. . .lost and alone. . .yet going through the motions day in and day out of just "getting by." Many of us have been discouraged over the years. Many of us have had setback after setback, wondering if things will ever work out in our favor. . .if the trials and tribulations will ever stop. We are in desperate need of hope and healing.

But first, we are in desperate need of repentance, forgiveness, and salvation. What we need is to admit that we are sinners, a fact many of us abhor. After all, if we are sinners then we must be doing something wrong, and if we are doing something wrong then where does our belief system lie? Our society tells us that virtually anything and every-thing is okay, and little is "wrong" in today's age of acceptance and tol-erance. How off track we have come! What we need is solid guidance. Someone to help get us back on track, to hold us accountable, to show us a new direction and bring us peace.

In 1990 I found peace; I found direction. I filled that empty place in my heart and soul with a relationship—*not* a religion. A relationship with Jesus Christ. Second Corinthians 5:17 touched my soul and became real to me: "Therefore, if anyone is in Christ, he is a new cre-ation; the old has gone, the new has come!" I was "new," and as I grew in the Lord, so did my desire to spread the Word.

I started writing *God Allows U-Turns* in the early 1990s as my per-sonal proclamation of what God had done in my life. By the end of 1999, it had grown into something much bigger. The year 2000 saw the God Allows U-Turns Project take flight. Today, the book you are holding in your hands is volume two in what we pray will be a long, long series of true short story collections. True stories of how God works in everyday life. True stories we pray will reach out and touch hearts and souls around the world.

Hearts and souls need to be touched. We are a hurting world. The wages of sin have taken their toll. Yet through it all, God is there. . .even when we choose not to believe. He alone has remained sovereign. He is the rock on which we can stand when our own knees become weak. The truth of God's plan is that "Jesus Christ is the same yesterday, today, and forever" (Hebrews 13:8 NKJV).

When I find myself traveling paths in my heart I know are wrong, I can turn around—safe in the knowledge that God will forgive me. No matter how many times I step off the path, I know in my heart that GOD ALLOWS U-TURNS.

And so, dear reader, I pray that no matter where you are in your walk of faith you will allow the messages of these stories to touch your heart and soul. That you will come to read these little slice-of-life messages as parables for our time.

I also pray that if the Lord touches your soul to come closer to Him you will read the pages at the back of this book that share how you can turn your life around.

Speaking of the "pages at the back of the book," please take a few minutes to read about the awesome outreach of the God Allows U-Turns Project. Our foundation is donating a percentage of proceeds from this book to several nonprofit faith-based organizations you can read more about at the back of the book. Additionally, you can read about future volumes and how *you* can send us your true short story to be included in a future volume. Also in the back is an invitation to participate in our free book giveaway. How would you like to win five free copies of *God Allows U-Turns* to give to family and friends? All you have to do is select your favorite stories from this volume and let us know what they are. A winner will be selected every month for one entire year after publication. Make sure to let us know your favorite stories! Remember, you can keep up to date on all that is happening in the God Allows U-Turns Project by visiting our web site at www.godallowsuturns.com.

In closing, the authors and contributors from around the world whose stories appear here today have opened their hearts and souls to us. They are warriors proclaiming their faith. Thank you for spending time with them. Thank you for sharing this book with other family and friends. And remember—we are all family—and that bond, combined with God's promises and direction for our lives, is our saving grace. Never forget that. Never forget that our God is a God of second chances and new beginnings, and never, ever forget that our GOD ALLOWS U-TURNS!

May God's peace, protection, and direction be with you always.

Your Sister in Christ,
ALLISON
editor@godallowsuturns.com
www.godallowsuturns.com

CHAPTER ONE

God's Love

We love because he first loved us.
1 John 4:19

CHICKEN WINGS AND COLLARD GREENS

Leanne Bright Cloudman, Wilmington, North Carolina

Somewhere out there is an elderly black woman who touched my heart in a genuinely special way. I want to thank her for allowing me to see how blessed I truly was, and to apologize for the way she was treated by a younger and much more foolish generation, of which I am at this moment, regrettably, a part. I never knew her name, but her face and her smile will remain in my memory forever.

My youngest son, Christopher, was about five years old. We had gone to the grocery store to pick up some things for his little sister's birthday dinner. My son and I were both caught up in the excitement of surprising my daughter with a cake and a special dinner. We gathered up what we needed and headed for the checkout counter. There was only one cashier, so we pulled up to wait. I was half listening to Christopher's endless, excited chatter and half planning my dinner when the cart in front of me caught my eye.

A woman I didn't recognize was slowly unloading the few simple items. She was barely five feet tall and very thin. I was surprised to catch a glimpse of muscles in her aged arms flexing as she lifted the groceries from her cart. Her round face held soft black eyes, and the bandanna on her head was a rainbow of reds, yellows, blues, and greens, all of which repeated in the dress that fell to inches above worn brown shoes that had places cut out on the sides so as not to rub raw the corns on her feet.

It made my heart ache, but more importantly, it opened my eyes. I looked down at my precious little boy and tousled his thick hair. I'd been feeling sorry for myself, because I'd gone without lunch all week to save enough to buy my daughter's birthday gift and special dinner supplies. Here was a woman whose entire week of groceries consisted of no more than a small bag of potatoes, a bag of cornmeal, a large bag of dried beans, a couple of onions, some fresh collard greens, two dented cans of tomato soup, and a quart of milk, reduced to half price because the expiration date was that day. In the center of these meager victuals was a huge package of chicken wings. That package of chicken wings created a bond between this gentle stranger and myself. I understood completely. Because most people consider wings a less than desirable part of a chicken, they are cheap. If you planned carefully and prepared them right, you could get several meals out of that one pack of meat.

The woman laid each of her items on the checkout counter as carefully as if they were made of crystal and might break if she weren't gentle with them. When she came to the package of chicken wings, she looked up at me and smiled like she'd known me forever, eyes shining. Then she laughed. The kind of laugh that starts deep down inside your heart and bubbles up and explodes like a song from the soul. She was going to take those few simple items home and turn them into a magnificent feast.

The checkout girl totaled the groceries and told the woman her bill was eighteen dollars and thirty-six cents. From a change purse she methodically counted out twelve one-dollar bills, then two dollars and fifty cents' worth of nickels, dimes, and quarters. The clerk stood there making exasperated faces and very impatiently told the woman she was three dollars and eighty-six cents short.

All the light went out of the soft eyes set deep in the shiny ebony face. She touched each of her items, trying to decide which one to put back. When her hand fell on the chicken wings, the most expensive item in her cart, she took a deep breath and handed them to the clerk, her whole body appearing to tremble in defeat. The clerk grabbed the package of chicken wings and, in her agitation, called rudely over the intercom that she had a void because the lady didn't have enough money.

It made me so angry. This radiant matriarch, denied the respect her years entitled her to, was reduced to bowing her head in shame and humiliation. I reached in my pocket and pulled out four one-dollar bills and handed them to the clerk while my son stood there in total disbelief. He knew we barely had enough to feed ourselves. I told the clerk there was no need to void the ticket. The lady was a friend of mine and I would lend her the balance. Cautiously, the woman took my hand and pushed the money gently back toward me, shaking her head. I told her it was all right; I was glad to help. She looked up at me and ever so softly said, "God bless you, Child."

I realized in that moment He already had. As this angelic grandmother patted my hand, a single tear slid down her time-weathered cheek. That was all the thanks I needed.

I never saw the woman again. For the next two days I didn't eat any lunch, but it was well worth it. In my mind, I'd picture that woman laughing while she fried her greens and chicken wings, and my heart was so full I forgot about my stomach.

I am sorry I was never given the opportunity to meet this woman again and get to know her. There is no doubt in my mind her life experiences would have told of countless episodes when the God she asked to bless me had done just that for others upon her simple request. My little family made do just fine without that four dollars, and the gift this wonderful stranger gave to me in reminding me of my faith was priceless.

I have since been blessed a hundred times over. God sent me help I didn't even know I needed, in the form of a gentle stranger. I have since come to believe that as long as you are trying to help yourself, when you really need it, God will send someone to help you. All you have to do is believe.

JOY IN D-7

by Malinda Fillingim, Roanoke Rapids, North Carolina

My brother Scott has taught me more about joy than any book, sermon, or class I have ever known. Scott is the most joyful person I know. In fact, when I tend to feel depressed, lonely, left out, or in some way sad, I think about Scott and I feel better.

Scott will never write a book, preach a sermon, or be famous. In fact, Scott will never walk, talk, feed himself, or do so many other things you and I might take for granted. Maybe that is part of the reason Scott is such a person of joy: He is also a person of gratitude.

Scott was born with a severe case of cerebral palsy back in the days when there was little intervention, treatment, or understanding of this birth defect. His body is very shriveled up, his legs unable to move, his body dependent upon many medicines to keep him pain-free and alive. I grew up pushing Scott around in a wheelchair, feeding him, bathing him, taking him to the bathroom. We had our usual sibling arguments, but he was and still is the most inspirational person I know.

One summer while I was in seminary, I worked as a summer missionary near Scott's place of residency in Charleston, South Carolina. Before work every morning I would visit Scott in his cottage, D-7, where he lived with about seven other boys. He and the other residents of this facility for handicapped persons would greet me with big smiles and open arms, ready to hug and be hugged. I'd read them stories, talk with them, and, of course, we would all sing. Our favorite song was always "Jesus Loves Me." We'd sing that song over and over and over until I could no longer sing. One day as we sang, I looked around me and saw several people in wheelchairs, some in casts, some bedridden, some with oxygen tanks, some severely handicapped in several ways. They all were singing this song with great conviction. I began to feel a sense of sadness, of wishing I could take away their pain and suffering. Then I began to wonder how they could think Jesus loved them, in light of all their problems. On that day I asked these folks who were now my friends how they knew Jesus loved them. They all began laughing at me, smiling and clapping.

"What's so funny?" I asked. One boy named Charlie told me, "You are funny. Of course Jesus loves me. And I know it because you told me and you love me so it must be true."

Scott looked at me proudly, as if I had just won the Olympics or some other grand prize. "Jesus loves me, this I know, for the Bible tells me so" is how the song really goes. But to these folks the song really means "Jesus loves me, this I know, because you show me love wherever we go." They were seeing Jesus through me. Love was their life source and I was the conduit of God's love.

I had come to give these people a blessing, to share some iota of joy with them, to impart some goodwill. But I was the one who walked away with blessings beyond compare. I did not hear about their pain, their inability to do so many things. I never once heard anyone complain or gripe about what they had to eat, what they had to wear, or how little money they had. But I did hear words of glee when the ice cream truck came, or someone volunteered to wash their hair, or take them for a walk. I heard words of gratitude when someone sent them a card, or held their hand, or washed their face. Love was about being accepting for who they were, of embracing the creation God made in each one of them. I was blessed to be in their presence, to reap some of their joy, to garnish some of their unconditional love for one another and others.

Blessings are not always the kind we see with the eyes. Some blessings can only be felt with the heart.

Jesus loves me, this I know, for the folks in Cottage D-7 showed me so.

*⁓ Make sure to read Malinda Fillingim's story, **"Bathroom Blessing,"** in volume one of* God Allows U-Turns: True Stories of Hope and Healing.

LOVE FIRST, TEACH SECOND

by Joan Clayton, Portales, New Mexico

"You're going to have Mary in your room?" a fellow teacher asked. Her voice conveyed apprehension as she added, "I feel sorry for you!"

"She's on medication, you know," another teacher warned. "You will be, too, before the year's over!"

Similar comments had fallen on my ears during my eighteen years of teaching. But usually these first-grade children would turn out to be normal in every respect. So I began the year with calm assurance that I could handle whatever came. Was I in for a surprise!

A few days before school started, Mary and her mother dropped by to "get acquainted." Golden blond hair fixed to perfection cascaded down the little girl's back. Large, beautiful blue eyes gazed into mine. Between the outbursts from Mary, which frequently interrupted the conversation between her mother and me, I learned that Mary needed medication for both hyperactivity and asthma. She would need to take one pill after lunch. Her mother agreed that the office would keep the medicine and I would send her for it every day after lunch. Mary's mother graciously volunteered as room mother. I was delighted.

Then came the first day of school.

Purses, tablets, marking pens, hair barrettes, gimmicks of all kinds—Mary dropped the whole assortment as she made her bouncy entrance. Every time I turned around, it seemed that some child was crawling under a table to retrieve Mary's loot.

Whispering seemed an impossibility to Mary. She frequently blurted out comments, disturbing the entire class. "The answer is ahhh. . .one. *NO, two. . .no, threeeeeeeeeeeee.*"

I knew the scene by heart. Scrubbing vigorously with her eraser usually tore the paper, and she would start the whole procedure with a fresh sheet of paper again. . .and again.

One day, completely exasperated, I voiced my complaints to the office secretary.

"Mary's medication doesn't seem to help at all."

"What medication?" the secretary questioned. "She hasn't been in for it since school started."

After that, I began sending a child with her on whom I could depend to see that she took her pill. Even with resumption of her daily medication, I still had to deal with Mary's frequent outbursts.

One day, after constant shushing, isolating, and reprimanding, I stopped the class and said, "All right, Mary, come to the front. Take all the time you need to talk, wiggle, or whatever, so you can settle down and we can get back to work." This drastic method had always worked before. The student, embarrassed, would stand silently and be more than happy to sit down and resume working.

But not Mary. At first she jumped up and down, growling like a caged bear. Then she pounded on the desks with her fists, screaming like Tarzan in the jungle. The children loved the show as Mary alternated between growling, screaming, and laughing. This encouraged her to show off even more.

After five minutes of these antics, I could stand no more. This little girl had outsmarted me, the teacher!

In the weeks that followed, I ran the gamut of rewards, praise, and reinforced positive behavior (when I could find any). Nothing seemed to work. At the end of one particularly harassing day, I dismissed the children and slumped in the chair behind my desk, totally defeated. I had tried everything.

Everything, that is, except prayer!

With my head on my desk, I prayed, "Lord, help me with this child. Show me the key. Where have I missed it?"

In utter exhaustion, I dozed off. When I awakened a few minutes later, my frustration and weariness had disappeared. Two words kept coming to my mind: *"Love her."*

I was well aware that those who are the hardest to love are often the ones who need it the most. But I thought I had worked through this and that I already loved her. Yet, those two words. . ."love her". . .lingered in my mind. And they were there when I awakened the next morning.

"Lord," I prayed, "I already love her, so I'm going to take those two words to mean that I'm to love her physically."

I hurried to school that morning, bursting with anticipation. God had answered, and I was eager to see His plan unfold.

When the bell rang, Mary bounded in with enough energy for the whole class. I gave her paper to write her spelling words on, and she jumped ten frog jumps to her seat. Then she began to write and spell out loud, "D-o-w-n. Deeee. . .ohhhh. . .double-yuuu. . .ennnnnnnnnn!"

"Mary, come to my desk, please," I said quietly.

With two hops, a skip, a side two-step, and three giant steps backward, Mary obeyed my command. Silently, I pulled her toward me and held her close. In my thoughts I was praying, *Lord, help this little child to calm down. Take away whatever is causing her hyperactivity.*

Sometimes these sessions would last five minutes with no one saying a word. It was just Mary and me holding each other. The other children watched silently and seemed to understand.

If Mary's behavior seemed to be getting out of control, we would stop and hug, just Mary and me, while the class waited patiently and lovingly. There were times we would do this four or five times a day.

One week later, Mary's reading teacher came running across the hall.

"Whatever has happened to Mary? She isn't the same child!"

"It's called 'pray and hug therapy,'" I explained. "I silently pray for her every day, and before I let her come to the reading class, I stop the children, hug her, and say a silent prayer."

"Well, don't ever stop!" the teacher exclaimed.

In just a few short weeks, Mary's behavior change was noticed by other staff members.

I knew in my heart that God was leading.

It is now spring. Last fall seems long ago. It's hard to think of Mary now as ever having had problems. She acts perfectly normal in every way. When she raises her hand to answer a question but instead says, "Teacher, I love you," I say a silent prayer of thanksgiving.

In a few minutes the bell will ring, and the children will come in. . . each with different needs. As I pass out their papers, I pray silently for these little lives that have blessed mine so abundantly.

Lord, bless this child today. Help me always to love first and teach second!

This is a good rule for all of us to follow.

⌐ *Make sure to read more great stories from Joan Clayton in volume one of* God Allows U-Turns: True Stories of Hope and Healing.

DOES GOD MOVE AWAY FROM US?

by Richard Bauman, West Covina, California

In the movie *The Horse Whisperer,* there is a scene where Pilgrim, the horse, escapes the confines of the corral and bolts blindly for open land. Instead of chasing after him, Robert Redford's character, Tom, shouts, "Let him go." Eventually Pilgrim tires and comes to stillness in a green, high meadow.

Tom doesn't rush out after Pilgrim. He casually catches up with him. He doesn't hurry up to the horse. Nor does he become angry and abusive toward the confused and terrified Pilgrim. He doesn't even call to the horse. He doesn't try to tempt the horse with food, to lure him back to the barn with him. He simply gives Pilgrim plenty of room.

He says nothing to the horse. He comes within a few hundred feet of the horse, but no closer. Tom does just one thing for Pilgrim—he sits patiently, watching him, his eyes fixed on Pilgrim. He sits in that meadow and never takes his eyes off the horse.

He doesn't say even one word. He doesn't inch toward the confused, psychologically crippled horse. He just sits and watches him, focusing his loving energy on that incredibly damaged animal.

Pilgrim was maimed through no fault of his own. The victim of human misjudgment and carelessness, he was horribly injured and wants nothing to do with people. Humans are his bane. They represent pain, suffering, and abandonment. Tom wants to help Pilgrim, but the horse doesn't understand that. All he knows is humans are synonymous with pain.

Tom has been blessed with insight into horses. He comprehends horses in a way few other persons do. He discerns the pain, the anguish, and the hatred Pilgrim has for him and all humans.

So Tom sits absolutely still—and waits. . .and watches—hour after hour. Ever so slowly, imperceptibly at first, the distance between Tom and Pilgrim starts to shrink. Without perceiving any significant movement, man and horse come closer together. Finally, Pilgrim is standing right in front of Tom. Only then does Tom rise—slowly, lovingly—to meet Pilgrim. Gently he reaches out and strokes the horse's face, touching him gently. He puts his cheek on Pilgrim's cheek, as if to hear the horse's pain. When Pilgrim finally senses Tom's trustworthiness, he is willing to walk alongside Tom and again return to the confines and the safety of the corral.

When that movie comes to mind, it is that scene of Tom sitting in the meadow waiting for Pilgrim that I see. Why? Because I can be like Pilgrim sometimes. I bolt from the safety of God's teachings, the discipline they require. Truth becomes too real for me. I run away from God; I flee His commandments. I charge off to higher ground, to what looks like greener pastures, so I can do what I think I have to do.

When I rush off into the wilderness of the world, or let its distractions obscure my connection with God, does He come running after me, calling my name, trying to coax me to return to Him? No! On the other hand, He never loses sight of me. He won't let me out of His view. He stays connected but at a safe distance.

For me, God's relationship with us is akin to Tom's relationship with Pilgrim. He sits and waits patiently for us to discover Him—most of the time. Sometimes God confronts us directly, but more often He is content, like Tom waiting for Pilgrim, to let us finally see Him again and return on our own to Him. He never loses sight of us. He sits and watches and waits ever so patiently for us to come to Him.

The wait might be days, weeks, years, or even decades before we even look up and see Him. Still, wait He does. Of course it would be faster for us, and for Him, if He would just come right to us and grab us. Instead, He just makes sure we have chances to see Him waiting for us.

Our movement back to God might be painfully slow, and barely perceptible, like Pilgrim's movement toward Tom. Sometimes we might move a little toward Him, and then circle back away from Him, ending farther away than when we started. Nonetheless, He keeps us in sight, aware that eventually we will look in His direction and see He is still waiting for us.

Why doesn't God usually come after us? Why does He sit and watch, unmoving? Perhaps because He knows the pain and fear we are in envelops us like a fog, and He has to be the steady One. He has to be the one permanent, unchanging thing in our lives. Whether we realize it or not, whether or not we want to admit it, we need Him to be fixed and unmoving.

When we can finally come to God with our pain, the pain He has seen forever but we are only learning to see, and we give it to Him, He will help us grieve over it and release it.

God sits and waits, because He knows the way we heal is not in isolation and aloneness. We heal through His comforting touch. And His comforting, healing touch, however, usually comes to us not just spiritually but through the hands and arms and hearts of other people. Those who sit, and watch, and wait in stillness, ready to embrace us once we permit ourselves to be embraced.

IT'S THE SIZE OF YOUR LOVE

by Joan Clayton, Portales, New Mexico

Christmas had come and gone, but the memories kept repeating a song of thankfulness in my heart. We were blessed to have had another Christmas with loved ones. The house our boys grew up in bulged at its seams. The long legs of the men in my household sprawled across the den floor as they relaxed in the warmth of the crackling fire in the fireplace. The crisp, cold, chilly night made everything perfect on Christmas.

We had a wonderful time of sharing stories about the love of Jesus, including His mighty works that had occurred in our lives this past year. In the wee hours of the night, our house became strangely quiet again. Those little boys who grew up so quickly were back in their own beds. The same familiar refrain from previous years echoed from grandchildren: "Good night, Mommy. Good night, Daddy. I love you." The same clock chimed its soothing sounds, blessing me that everyone was home once more.

Our house is too small when they come back home. Grandchildren sleep in sleeping bags on the floor, and people are snoring all over the place. The dining room is also too small, but hungry people don't seem to mind. It's all about love and family.

I apologized for the lack of room, but Connie, our middle son's wife, said something that I will hold in my heart forever: "It isn't the size of your house. It's the size of your love!"

The thirteenth chapter of 1 Corinthians encourages and inspires me to strive to have that kind of love. The chapter ends with verse 13: "There are three things that remain—faith, hope, and love—and the greatest of these is love" (TLB).

Think of the joy of seeing your children when they have been away a long time. Your joy can hardly be contained. God is like that. Hearts who turn to Him bring great joy. Malachi 1:2 (TLB) simply states:

"I have loved you." What a profound truth! It's hard to understand.

It isn't the size of the house, possessions, or career. It isn't the fame or fortune one has. One cannot work his way to heaven. The gift of salvation is a free gift. It is a gift of love from the heart of God. He only asks for our love and faithfulness in return.

God wanted us and He made us in His image. We are the object of His incredible love. This love goes beyond anything that we can fathom. God is love and He loves so much that He sacrificed His only Son. I could not have done that. I could not have sent my only son to die a cruel death for the sins of mankind.

The next time you feel unloved, think about the love that God has for you. God never runs out of love. His love never ends. It is eternal. It's like my beautiful daughter-in-law said: "It isn't the size of your house, but the size of your love."

⌐ Make sure to read more great stories from Joan Clayton in volume one of God Allows U-Turns: True Stories of Hope and Healing.

GOOD WORDS AND REFLECTFUL PAUSES

by Michele Howe, LaSalle, Michigan

Each evening, I make it my aim to spend about an hour sitting alone and reading a good book. Depending upon the season of the year, I'll either choose a cozy chair on our enclosed porch, which overlooks the fields all around us, or I'll jump into my bathing suit and sit in the hot tub outside my bedroom. There, too, I have everything necessary for physical, spiritual, and emotional rejuvenation.

I take some time to relax and reflect on the day before I open my book. I clear my head of unwanted interruptions, distractions, sometimes even fretful worries. I look around at God's wondrous world and marvel that by His word alone everything is held in place. I see the trees, the fields, and flowers. I hear the geese flying overhead. I smell the faint scents of seasonal changes. I can feel the brisk chill in the air or the warmth of the summer sun upon my face. In every season, I find Him present and ready to teach me something more about His character and grace.

Once I've soaked in all of the goodness of nature, I turn my thoughts to whatever written word of encouragement or instruction I've brought along. Sometimes I read the Bible, other times a devotional. Maybe even a fictional tale. Whatever book I choose, I'm ready to learn, absorb, and contemplate the truths found in its pages. After a time, I close my book and then take a few moments to ask God to help me take a portion of His Truth with me for the remainder of the day. In solitude with God's created world and with the written word, I find a private place of retreat and renewal each and every day. By His command, the natural world around me speaks to me of His enduring love for me. By the words He has inspired others to write, God speaks to me of His never-ending commitment to me.

Once I receive these gifts from His hand, I am ready to become the giver of gifts to those around me.

~ *Make sure to read Michele Howe's story,* **"Laundry Lines and Broken Clothespins,"** *in volume one of* God Allows U-Turns: True Stories of Hope and Healing.

CHAPTER TWO

Tales of Triumph

I know what it is to be in need, and I know what it is to have plenty.
I have learned the secret of being content in any and every situation,
whether well fed or hungry, whether living in plenty or in want.
I can do everything through him who gives me strength.
PHILIPPIANS 4:12–13

A SECRET CODE

by Sara A. DuBose, Montgomery, Alabama

"A code?" Bob asked.

"Sure, why not?" Sonny answered. "You ask the questions and I'll knock out the answers on the telephone receiver. Look: If it's yes, I'll knock three times; and if it's no, I'll knock once, like this."

Sonny Paterson rapped the receiver.

"Roger. I read you loud and clear," Bob said. "I'll call you Tuesday afternoon around five o'clock. Now, before we hang up let's pray."

The prayer was short, but as Bob prayed, Sonny tried to commit the next few days to God. The flight from Montgomery to Houston would take no longer than the surgery—about three hours. But coming out of the operating room, Sonny would be minus a voice box, his communication cut to a knock, a nod, or a piece of paper and pencil. Later, Sonny might want special laryngeal speech lessons, but for now his one objective was to have the Texas surgeon cut his cancer away.

"Amen," Bob said.

"Amen," Sonny replied. "I'll be waiting to hear from you on Tuesday."

Sonny Paterson—a prominent businessman and active layman in the church—had only three more days to talk. How could he speak everything on his mind? How could he tell his wife and family how much they meant to him? There would still be communication, but what if he couldn't learn the tricky speech method the physician described?

Sonny tried to shut off the pessimism. He'd had troubles before, and God had never let him down. At the same time, Sonny knew that a person's heart can accept something, while his mind and body still want to rebel.

Tuesday came. The papers were in order. Blood pressure, temperature, pulse—all checked and found normal. Waiting, saying good-bye, rolling to the operating room on a stretcher. Then nothing, until waking up with a dry, hollow feeling of having something missing. Smiles, hand-holding. It was over, the offending cancer removed.

The ring came later. Sonny checked his watch and reached for the phone. It was five o'clock.

"Sonny? Bob Strong. Is it all over?"

Knock, knock, knock, came the reply.

"Are you in much pain?"

Knock.

"Sonny, I have one more question. Has God stood with you? Have you felt His grace and presence through all this?"

There was a pause, and then it started. Not once, not three times, but again and again and again and again came the knocking until Bob Strong closed the conversation with another loud "Amen."

A HEART TO GIVE

by John Patterson as told to Louise Tucker Jones, Edmond, Oklahoma

As I lay in bed on Thanksgiving Day in 1989, my body racked with pain, I found little to be thankful for. Some months earlier I had broken my foot. Having been a world-champion steer wrestler on the rodeo circuit in my early years, I certainly didn't worry over broken bones. The main problem was the inconvenience of the cast. But as the weeks went by, I began to experience intense pain. Finally, the cast was cut away and the source of pain revealed. Somehow the cast had cut the bottom of my foot, and since I was a diabetic, gangrene had quickly set in. After several days of intravenous antibiotics, I went home, but the wound never healed. Now the searing, throbbing pain was unbearable, and my temperature was escalating. I knew what the next step would be.

The following morning an emergency surgical team prepared to amputate my right leg, just below the knee. Though I had protested in the beginning, now I just wanted to live and to be out of pain. After the surgery, I gradually moved from a wheelchair to crutches and often hopped around on my good leg until a blister appeared on my foot. Six months later, my left leg had to be amputated. If I felt sorry for myself with the first amputation, it was nothing compared to the anger and rage I now experienced.

When I was twelve years old, I had joined a little country church and thought that took care of my religion. I didn't talk to God the way some people claimed to do. I took care of myself and figured most folks would be better off if they did the same. What I learned about God growing up was that He was to be feared, and I had experienced enough fear in my own home. I certainly didn't need more from some deity.

But now, as a grown man, trying to cope with two "stubs" instead of legs, I even lost my fear of God. As I sat in the middle of the bathroom floor, unable to raise myself up, I cursed God violently. So what if He struck me dead with lightning; could that be much worse? Maybe I wasn't the best person in the world, but I didn't deserve this.

Eventually I was fitted with two prostheses and spent time in rehab learning to walk again. As my muscle mass and weight decreased, my own determination to walk increased, and I continued my tirades against God. Who needed Him anyway? I could take care of myself, just like I had always done.

By 1995 I was back to a fairly normal lifestyle with a good job, when I began to have chest pains. The pain was familiar. When I was thirty-one years old, I'd had quintuple heart bypass surgery. Years later, stents were placed in the arteries. What else could they possibly repair? After spending a few days in the hospital on pain medication, I went home. The pain returned and didn't go away. I couldn't even walk from one end of the living room to the other without collapsing in total exhaustion. Finally, the doctor recommended a heart transplant even though my medical problems posed a great risk. Having been a gambler in my rodeo days, I didn't like the odds they were giving me, but I saw no other option.

The first step was being accepted by a transplant team, which was no easy task. As a diabetic and double amputee, some teams wouldn't even consider me. And even if I were accepted, I would have to go on a waiting list, which could take months or years. And if I was lucky and received a heart, there were no guarantees that the surgery would work.

When I'd had the bypass surgery years earlier, I was put on a heart-lung machine to keep my heart pumping during surgery, then an electrical impulse restarted my heart. But this would be different. My diseased heart would be removed and someone else's heart would be placed in my body. It didn't take a genius to figure out that the only One who could make a brand-new heart start beating was almighty God, and I figured I had alienated Him completely when I cursed Him. I truly didn't think I even had the right to ask Him for help.

But my wife, a wonderful Christian woman, along with the pastor and friends from her church, had a different idea. They gradually convinced me that God was full of love and forgiveness, not anger. That was a new concept for me. How could anyone, especially God, love me enough to forgive me for the years I had ignored Him and the things I had said? But slowly, as I read and studied my Bible, I found a God that was totally different from the judgmental one of my youth.

This was a God of love, peace, joy, and even healing. This was not a God to fear. This was Someone I could trust and believe. To say I was surprised by His love would not be sufficient. I was completely overwhelmed. I asked God over and over to forgive me and told Him whatever life I had left, no matter how much or how little, I wanted it to count for Him.

Eventually I was accepted as a transplant candidate, and on the day after Christmas I went into the hospital to wait for a new heart. It was like living with life and death at the same time. One minute I thought of being healthy again; the next minute the reality that I might die surfaced.

Finally, on January 22, 1996, a heart was available. The doctor told me to get my family together. We called our pastor, friends, and family and prayed together. I was prepared for surgery and felt complete peace. I had given everything to God. He was in control no matter what happened.

Suddenly, the doctor came in and told us they had a problem. He didn't seem to know how to approach us. Finally, he said, "We have a seventeen-year-old boy on a ventilator that probably won't make it through the night without a heart." He paused, then asked if I would consider giving the boy the heart. He also emphasized that the heart was originally intended for me and it would be my choice. I could keep it or give it away, not knowing when another heart would become available or how long my body would make it without one.

Talk about a roller coaster of emotions. From the moment I was notified, I had gone from disbelief, to elation, to apprehension, to acceptance, and now I wasn't sure what I was feeling. How do you choose who lives or dies? It was both the toughest and the easiest decision I ever made. The tough part was knowing what my family would go through if I didn't receive another heart. I didn't want to leave my wife a widow. I wanted to live. I wanted to see my grandchildren grow up.

The easy part was knowing who needed the heart most. And it wasn't just about the physical body. My faith in God had intensified over the last months. I knew I was going to heaven when I died, but I didn't know about that boy. Was he a believer? If he lived, it might give me a chance to tell him about God and share His love. And didn't a seventeen year old deserve life more than a forty-nine-year-old double-amputee diabetic?

The young man survived the surgery; and one week later I received my new heart, an even better physiological match for my body than the previous one. I was even able to share God's love with the young man's family.

That was five years ago, and today I feel great. In fact, I'm probably healthier than many people my age. It takes extra energy for me to walk, but I enjoy going places and meeting people. And I wear shorts everywhere I go, no matter what the season or weather. I want people to see my prostheses and ask questions so I can tell them about my medical miracles. When they ask, I tell them that God gave me new legs so I could walk with Him. Then I explain how He gave me two new hearts—this physical heart transplanted into my chest cavity and a spiritual one deep in my soul that overflows with His love.

That's my greatest miracle, and I plan to share it with everyone I meet.

THE GIFT—CONFESSIONS OF A SURROGATE MOTHER

by Carrie Mikolajczyk-Russell, Toledo, Ohio

The last time I gave a gift such as this it was a wintry day in December 1999. The twins, Ryan and Alexa, came into this world to be received by their parents with all the love a heart can hold. I knew that the gratitude of those parents would forever hold a place in my heart.

And now I had heard my calling again. The embryo transfer had been successful. God had blessed me with the ability to carry yet another child for yet another couple. Today was the day we had all waited for so anxiously.

This, the morning of the birth, we all met for breakfast. Tim and Lisa, the parents-to-be, greeted us with hugs. Tim is a pediatrician and Lisa is an OB-GYN. They had endured years of heartache in their quest to have a child. Today there was no evidence of that. There was only excitement and joy for what was about to take place.

On the way to the hospital, my husband held my hand with unspoken understanding. These moments were very precious to me.

They were my final moments with this baby who had touched my heart in so many ways. He had his very own personality, this child that slept with me and woke with me. He made me laugh when he was active. I knew I would miss his presence, as I had missed the twins. But now it was time to close this chapter. It was time to create a family. So, with my husband's hand in mine, we made our way to the hospital with a smile in our hearts. It was time to assist God in uniting a loving couple with their child.

Labor was induced at 1:30 P.M. A short while later, each contraction was strong enough to bring tears to my eyes. Lisa sat next to me expressing her regret for my discomfort. I reminded myself of how small a price tag it was, knowing that she would have given anything to be sitting in the bed I was perched on, feeling each wave of pain. It was shortly after five o'clock when I prepared for the first push. I had no idea I would have two more agonizing hours of labor.

By 7:00 P.M. I was exhausted and my doctor was looking anxious. Convinced that I could go no further, I wanted to give up, but I felt conflicted. All through my pregnancy I prayed each night for the strength and ability to carry this baby to term. Every night I would say to God, "I know I can do this but not without You." It was now, in my darkest, weakest hour, that I knew I had to depend upon Him. I closed my eyes and prayed. "God, please help me to bring forth this child. I can do it but not without You."

The next push was not "the one" and neither was the next. I was not discouraged. I would not lose my faith in my ability to do this and found myself looking forward to the next contraction. When it came, I repeated my prayer. Almost instantly I felt the baby making progress. He was coming!

When I pushed for the last time, all shed tears of joy. All that mattered to me now was seeing this woman whom I had come to love so much receive her child. I wanted to see a father gaze upon his firstborn son. I wanted to see what I had achieved with God's help.

As Lisa stepped forward to claim her son, he was gently placed in her arms while she cried tears that washed away years of pain and emptiness. Tim had come up behind Lisa with tears of his own. They were a family at last.

I thought to myself, *Look what God chose me to do.* I could feel God was smiling at me as I looked over at Tim and Lisa again. This is what it was all about. Some people go their entire lives and never get to see what I saw in those moments. I've been blessed with seeing it twice.

So many people ask surrogate mothers "why?" Why would you do this for someone? These moments are the answer to those questions. If I had a bottle and could capture these moments, it would make it so easy to explain to all those that judge us unfairly. I have these memories that will never fade. They leave an imprint in my mind, my heart, and my soul that can never be erased.

Two days later, it was time to leave the hospital. I held Harrison for the last time. I told him to be a good boy, to always remember how special he is, and that I would see him later on in the year. I told him how proud I was to have been chosen to give him life and then I said good-bye.

I was filled with satisfaction, and I thanked God once more for my own children, my fertility, and my ability to be a surrogate mother. I walked out of the hospital that day with my children's hands in mine, fully aware of the gift that I clasped in each hand. The sun shone down upon my face, and I looked at everything as if I were seeing it for the first time.

THE EXTRAORDINARY FAITH OF A DUNG CATCHER

as told to Sharon Doorasamy, Westville, South Africa

When I was a boy growing up in South Africa, I prided myself on being the best dung catcher on the sugar cane estate where my father was a laborer. To achieve this high position required two important attributes: an ability to run fast, which I could do, and an understanding of the nature of cows, which I had.

We needed the cow dung to keep down the dust in our dirt-floored cinder block house. We would mix the dung with water and splatter it onto the ground to seal the dirt. So, at least once a week I ventured into the fields to collect fresh dung, not old dry dung, left to cool on the ground with flies on it. However, to get fresh dung you must pay close attention to when a cow picks up its tail. So when I spotted a tail lifting up, I'd dash to the cow with my bucket and try to catch the dung before it hit the ground.

It didn't bother me that we were poor until I started high school. It became clear to me that the teachers favored the students from "good" homes. I began to compare myself to other children, who wore nice clothes, ate bologna sandwiches, and brought their lunches in neat bags with plastic ties. I ate leftovers from dinner, usually beans or potatoes, smashed between two slices of bread. My mother wrapped my sandwiches in newspaper.

Every evening at our home, my mother gathered us together for family worship. She couldn't read very well, so one of us children read the Scripture. She chose it. We read it. The Scripture one night was from Jeremiah 29:11, in which the Lord says, "For I know the plans I have for you. . .plans to prosper you and not to harm you, plans to give you hope and a future."

I was a different person after that night. I never again compared myself to anyone. With the Lord's promise as a comfort and shield, I began to excel in my schoolwork and my Christian walk.

I graduated from high school but had no money to go to university. Since these were the days of apartheid, it seemed that I had no reason to hope. Yet, I was full of hope. I believed in God's promise to prosper me and give me a future. And He did, by way of a missionary who passed my way. This American missionary paid my first semester tuition.

Thereafter, I won a series of scholarships and awards, which covered the cost of tuition for seven years of full-time study. I was even awarded a Fulbright scholarship to study environmental law at American University in Washington, D.C.

Today, my life is far different from my poor beginnings. I'm an environmental lawyer. It is through God's grace that I am what I am. How else does one explain how a boy whose parents could not afford to buy him a fifty-cent ball has achieved what I have?

The best dung catcher ever, I am living testimony to the truth that "in all things God works for the good of those who love him" (Romans 8:28).

FIVE MINUTES TO LIVE

by Jill Lauritzen Zimanek, Athens, Georgia

"Jill, this is what we're going to do. We're going to pump your stomach, then we're going to give you an alcohol drip, which will be like a triple cocktail in an IV. But I have to tell you. . .this could kill you. And if it doesn't, you could go blind or have kidney damage," he said, matter-of-factly. Then he gave me five minutes to say good-bye.

Try to take that one in. Minutes before, I had been completely healthy and now a doctor was telling me the sand in my hourglass was running out. . .fast.

Returning from our Christmas vacation with family in Pittsburgh, I had accidentally ingested methanol, a chemical so toxic that four teaspoons is fatal, according to Poison Control. Our windshield wiper fluid had frozen under the hood, so we had put some fluid in a Gatorade bottle to squirt periodically on our windshield as we drove. While reading to my husband, I inadvertently grabbed the wrong Gatorade bottle and chugged down. When I felt the burning in my chest, I realized what I had done. I drank approximately a half cup of liquid that contained the chemical, maybe more. I immediately grabbed the water and drank that down while my husband found a gas station to ask for directions to the nearest hospital.

Within minutes, I was explaining to hospital personnel what had happened. Nurses looked at me sympathetically and patted my leg. Then the doctor came in and laid it on the line for me. While my husband ran out to tell our children what was happening, the nurses came in to insert a tube through my nose into my stomach.

That's when the doctor told me I needed to see my children to say good-bye. . .just in case. I told him I didn't want them to see me like this, but he said they needed to.

They came into the room, crying, while their daddy held them. The tube made it difficult to speak, but it was harder to know what to say. How could I sum up the feelings I had for my family in five minutes? I started to cry, which made my throat hurt even worse.

"If Mommy dies," I started slowly, "where am I going?"

"To heaven," my daughter said, sobbing.

"That's right," I said slowly. "And where did Mommy say she'd be in heaven?"

"With arms wide open at the gate waiting for us," they said together.

We held hands and held each other as best we could. I took a heart-shaped piece of shell my son had given me years ago at the beach from my purse and held it tight in my hand. "See," I said, showing it to them. "I'll have this with me the whole time and be thinking of you." Knowing I could lose my sight at any moment, I studied their faces. I wanted their images to be the last I'd see.

I thought of my mother and father, whom I so desperately wanted to hug. I thought of my sister and brother, my nephews and nieces. I thought of friends. . . . I would never get to tell them how much they meant to me. I felt ripped apart from the inside.

Moments later I was taken by ambulance to another hospital, on a continuous alcohol drip. I was the only legal drunk in West Virginia.

I think my husband had made four telephone calls: one to my family, one to his family, one to a friend in Green Bay, and one to a friend in Athens. Just those four contacts resulted in literally hundreds of people being called. I was frantically put on prayer chains around the country.

If the Lord had plans to take me or have me suffer some of the horrendous side effects, with all those prayers going out He must have changed His mind.

Twenty-four hours later, every test came back negative. My vision was not impaired. My kidneys and liver were fine. I was alive. I was alive and unharmed. As my recovery became more assured, I became the hospital joke, especially when they ran out of alcohol. Nurses ran around asking if anyone had alcohol hidden in their lockers that they could pour into my IV. And I can't tell you how many "alcohol drip" jokes I've heard since.

It's hard for me to think about what I went through emotionally, but I think it was a lesson for me. As a family, we've had a number of hardships during the last two years. I remember wishing God would just come for me. I actually prayed for it. I think God wanted me to realize what I'd be leaving behind if He answered my prayer. I can't tell you how grateful I am for that lesson. Now I know I'm not ready to go. Not yet.

I'm not going to live happily ever after. No one does. But I'm living. And as long as the good Lord doesn't want me just yet, I'm going to keep on living, and laughing, and crying, and loving. I'm going to hold my children and look at their faces and watch them grow for as long as I can. And I'm going to make sure the ones I love—particularly my husband, who so strongly faced the what-ifs with such compassion and bravery— will know how much they mean to me. . .so that I won't need five minutes ever again.

JEREMY, MY TEACHER

by Joan Clayton, Portales, New Mexico

I met Jeremy when he started first grade. I was his teacher. He immediately won my heart with his upbeat spirit and unfailing courage. You see, Jeremy had juvenile rheumatoid arthritis, a terrible disease, especially in one so young.

With braces on his legs, walking was a daily trial for Jeremy. Whether it was walking down the hall to music class, across the street to the cafeteria, or even out to the playground, Jeremy was always exhausted by the time he got there. One day I quietly asked Jeremy if I might carry him. I didn't want to embarrass him or call special attention to him, but when he said yes, he seemed greatly relieved. I was thankful, too! What better way to show my gratitude for three strong healthy boys of my own!

In the days and weeks that followed, I marveled at this little boy's ability to bravely face each day, one day at a time. "Teacher, it hurts so bad," he would say. "But I am thankful that I'm as well as I am. Lots of kids I've seen in the hospitals aren't as blessed." What a truly wonderful character this child had.

One day after carrying him out to the playground, Jeremy asked if he might please stay in the room at recess. Although the children were protective of him, the rowdiness of their running here and there made Jeremy nervous. It was hard for him to keep his balance, and he worried that a child might accidentally knock him down. The fall weather was getting too cold for him anyway, so I agreed that this was probably a good idea.

Before going out, I made sure I left him with plenty of markers, crayons, pencils, and paper during recess. When we returned each day, the children would gather around Jeremy with sighs and gasps at the pictures he had made. For what Jeremy's little body and legs could not do, his hands and brain made up for. He had an extraordinary gift for art, illustration, and graphics. His perspective was keen for one so young, and a specialty of his was drawing airplanes and tanks.

The children were always pressing him for this one and that one. Jeremy's pictures were so popular that he devised a unique way to handle the supply and demand. He charged ten cents a picture for everyone except me. He gave me his special ones, always signed "I love you" by Jeremy.

I prayed every night for Jeremy. I desperately wanted Jeremy to walk like the other boys and girls. One night I dreamed he was running down the hall as fast as any of the other children. Like any other teacher, I called out to him, "No running in the hall, Jeremy. We walk; remember that, please." How I so prayed that someday he could be just like all the other children.

Jeremy excelled in every subject, despite living with his pain. He made the top score in my class. All too soon the year I had with Jeremy was over. I was very happy that second grade was just across the hall so I still got a chance to see him every day and still be a little part of his life. I continued praying to God to someday help him heal.

From third grade on, Jeremy was in a different part of the building, and I rarely had a chance to see him. So I was really thrilled that while he was in the sixth grade he invited me to his baptismal service. Several years later, when I heard through a fellow teacher that Jeremy had fallen and broken his leg, I could only pray harder. I continued praying all through the next nine years that passed by quickly.

One day I was standing in line at the grocery store when I felt a tap on my shoulder. When I turned around I found myself staring directly into Jeremy's face! "Jeremy, it's you! You're all grown up! You're walking! You're walking!" He grinned as I cried and hugged him tight. Jeremy was in high school now, and I was seeing him walk normally for the first time.

Jeremy finished high school and college. As I watched him walk across the stage that graduation night and receive his college degree with honors, I was immediately taken back to his first grade classroom. The courage and faith I had seen in that little first grader had persevered and had overcome. Jeremy's indomitable spirit had faced one of life's hardest obstacles and had won.

Jeremy was hired by a very prestigious company and given a high position in computer graphics. I could have already told you that, because I knew it would happen when he was in my first grade class!

On May 29 I saw Jeremy walk down the aisle on his wedding day, with his beautiful bride by his side. Today I received this letter from him:

> *Dear Mrs. Clayton,*
> *You've always been very special to me and I was proud that you were at my wedding. Becky and I want to say "thank you" for the gifts and encouragement. Our children are going to hear lots of stories about you!*
>
> *Love, Jeremy*

I shall always be grateful for Jeremy and the lesson he taught me. Instead of my student, he became my teacher. He taught me the greatest lesson of all: The faith-filled, courageous, indomitable human spirit can overcome impossible odds, because with God, all things are possible!

⌐ Make sure to read more great stories from Joan Clayton in volume one of God Allows U-Turns: True Stories of Hope and Healing.

WHINE OR SHINE?

by Ronda Sturgill, Shalimar, Florida

It was a beautiful New England fall day. The cloudless sky was the prettiest shade of blue that I have ever seen. The warmth of the sunshine was in stark contrast to the cool, crisp October air, and the foliage was at its peak, setting the woods ablaze with bright shades of orange, red, and yellow.

When my friend Joyce asked me to go horseback riding with her that afternoon, I could hardly say no. Oh, I had lots of homework to do, but that could wait. With winter quickly approaching, we both knew that this day would be the last time we would be able to go riding until the following spring. I had always loved horses and did anything I could to be around them. I had never outgrown my love for horses, even as I entered my second year of nursing school at the age of eighteen.

When we arrived at the stables, we were given horses that, according to the stable owner, would try to outrun each other. Since neither one of us were beginning riders, we thought this would only give us a more exciting ride. As we were getting ready to set out on the trails, a man suddenly appeared at the stables and wanted to ride with us. A little reluctant at first, we agreed to let him come with us. Soon Joyce, Bob, and myself went galloping merrily off into the woods.

The stable owner was right about the horses; they did try to outrun each other. From the very beginning, I had trouble controlling my horse. He kept on running off the path and into the thick forest. As we rounded the last turn in the trail that led back to the barn, my horse definitely wanted to be the first one to get there. He charged ahead, totally out of control.

I was holding on for dear life as we approached a large puddle in the path. Instead of running through the puddle, he quickly and unexpectedly swerved to the right. The momentum threw me into the air with tremendous force. I was like a rag doll as I somersaulted out of the saddle. The trees circled above me as I crashed violently against one of them and fell to the ground.

My legs felt odd, and when I sat up to look at them, I realized they were numb. They were spread apart and I could not move them back together. We had just been studying anatomy and physiology in nursing school so I knew exactly what had happened to me.

Oh, no, I thought, *I broke my back and severed my spinal cord.*

"Joyce, Joyce," I moaned, "why couldn't I have died? I'm paralyzed from the waist down." I was horrified to think that I would never be able to walk again.

"You don't know that," she replied.

Bob rode ahead to get the ambulance. As she staunched the blood from a cut on my head, Joyce began asking me simple questions to see if I was disoriented. I was not in much pain.

Staring at the ceiling of the ambulance on the way to the hospital, I was amazed at the peace I felt. There was no panic, no hysteria, not even much pain. Just peace. I knew that I was in God's hands and that God is a good and loving God.

This is it, I thought. *This is what I've been prepared for.* Ever since I was a little girl, I've felt that something was going to happen to me. I never could put my finger on it, but every so often, a particular feeling would come over me that made me think that one day I might become physically challenged.

I have a very vivid memory of a scene from an old World War II movie in which a doctor tells family members that their husbands, fathers, sons, and brothers have been injured in combat and they are now paraplegics. The word "paraplegic" never left my mind from that moment on. I noticed people with disabilities. I had always admired their courage and determination.

But as I lay in the ambulance, foremost in my mind was the party I had attended with some friends the previous evening. I didn't know anyone there, but as I looked over the crowd I saw a young man sitting in a wheelchair. Standing beside him was a girlfriend, leaning on his wheelchair. I was struck by how comfortable both of these people were with his disability. They were laughing and having a grand time.

"Look at that," I said to one of my friends. "If anything ever happens to me that I should end up in a wheelchair, I want to be just like him. I'm not going to let it get me down. I'm not going to be depressed and angry. I'm going to get on with my life."

Well, I thought as I lay there in the ambulance, *I guess I have the chance to live up to those words!*

In the emergency room, the nurses quickly began to cut off my clothes, keeping me as still as possible. Before I went into surgery, I asked the doctor if I would ever be able to walk again. I'll never forget his kindness to me at that moment.

"I don't know," he said, gently cradling my hand in his. "We'll know more after surgery."

But in my heart, I knew the answer. I was never going to walk again.

Joyce called the school to let them know what happened. They called my parents in Delaware, who immediately started the eight-hour drive to Massachusetts. Friends began to arrive at the hospital. What was going to happen to me now? Would I ever become a nurse? Would I have to leave my friends in Massachusetts?

The first night of my accident I just wanted to die. I tried to die. The enormity of everything was beginning to set in. What was left of my life that was worth living? All I ever wanted to be was a nurse; that would never happen now. I would never get married; I would never have children. There was no hope, nothing to look forward to—just total despair. I would be pushed around in a wheelchair for the rest of my life, helpless. I couldn't sit up. I could not dress myself. I was an infant in an eighteen-year-old body!

A nurse came into my room later that evening and noticed that I was slipping into a deep depression.

"Ronda," she said, "you can't do this. If you don't want to live for yourself, think about your parents. They are wonderful people who will do everything they can to help you get your life back together again. But if you give up and die, they will be even more heartbroken than they are right now."

She was right. My parents were wonderful people. And at that moment they were in as much, if not more, pain than I was. For their sake, I had to let them know that I was going to be okay. Lying there in silence, it began to dawn on me that my life was not the only one that would be changed forever; so would my sisters' and my parents'.

I thought about the choices I had. As I look back on it now, it seems clear to me that there were only two: Quite simply, I could either whine or shine!

Realizing that whining and complaining was not going to change or help my situation, I decided that night to work very hard to put my life back together again. I chose to use my energy in a positive and constructive way to rebuild my life.

Did I ever get angry? Oh, yes. Did I ever get frustrated? You bet. Was I ever scared? Absolutely! But I never doubted God's love for me, nor did I ever equate His love for me with my circumstances. I knew that if I trusted and depended on God, He would help me overcome my anger, frustration, and fears.

Indeed, He did exactly that!

Twenty-eight years later finds me happily married to an Air Force chaplain, a proud parent of an eighteen-year-old son, the owner of a seminar company, and on the brink of a viable speaking ministry.

As I look back on the day of my accident, I know God was with me. And I believe that if He could have spoken to me in an audible voice, He would have said something like this:

"Ronda, it's time. I've prepared you and you are ready. I'm about to take you through the fire. Your life will change forever, but you will be a testament of My love, My grace, and My power. When your body hits that tree and you fall to the ground, I will be there to catch you; you will be falling into My arms and I will carry you out of the woods."

In Isaiah 43, verses 2 and 5, the Lord says, "When you pass through the waters, I will be with you; and when you pass through the rivers, they will not sweep over you. When you walk through the fire, you will not be burned; the flames will not set you ablaze. . . . Do not be afraid, for I am with you."

When I am faced with difficult circumstances today, I know that I am never alone. I still have to make the choice of whether I will whine or shine. But when I look back on my past and see how God's love has strengthened me, and how His grace has sustained me, it's never too hard to make the choice to shine instead of whine.

∼ Make sure to read Ronda Sturgill's story, "A Mom Who Uses a Wheelchair," in volume one of God Allows U-Turns: True Stories of Hope and Healing.

THE CROSS ON THE CHALKBOARD

by Mary Ellen Gudeman, Fort Wayne, Indiana

To my relief, the bell rang. It was a sweltering hot and humid day. I sighed as I stuffed my teaching materials into my briefcase. How could I expect these Japanese students with so little understanding of the Bible to comprehend the message of the Cross in a language that was not their own?

As I turned to erase the chalkboard, I almost bumped into a student who was standing beside me. I apologized in Japanese to the lanky young man. Looking down, he shuffled his feet from side to side. I vaguely remembered his slipping into the back of the classroom halfway through the lesson.

By custom not daring to look into my face, he stammered, "Speak Japanese, okay?" I assured him it was okay.

"Can that man help me?" he asked as he pointed to the cross I was about to erase from the chalkboard.

"He most certainly can!" I replied.

"I have a problem in my heart," the student blurted out. "I would like to speak with you about Him." His name was Tsuji-san. We made arrangements to meet the following Tuesday.

From Friday to Tuesday, I wondered if Tsuji-san would have the courage to show up for our meeting. But he came at the appointed time, and bit by bit he related his story to me.

He had come from the mountains of Fukui-ken. Not always able to express himself verbally, he had kept a diary. Then, before coming to

Osaka to enter Kansai University, his mountain home had caught fire and had burned to the ground. The family had saved the Buddhist altar, but Tsuji-san's diary lay ruined in the ashes. So many thoughts and dreams had been recorded in that diary. Then his closest friend in high school took his own life when he failed the university entrance exam. Tsuji-san managed to pass the stiff exams to enter this choice university. But now, in spite of this accomplishment, a shadow had crept over his life.

The big city had held many charms that distracted him from his loneliness and despair. But they never filled the emptiness in his heart.

"But Tsuji-san, there is a great God who has a wonderful plan for your life," I told him, wondering how I could communicate some hope to this dejected young man. "Tell me," I said, "why did you come only once to the Bible class on Fridays?"

"Well, to tell you the truth, I wasn't interested in the Bible," he replied. "But last Friday I decided to come to the final Bible class." He paused, and then added with painful effort, "I decided to attend and then. . .and then take my life. But when you drew that cross on the chalkboard," he recalled, "you told us, 'You are loved by Someone—Someone who died on the cross for you. . . .'" His voice trailed off in a sob.

I sat there staring at him. Could it be that although he heard just a portion of the gospel for the first time, and in a foreign language, he really understood it? The message of the Cross—represented on the chalkboard that day—had spoken to Tsuji-san's heart.

Before he left that evening, Tsuji-san fully understood that God loved him, and he had placed his trust in Christ. Later he sent me a long letter. He wrote: "For the first time I know why I am living. Returning home tonight, I flung myself down on my futon and prayed for the first time, 'God, I'm sorry.'" He added, "My joy was so great I cried for over an hour."

During his college days, he attended our church in Osaka. Tsuji-san's faith grew as he studied the Bible. He loved children and poured himself into teaching Sunday school. Later he led Bible studies for the youth group and also counseled at Bible camp in the summers. Tsuji-san often returned to his mountain home to share the message of the Cross with his mother. One day she also believed.

When he had entered his junior year of college, I returned with him to Katsuyama-shi near his home. He wanted to visit his old high school and tell the students there about the Cross. The question was whether or not the school would permit it. In an unexpected gesture of welcome, the teacher told him he could say whatever he wished. I was amazed that a public school would permit such liberty in speaking. Tsuji-san related his classmate's suicide and then Tsuji-san's own search for meaning in life.

"Jesus died for you," he said as he drew the cross on the chalkboard and explained God's love to the students. I could almost hear him repeating the same Bible lesson I had taught in his university club. That evening a number of high school students, along with their teacher, attended the tiny village church!

After graduation from his university, Tsuji-san became engaged to Miyako-san, a young woman in the church in Osaka. He believed God wanted him to return to the mountains of Fukui-ken to live with his bride-to-be. They established a Christian home in Fukui-shi. Shortly after marrying, they invited their neighbors into their living room for a Bible study.

Over the years, I would occasionally meet Tsuji-san when he and his wife and children visited Osaka. On one particular visit when he was alone, he telephoned me.

"Do you still go to Kansai University for the Bible class?" he asked.

I told him I did.

He stammered, "I'd. . .I'd like to sit again in that classroom where you drew the cross on the chalkboard."

I remembered that hot, sultry day at Kansai University many years before, when all but one of the students of the club had gone off to class. When the cross is lifted up—wherever, whenever—even on a chalkboard, people will be drawn to Jesus, and the good news will spread in any tongue.

CHAPTER THREE

Love One Another

*Dear children, let us not love with words or tongue
but with actions and in truth.*
1 JOHN 3:18

A DAY IN A LIFE

by Elaine Ingalls Hogg, Port Hawkesbury, Nova Scotia, Canada

When I first entered the hospital room, my patient's family was ministering to her needs. It was lunchtime, so I offered to sit with her and give her loved ones a break for the afternoon.

From her bed, Marie heard my voice and beckoned me over. She wanted to give me a hug. This had become our way of greeting and saying good-bye for the last number of weeks since I had been assigned as her palliative care volunteer. I leaned over the bed rails that in her mind, at least, had come to signify the boundaries of her personal prison.

She then whispered, "I'm happy now, not anxious anymore."

This was an important change for her. Prior to this she had said she felt like she was climbing a mountain or crossing a parched desert.

I placed my chair beside her bed and took her hand as her family slipped from the room for a much-needed break in the long vigil. For the next half hour, she rested while I held her hand and hummed or softly sang familiar hymns. Only a few weeks ago at Thanksgiving, she had sung the hymns along with me. Today, I wasn't even certain she heard them.

She woke just as I had finished the chorus of "This Is Holy Ground."

"The angels are all around today," she said. "Pretty soon you won't have to look after me."

Moments of silence came again. The room was quiet except for the sounds of uneven, labored breathing. Suddenly, her big brown eyes opened again and words tumbled out of parched lips.

"Paradise—it will soon be over. I'm so happy for how everything is now. Life is beautiful. Talk to me, Elaine."

As had been our custom, I shared some family news, before she drifted off to sleep once more.

Quiet engulfed the room again for a long period. Then, once again

I heard a tiny mumble. She was growing so very weak. I put my head closer and gave her my undivided attention. These are the words I heard:

"A beautiful place—I am seeing a beautiful place."

I took her hand once again, thanking God I could be with her at this most holy time.

Then once more she spoke: "The time is coming."

I studied her for a moment, then said truthfully, "Oh, Marie, it will be hard for me. We've become so close these past few weeks. But we know God has promised that we'll see each other again, my dear friend."

She smiled then whispered, "I knew you would catch on to what I meant. Elaine, please write my story so others won't be afraid of death."

Early in our relationship we both had acknowledged that our inner strength came from our faith in God. In fact, on our very first visit she asked me if I knew any Scripture that I could quote, for she missed not being able to go to church. That day, my mind had gone back to one of my favorite Scriptures, one of the first that I remember printing out in an orange-covered notebook. I quoted:

" 'Do not let your hearts be troubled. Trust in God; trust also in me. In my Father's house are many rooms; if it were not so, I would have told you. I am going there to prepare a place for you. And if I go and prepare a place for you, I will come back and take you to be with me that you also may be where I am. You know the way to the place where I am going. . . . I am the way and the truth and the life. No one comes to the Father except through me' " (John 14:1–4, 6).

The curtains of night were still drawn around that little hospital room as I held my friend's hand while she crossed to the other side. After a long illness, my friend had finally passed away. It was a bittersweet time.

I made my way out of the hospital and crawled into my little car. The car lights pierced the darkness, yet the heaviness in my heart made breathing difficult and concentrating on the road even more so. Just before I reached home, the sky began to pull back its curtain and fill with light. I stopped the car and sat alone for a few minutes.

As I watched the eastern sky, a flock of geese flew overhead, honking encouragement to their leader as they made their way in the dawn's early light. The sky in front of me opened up to a glorious red and golden sunrise. It filled the sky, reflecting its beautiful colors on the blue lake below. It made soft golden touches on the green grass, but most of all it touched my heart.

My friend was no longer in pain; she was no longer alone. She was now in peace, and this display of nature's beauty had been given to those of us who loved her but were left behind for a little longer to carry on her acts of kindness here.

"Good-bye, Marie," I whispered. "Good-bye, my friend." And I knew where she had gone.

GRAMMA JAN

by Jan Coleman, Auburn, California

I hadn't expected her to be at the park that afternoon. I found myself resentfully wondering why she had to come at all. Couldn't I be the only Gramma this day? I'd waited five years to know this child.

Grace touched my arm softly. "I've thought about you so much these last few years." She had been constantly in my mind, too—the woman who is grandmother to my daughter's child.

I thought back to the morning when Amy announced her pregnancy. She was seventeen. Being a single mom myself, I had struggled solo through all her rebellious episodes. Until that day I thought we were past the worst.

"I'm going to place the baby for adoption," she said. "Will you help me choose the parents?" she asked. My heart jumped. I felt relieved that she was choosing life and two loving parents for this child.

I was confident it was the right thing. "God will bless you for this, Amy," I said assuredly, drawing her close.

In the quiet of Amy's bedroom, we sat cross-legged on the floor reading the couples' profiles. I prayed for the Lord to give us discernment.

We each rated the couples on a piece of paper and compared notes. "I can't believe we both picked Keith and Leslie for number one!" Amy said with delight. She had interviewed the top three but was instantly attached to Keith and Leslie. The papers were signed shortly thereafter.

It wasn't until the ultrasound revealed that the baby budding inside Amy was a girl that the import of it all finally hit me. I could suddenly envision a precious infant looking exactly like Amy with big, brown, curious eyes. *You'll be okay,* I told myself. *This kaleidoscope of emotions is normal.* Leslie then assured me, "We want you to be a part of this child's life." What role could I possibly have? Leslie's mother had waited sixty-three years to spoil her only grandchild. How much would she want me hanging around?

In Amy's eighth month her boyfriend jilted her. She and the adoption agreement totally fell apart. "I can't do this," she said. "I'm keeping this baby. She's all I have."

I knew she was changing her mind out of desperation. She was so young, so tender, so bruised, not ready to be a mother. Stubbornly, she laid out her plan. Collect state aid for awhile, live at home, and find some job training. Would I help her, she wanted to know?

It was so tempting. I was a single mom with a good job. I could afford to help Amy and offer so much to the granddaughter I loved so much already.

I wrestled for days. I remembered all the times I rescued Amy from her consequences, trying to shield her from her mistakes, trying to make up for the loss of her father. I remembered David's prayer in Psalm 86:11: "Lord. . .give me an undivided heart." I asked God, "What is right in *Your* eyes for this situation?"

God reminded me that faith is doing the right thing regardless of the circumstances, knowing He will turn it to good in the end.

The right thing.

I knew what that was, but would it turn Amy from me? Would I lose her, too?

"I love you, Amy," I told her. "This is your decision, and I'll support you in it, but you must find a way to support this child on your own."

She was so angry with me she didn't say a word to me until the day she went into labor. Then she asked me to be in the delivery room with her. After Nikki was born, I went right home, unable to sort out my feelings. I spent almost all night on my knees.

The phone rang early the next morning. "Something's wrong with her," Amy sobbed. "They're putting her in an incubator. Oh, Mom, I've been praying to God all night. I'm so confused. I love her so much."

Nikki rallied and the crisis ended, but it gave God time to work in Amy's heart. "I've prayed about this, Mom, and I'm calling Keith and Leslie right now. I know it's the right thing. It's God's best for her." Our tears were bittersweet.

Needing to say good-bye, Amy brought her daughter home for one week. Those were special days to make memories with her first child: hold her, sing to her, write her a loving letter, and then let her go. I couldn't get too close. I was afraid that embracing this child would only increase my sorrow when she left us.

When that day came, Amy could not stop weeping. We went straight to the Bible, to 1 Samuel. We talked about Samuel's birth being a testimony to the faith of a mother. "It wasn't easy for Hannah to give him up to be raised by someone else," I said. Hannah was blessed with more children to take the place of the one for whom she prayed.

Just after Nikki's first birthday, Keith's job transferred him from California to Florida. Sure, I would get pictures and videos, but how would she ever know me at three thousand miles away? And as the years went by, the pain grew with every photo I received. Nikki was the image of my daughter. I felt so cheated. I was so angry with God.

When Nikki was five years old, the family made their first trip back to California. Could I meet them at the park, I was asked? All the way down the freeway, I selfishly hoped Grace would not be there. I didn't want competition for Nikki's attention. How would she respond to a woman she didn't know? "She knows she's adopted," Leslie had told me on the phone. "We're not sure how much she understands, but you are her Gramma Jan."

She was a delightful, loving child. We played hide-and-seek and fed the ducks. She sat on my lap, and I fixed her ponytail, while Grace sat quietly in the background. I was ashamed of my attitude.

At the end of the day Grace took me aside. "You've done better than I thought you would, Jan. I know how hard this must be for you. She's a special child. She's such a blessing to me. Thank you," she said, squeezing my hand.

Tears stung my eyes. She was thanking me! Because Nikki was her gift from God, a gift that came through me. I had missed Grace's joy because I focused on my loss, instead of the good that had come from it. I had forgotten that God ordained this adoption. He has a plan for Nikki's life, and He chose the part that I will play in it.

I glanced back at Nikki and said, "Thank *you*, Grace, for having room in your heart to let me be 'Gramma Jan.' "

⌐ Make sure to read Jan Coleman's story, "Miracle in the Rain," in volume one of God Allows U-Turns: True Stories of Hope and Healing.

THE NEIGHBORS NEXT DOOR

by Karen Strand, Lacey, Washington

It's Saturday morning. Sunlight falls into my bedroom, drawing my eyes to the soft pastels of my wallpaper, then to the window where I can see the peak of the rooftop next door. The Coles' rooftop. My thoughts turn to the latest neighborhood news: Kristy has had her baby.

Kristy. Fifteen years old and an unwed mother. Although the Coles have lived next door for several months, I don't know them. But I have heard that Kristy's stepdad, Ron, has an eight-year-old son, Chad, from a previous marriage. And that Kristy's mom, Sue, has a teenage son, Todd, from her first marriage. Next there's two-year-old Scott, who was born to Ron and Sue. Now Kristy has made Sue a grandmother. Does that make Ron a grandfather? Or is he a step-grandparent? Or is there such a thing?

Intrigued by the relationships next door, I envision a time when Kristy is explaining who is whom to Baby.

I slowly shake my head in disgust.

My husband wakes up, fluffs his pillow, and asks what's for breakfast. At the same time, I hear eight-year-old Julie bounding downstairs for morning cartoons. I roll out of bed and head for the shower. After breakfast I load the dishwasher, wipe off the counters, and work on a sewing project I'd started. Julie taps on the door.

"There's something I want to show you," she murmurs. Clearing a space, she lays down a piece of notebook paper folded in half like a greeting card. On the front is a crayoned rainbow. On the inside are large, red letters:

DEAR KRISTY, I'M HAPPY YOU HAD A BABY.

JESSICA IS A PRETTY NAME.

Hmm, I muse. *Jessica. So it's a girl. . . .* Underneath is the drawing of a smiling, toothless baby and the words GOD LOVES YOU. It's signed, "Love from your next-door neighbor, Julie."

After my daughter leaves the room, I lean on the sewing table, chin in hand, and think about this. Then I go looking for my daughter.

"Don't give it to her yet," I say. "Would you like to get a little gift, too?"

"Yeah, Mom!"

We drive to K-Mart where we buy a silly yellow duck wearing a blue hat.

When we return home, Julie wraps the duck, tapes the card on top, and we take it next door. As we wait on the porch, I'm surprised that I never noticed the pretty welcome sign. But then, I've made no effort to become acquainted with Sue at all. She has so many family members, while I've been married to the same man for over fifteen years. I'm just unable to identify with Sue's kind of life.

When Sue answers the door—that is, I think it's Sue—I am embarrassed at having to introduce myself.

"Karen, from next door. This is my daughter, Julie."

Sue, wearing her dark curly hair in a ponytail and dressed in jeans and a flannel shirt, looks quite normal. She smiles warmly and invites us in to see the baby. Kristy is on the couch, cuddling and kissing her precious bundle. Julie hands Kristy the duck and asks to hold Jessica, while I apologize.

"I'm sorry I haven't come over to meet you before now. Just busy. You know how it is."

Sue laughs and offers me a cup of coffee. I look around the room and am surprised at the cozy atmosphere. But what had I expected to see? Purple gremlins poking out of the corners, with a big sign that reads "Weird Family Lives Here"? A basket of yellow daisies rests on a side table, and on the wall above it hangs a creatively arranged collection of photos. Pictures of Sue and Ron. Kristy and Todd. Chad. Scott. And I know that a space is reserved for Jessica.

Over coffee and a crescent roll I learn more about Sue, and our woman talk turns to personal stuff—the kind where you feel so comfortable with someone you can tell her you hide candy bars in the linen closet.

"I never thought divorce would be a part of my life," Sue says. "We were married for ten years when my husband just up and left. Fell in love at the water cooler."

Ron, I learn, has been widowed for four years. "Breast cancer," Sue explains. "It was awfully hard on him." She gives a deep sigh.

"I don't know if it was the divorce, or what, but Kristy's been a real handful, lately. Now. . .” She motions to Kristy, who is fussing over the baby.

My throat begins to feel tight and funny, making it hard to swallow.

This wasn't at all what I had imagined. Suddenly I don't like myself very much.

When it's time to leave, Sue and I plan to get together again. Julie skips home across the yard, unaware that her simple, nonjudgmental act has caused a major turnabout in my judgmental heart.

After going inside, curiosity makes me reach for my Bible to look up verses with "neighbor" in them. I stop at Proverbs 11:12: "A man who lacks judgment derides his neighbor, but a man of understanding holds his tongue."

"God loves you," Julie had printed at the bottom of the card. And He does, indeed. Sue. Ron. Kristy. Todd. Chad. Scott. Jessica. Me. People.

I go to the kitchen, get out the large blue bowl, and stir up a batch of chocolate chip cookies. Sometimes it's never too late to welcome people to the neighborhood.

TIME MANAGEMENT

by Esther M. Bailey, Phoenix, Arizona

I had more than enough work of my own to do. Progress on my curriculum assignment was slow, and I was beginning to suffer from burnout. For the first time in my life I had recently been forced to decline a writing assignment. I had neither the time nor the inclination to write a speech. So when the prison chaplain said to me, "If you have any ideas on volunteering, I could use some help. . . ," I had no intention of getting involved. Besides, what did I know about volunteering?

Then, just when I thought the subject was closed, Scriptures that might encourage volunteer work began to flash through my mind. Could I work up a few ideas in a couple of weeks or whenever the speech was scheduled? I wondered.

I recalled a story I once read about Dr. Norman Vincent Peale when he was just a young pastor grappling with financial woes. When he could not find a solution to the problem, he asked his wife, Ruth, for advice.

"I'll tell you what we're going to do," she said in her perky style. "We're going to start tithing."

A shocked Norman shook his head. "You don't understand," he said. "We can't even pay our bills." Ruth persisted, however.

"Don't you see, Norman? We're not taking out God's portion first; so He isn't helping us manage our finances."

After some discussion, Peale decided to give his wife's theory a try.

Soon he learned the truth of the paradox taught by Jesus: "For whoever wants to save his life will lose it, but whoever loses his life for me will find it" (Matthew 16:25).

Why, I asked myself, did that particular story come to my mind at that time? I did not need a lesson on tithing. Then suddenly I caught the connection. Perhaps the same principle held true for time as well as for money. If I spent my time on God's work, maybe He could help me with the problems I seemed to have trying to get everything else done.

I called the chaplain the following day. He explained his ideas and what he wanted from me. I began to feel inspiration coming on.

"When do you need this?" I asked. I was unprepared for his answer.

"Tomorrow night," he said with something of an apology in his voice.

Even with a one-day deadline, I felt it was too late to back out.

"Lord, I think You got me into this. If You want me to come through for Marvin, You'll have to help me fast," I prayed.

Although I depend upon God to help me with every project, sometimes I struggle for an hour or so to complete a paragraph or even a sentence.

This was no less difficult to start, but, after the first couple of paragraphs, words began to flow. In a record four hours I finished my task.

At church the following Sunday, Marvin reported good news. Not only had his speech gone well, he received two invitations to speak for other occasions. I was delighted for him.

In addition, I found that instead of sapping my mental energy, the diversion had inspired me with fresh zeal to generate creative ideas.

Shifting my focus proved to be an effective antidote for the burnout I was suffering. I finished my assignment nine days ahead of my projected goal.

So the next time I feel called to participate in a worthy endeavor, I hope I remember a principle of time management: God more than makes up for time given in His service.

~ *Make sure to read more great stories by Esther Bailey in volume one of* God Allows U-Turns: True Stories of Hope and Healing.

THE PRE-DAWN TEST

by Elaine Cunningham, Wenatchee, Washington

R-r-r-ring. Was that the doorbell? I looked at the clock. Five-thirty A.M. Who could be ringing our parsonage doorbell this early?

My husband rolled out of bed and went to the front door. I heard a mumble of voices, and then he returned.

"Honey, could you get up? A hungry tramp needs some breakfast."

I groaned. Not only was it black as night outside, I knew our refrigerator looked like Mother Hubbard's cupboard.

"It's a poor time to feed anyone. You know we're moving next week. I've cleaned out the fridge and most of the cupboards."

"Well, see what you can find. He looks desperate."

I scrambled out of bed, threw on my bathrobe, and headed for the kitchen. There, in a chair in the corner, sat the most pitiful piece of humanity I'd seen in years. A tattered felt hat hid his eyes. An old scarf covered the rest of his face. His long, ragged coat dragged the floor.

"Would you like to take off your coat?" I asked.

"No," he mumbled through the scarf. His body shook. "I'm c–c–cold."

I opened the refrigerator door. *Hmmmm.* A few slices of bacon would have to do. *Maybe there's an egg left.* I found three. I took a frying pan out of the cupboard and turned on the front burner on the stove. As I opened the package of bacon and peeled off two slices, I glanced again at the man.

He still sat bundled up, shaking with cold, or palsy, or something. Poor old soul. Maybe this is one of the least ones Jesus said we should befriend. You couldn't get much more least than this one.

I turned back to the stove and laid the limp slices of bacon in the skillet. They sizzled as they hit the hot pan. This was probably the first good meal this old fellow had had in awhile. I prayed for him silently as I concentrated on turning over the bacon slices.

Suddenly, the man in the corner leaped from his chair, ran toward me, and threw his arms around me.

"Mom!" he yelled, as he threw off his hat and scarf.

My heart pounded with fright, then relief, then laughter, as I looked into the mischievous eyes of my son who was supposed to be away at college in Kansas City, not posing as a vagabond in Indiana.

"You passed the test, Mom," he said, as he continued to hug me. "I thought I'd surprise you and drop in as a tramp and see if you would feed me early in the morning. I drove all night to get here."

"Well, you certainly surprised me—almost gave me a heart attack. You're lucky I didn't crack you on the head with the frying pan!"

Later, after my heart stopped pounding, I reflected on my son's test and realized what a good reminder it was to be ready to help the needy for Jesus' sake, even at 5:30 A.M.

Next time, though, I'll watch closely for a twinkle in the eye—just in case.

THE PRIVILEGED LIFE

by Debbye L. Butler, Indianapolis, Indiana

I was fortunate to be handed a wonderful life on a silver platter. I didn't travel or study abroad, couldn't recognize the difference between imitation and fine Italian marble, and I will never have a hospital wing, educational scholarship, or philanthropic foundation named after me. Still, mine is a privileged life.

Society labels my kind of family unit "blue-collar." My dad's education went no further than his senior year of high school. A factory worker for one of the major U.S. automakers, his wages were measured in hours worked and stretched like a brittle rubber band. To make ends meet, Dad never turned down overtime. He even worked the midnight shift and often pulled double shifts on little sleep.

Mom rationed and recycled everything even before it was in vogue to do so. I wore hand-me-downs often, which was interesting, since only my brother's clothes fit me.

I learned at an early age the discipline required to stretch a dollar. I learned to love people who were different. I learned responsibility. Most importantly, I learned to lean on God in the darkest moments of my childhood.

Now I face a new juncture in this privileged life as I care for my parents, both of whom have serious health conditions.

My sixty-six-year-old mother is a breast cancer survivor, an epileptic, and the victim of a stroke that impaired her vision and walking. When she was hospitalized for that stroke for four days, I could not keep my frightened, feeble father in his own bed. At 1:30 A.M. on the first night, my dad and I sat in their living room praying aloud—a first in our history beyond holiday mealtime prayers. We prayed for courage, comfort, and healing. I remain thankful for that night of lost sleep.

My dad is not just physically frail. Vascular dementia and some stage of Alzheimer's are ravaging his thought processes. The doctor says Dad's like a twelve- to eighteen-month-old baby now. For this moment in time, with my mother stabilized, my father is the one more in need of extra attention.

He is deteriorating rapidly, unable to do anything which he once took great pride in or did with ease. Our roles are now reversed. Instead of Dad loosening a tight peanut butter jar lid for me, I do it for him. He struggles to do simple things like button a shirt or shave his once smooth, always groomed, cheery cheeks.

The first time I shaved my disheveled, disoriented father, tears streamed down his cheek, but we persevered. We move him gently to each ensuing level of dependency. Most recently, I bathed him—my father. He gratefully said how good it felt to have his back washed. God's grace surrounded us.

My life is indeed a privileged one. Privileged because my father trusts me enough to let me cross boundaries that separate dads and daughters. Privileged because as I bathed him from head to toe, I remembered Jesus washing His disciples' feet. I was honored to be placed in a circumstance that somewhat modeled Christ's ministry of love, sacrifice, and obedience. Christ said we should follow His example.

It is a privilege, and one for which I will be forever grateful.

THE SONG

by Sharon R. Haynes, Chardon, Ohio

When Martha and Betty were in their seventies, Alzheimer's disease brought these two strangers together. Their common love for reading, music, and grandkids made them fast friends.

Martha, a kind Jewish lady, and Betty, a very refined Catholic, happened to have rooms next to each other. I don't think they ever considered their differences. They were neighbors in the same battle and learned to fight that battle together.

I worked and prayed in the residential setting where Martha and Betty spent their last few years of life. It was a lovely place for patients in the early to middle stages of Alzheimer's disease. Often I would find these friends exclaiming over a new batch of pictures of grandkids, or walking arm in arm in the flower gardens.

These two brave women did not quit living just because life had become difficult. They continued to find enjoyment in everyday activities. If some weeds were spotted in one of the flower beds, neither Martha nor Betty was afraid to get her hands dirty. Of course, when they were ready to get back on their feet, they usually would need a little assistance. But then, in part, that's what I was there for.

Every afternoon, the residents and staff would gather around the piano to sing favorite oldies songs. Each day Betty would request "You Are My Sunshine." The residents, with smiles and delight, sang this well-loved song.

Betty's health began to fail shortly after her first year with us. Having sung her heart out one afternoon, she needed my assistance to get back to her room. I helped her lie down and sat on the bed next to her. I sensed a prompting of God's Spirit to express to Betty how much she meant to me.

"And you mean more to me than bacon and eggs," she told me. We both laughed. Sometimes Alzheimer's patients have trouble expressing just what they're thinking, but having spent so much time together, we both knew what she was trying to say.

I know that God is always near, but His Spirit was especially evident in the room at that moment. I believed He was leading me to share more with Betty than I had before. Asking her permission, I read a psalm. I spoke with her about the Shepherd and explained her need for a Savior. As she lay aged and weak upon her bed that day, Betty said, "I need a Shepherd, and I want to know the Savior." Although her body was weak, Betty had fervor in her eyes as she confessed, "I am an old sinner, Lord. Please be my Savior and forgive me for ignoring You for so many years." Then I bent and gently gathered this little lady in my arms and with joy welcomed her into the family of God.

The next day Betty complained of both stomach and back pain. A short time later, her doctor diagnosed stomach cancer. Martha was beside herself. She had lost so much, her husband, her home and independence. Now she realized she was losing her friend—the one with whom she had come to enjoy sharing the end of her life. Betty was rarely conscious. It wasn't very long before she had to be transferred to a chronic care unit.

Martha had not seen her in weeks and would pace restlessly around the facility as if she had lost her best friend. And she had. I was surprised that after a couple of weeks Martha still missed Betty. Usually, out of sight is out of mind for an Alzheimer's patient. Maybe it was the familiarity of the now-empty room next door, or hearing that one special song each afternoon, but Martha would ask daily, "How's my friend? How's Betty?" One day my supervisor suggested I take Martha to the chronic care unit to see Betty.

After standing by her friend's bedside for a moment, Martha began to stroke Betty's frail hand and speak to her gently. The seconds slipped by, but Betty did not respond. The pained look on Martha's face broke my heart. Maybe this was not such a good idea after all. *Lord, You know how much Martha loves Betty. Help Betty to sense her love. Please bless Martha with a sign.* Then a thought came to mind: "Martha, before we leave, let's sing 'You Are My Sunshine' to Betty." Martha's eyes lit up, and we began softly singing, "You are my sunshine, my only sunshine. You make me happy when skies are gray. . . ."

Just then, a weak, raspy sound came from the bed, bringing a catch to our breath and instant tears to our eyes. In a quavering voice, with her eyes still closed, Betty was singing, "You'll never know, Dear, how much I love you; please don't take my sunshine away."

That moment with Betty was just what Martha needed. As we walked back to our building, Martha's eyes glowed with a peace and contentment I had not seen in her for weeks. But she was not the only one deeply affected by that experience. I was left with a sense of awe— much like what Job may have felt when he said, "Surely I spoke of things I did not understand, things too wonderful for me to know" (Job 42:3).

That afternoon left me convinced of the soul's need and desire to communicate on some level; and I recognized the goodness and mercy of our God in making a way. A sense of gratitude rose up in my spirit. Truly we serve a gentle Shepherd and a compassionate Father.

Betty died a few weeks later. As often as I think of her, and our private afternoon sing, I recall Colossians 2:2 (KJV), "That their hearts might be comforted, being knit together in love." And so they were.

LOVE EXTRAVAGANTLY

by Marita Littauer, Albuquerque, New Mexico

When I was writing the chapter called "Celebrate Your Path," on the value of a mission statement, for my book *You've Got What It Takes!* I looked at my own life. I realized that I had a defining statement or theme for my professional ventures, but I did not have a personal one. I knew how valuable my professional statements were, so I could easily see the importance of a personal one. I was recommending this to my readers, but I did not have one myself. I mulled this over in my mind for several days. I focused on the need for a personal purpose statement, the "path" of my personal life.

I had been attending a women's Bible study on the book of Ephesians at my church. As a part of my personal preparation for the study, I had been reading the chapter covered each week in several different versions of the Bible. The night before class I read Ephesians 5 in *The Message*. I wasn't looking for a personal mission statement, although it had been in the back of my mind. I was simply preparing for the lesson the next day.

But, as I read, this verse jumped out at me, and I instantly knew it was my personal "path"—at least for now. "Observe how Christ loved us. His love was not cautious but extravagant. He didn't love in order to get something from us but to give everything of himself to us. Love like that." As I read that, I knew that my personal mission is to love my husband with extravagance, not to get, but to give everything of myself. As I cook breakfast or dinner, as I do the dishes, as I do the laundry— all of these things are something of myself I can give, not expecting to get in return. My husband has had a rough time recently. He is not in a place to be able to give much. But I am. I have written that verse out on my mirror in the bathroom to remind me that that is my mission.

I find that I have to frequently repeat this mantra to myself, as it is contrary to my human nature.

Shortly after taking on this idea of loving extravagantly, I had to put it to the test. Chuck has a large radio-controlled model airplane that has been a part of his life for over twenty years. He built it and has too much of himself invested in it to risk flying it. With a five-foot wingspan, you cannot just tuck it anyplace. In our current home, it hangs up near the peak of the cathedral ceiling in the family room. It is bright red with Red Baron-like decals. It is sure to be noticed. Since it is important to Chuck, I have accepted it as a conversation piece—and you can be sure it is! It has traveled with us to eight different houses.

Recently he took the airplane down to take to a model airplane show. He spent hours cleaning off the accumulated dust that had firmly attached itself to every surface. The plane was very popular at the show and he discovered how valuable it really is. Before he put it back on its hook, he wanted to protect it. He covered the body and wings with plastic dry cleaning bags, advertising and all.

I like my home to look like a showplace, so you can imagine that even having the airplane there is an act of compromise and love. Having it covered with baggy dry cleaning bags with words on them required something altogether different.

"I'll never be able to entertain again," I wailed. After my outburst, which I knew was an overreaction, I went outside and trimmed my roses. As I took a deep breath, "love extravagantly" came to mind. Does it really matter if the airplane has a bag over it? What is more important, that my husband be happy or that I have a lovely home? Hmm. . . that was tough. "Love extravagantly," I told myself. I came back in and apologized—ready to accept the dry cleaning bags. Meanwhile, he had decided that I was right and it was really ugly. He took the plane down, removed the dry cleaning bags, and was replacing them with clear plastic wrap that clings tightly to every curve and doesn't even show!

Ah, the power of a personal mission statement—not cautious but extravagant, not to get but to give. Love extravagantly; Christ encourages us to do no less.

CHICKEN AND CHECKS

by Karen O'Connor, San Diego, California

"During my active ministry, I always started my day with prayer in my study," said my husband's cousin Harry, a retired minister. "I liked to sit, palms face up in a gesture of openness. Before closing, I thanked the Lord for all His blessings and then asked Him to direct me throughout the day."

One Thursday morning, just after Harry finished praying, the word "chicken" came to his mind. "I wondered what that was about," he said, "so I thought, all right, I'll order chicken and see where it leads."

He reached for the phone to call Redman's Barbecue, where he had placed many orders in the past, when suddenly he remembered that Redman's barbecued chicken only on Tuesdays. But still the urge to order wouldn't go away.

Harry called anyway, expecting the usual response, but the cook surprised him. "As a matter of fact," he said, "the chickens came in later than usual so we cooked 'em today!"

Harry drove right over to Redman's and bought twelve fresh chickens right off the spit. "The number twelve just popped out of my mouth," he said with a chuckle. "I wasn't sure even then what this was all about. He put the chickens in his car and began driving. He didn't have a plan. But as he drove he felt an urge to turn onto this street, or into that driveway, sometimes as far away as two miles. "I stopped at whatever house I was drawn to," said Harry, "five in all."

The amazing part of this story is that everyone Harry encountered said they had been praying for food, for money, for provision. Each man and woman he met was desperate in some way.

"At the first house," said Harry, "a man had just come home from the hospital. He and his wife were in their eighties. She had a heart condition so was unable to cook or shop without help." They were in need of food that very day.

"Next, I met a woman with three children whose husband had left the family. She had no food and no money. She was really desperate. I left her twenty dollars and two chickens."

At the third house, Harry left a couple of chickens for a couple who was ill. The husband was a retired school principal with heart and visual problems, and his wife was suffering with the flu.

Harry pulled into another driveway, walked up to the front door, and there he met a man who had lost his job two months before. "I left him a couple of chickens as well as money for food."

The last family needed repairs to their house, and they didn't have enough food, "but they had been too proud to ask for help," said Harry.

"By the time I drove home, I realized I had no more chickens," he added. "My wife had the flu and I had offered to cook dinner that night. When she asked me what we were having, I told her what had happened.

"I planned on barbecue chicken," I said, "but they're all gone."

Harry opened the pantry, looked around, then turned to Anne and said with a chuckle, "Looks like it's Dinty Moore stew and crackers!"

While eating, both had tears in their eyes over how God had used Harry that day. Anne suggested they stop and give thanks to the Lord. They joined hands and sang the Doxology. "Praise God from whom all blessings flow. Praise Him all creatures here below. Praise Him above ye heavenly hosts. Praise Father, Son, and Holy Ghost."

"Then I delivered the last bit of news," Harry said, a wry smile crossing his lips. "I told Anne that the money I had set aside for a movie the next night had gone to the woman with three children who was desperate for food."

Anne was all right with that, too. She and Harry dried their eyes, picked up their forks, and dug into their canned stew—one of the best meals they had shared in a long time!

CHAPTER FOUR

Angels Among Us

Keep on loving each other as brothers.
Do not forget to entertain strangers,
for by so doing some people have entertained angels
without knowing it.
HEBREWS 13:1–2

THE GUARDIAN ANGEL

by Renie Szilak Burghardt, Doniphan, Missouri

The first time I saw my guardian angel, he was pointing a machine gun at us. It was early spring of 1945, and my grandparents and I had just emerged from a bunker where we had spent a terror-filled night.

I was nine years old then and lived in Hungary; and World War II was playing havoc with our lives. My grandparents, who were raising me, and I had been on the road in our horse-drawn wagon for many months, searching for a safe place. We had left behind the village of our birth in the Bacska region because Tito and his Communist partisans (guerillas) were closing in on the region.

By day, we'd move swiftly, ready to jump out and take cover in a ditch if warplanes were approaching. By night, we camped with other refuge-seekers, along the roadside. I usually lay bundled up in my feather bed in the back of the wagon, cradling my cat. War was almost all I had known during my nine years; there seemed to be no safe place to be found.

After the Christmas of 1944, when we were almost killed in a bombing in the city we were in at the time, Grandfather decided that a rural area would be safer. So we moved to one in upper Hungary and settled in a small house that had an old cemetery as its neighbor. Here, Grandfather, with the help of some distant neighbors, built a bunker in a flat area behind the house. And on that early spring day in 1945, we spent the entire night in the bunker.

Warplanes buzzed, tanks thundered, and bombs exploded over our heads all night, but finally at dawn everything grew deathly still. Grandfather decided that it would be safe to go back to our house. Cautiously, we crept out into the light of early dawn and headed toward the house. The brush crackled under our feet as we walked past the cemetery. I shivered, holding on to my cat tightly. He had spent the night in the bunker with us.

Suddenly there was a rustle in the bushes just ahead. Two men jumped out and pointed machine guns directly at us.

"*Stoi!*" one of the men shouted. Since we were from an area where both Serbian and Hungarian had been spoken, we knew the word meant "Stop!"

"Russians!" Grandfather whispered. "Stand very still, and keep quiet."

But I was already running after my cat. She had leaped out of my arms when the soldier shouted, so I darted between the soldiers and scooped her up. The younger of the two soldiers, tall and dark-haired, approached me. I cringed, holding Paprika against my chest. The soldier reached out and petted her.

"I have a little girl about your age back in Russia, and she has a cat just like this one," he said, gently tugging one of my blond braids. "And she has long braids, too, just like you." I looked up into a pair of kind brown eyes, and my fear vanished. Grandfather and Grandmother sighed in relief.

Well, both soldiers came back to the house with us and shared in our meager breakfast. We found out from them that the Soviet occupation of Hungary was in progress.

Many atrocities occurred in our area, as well as throughout our country in the following months, but because the young Russian soldier took a liking to me, we were spared. He came to visit often, bringing little treats along for Paprika and me, and always talked longingly of his own little girl. I loved his visits, yet I was terrified of the Russians in general. Then one day, almost a year later, he had some news.

"I've been transferred to another area, *Malka* (Little One), so I won't be able to come and visit anymore. But I have a gift for you," he said, taking something out of his pocket. It was a necklace with a beautiful turquoise Russian Orthodox cross on it. He placed it around my neck. "You wear this at all times, *Malka*. God will protect you from harm." I hugged him tight and then watched him drive away, tears welling in my eyes.

World War II was over, but for the people of Hungary, a life of bondage was at hand. Many men who had been involved in politics or deemed undesirable were being rounded up by the secret police, never to be seen again. Not long after, the knock on the door we dreaded came. They came to take my grandfather away. Fortunately, Grandfather managed to sneak out through a window and go into hiding. Then it was just Grandma and me, trying to survive as best we could. When my cat died, life truly seemed unbearable. Sometimes I would finger the cross my Russian guardian angel had given me, and wonder where he was. Was he back home with his own daughter? Did he remember me?

The time passed in a haze of anxiety and depression. Then, in the fall of 1947, a man came to get us in the middle of the night. He said he would take us to the Austrian border, and we'd be reunited with my grandfather. We traveled all night to a place where the ethnic Germans of Hungary were being loaded into transport trucks and expelled from Hungary. The man would give us counterfeit papers so we could all cross the border to freedom. When we arrived, a weary-looking man with a thick, scraggly beard and a knit cap pulled low over his forehead was waiting for us.

"Grandpa!" I cried out, rushing into his arms. It was so wonderful to see him again.

Then we walked toward the transport truck loaded with dozens of people and got on, fake papers in hand. I knew if we were found out, it would mean Grandpa would get hauled off to prison, and worse yet, he might even be executed. I glanced toward the Russian soldiers who were coming closer to inspect the papers, and I prayed to God to keep us safe.

Then I looked up as a guard boarded the truck. I caught my breath.

"Grandpa," I whispered. "Look, it's my soldier, Ivan! He is checking this truck." I wanted to leap up and run to him, but Grandpa shushed me cautiously.

"Maybe he won't recognize us," he whispered, pulling the knit cap further down his forehead.

Then he was before us. My grandfather handed over our papers without looking up. I leaned closer and put my hand protectively on his shoulder while I peered cautiously at Ivan, hoping to see the old kind sparkle in his eyes. But he was intent upon the papers, his expression grave. I didn't dare to breathe. At last he handed the papers back to Grandpa.

"Everything is in order in this vehicle," he announced. Then, winking at me, he got down, and in an instant the truck began to move on. I looked over my shoulder and caught my guardian angel's eye. "Thank you," I mouthed the words, holding up the cross hanging around my neck. He nodded discreetly, then quickly turned and walked away. As we crossed the border to safety, we all breathed a sigh of relief.

Although we had suffered much sadness during the war, one blessing will always stay with me: the memory of a kind soldier who turned my fear to faith and showed me that God's compassion can be found anywhere, even in the eyes of an enemy.

CROSSINGS

by Carol McAdoo Rehme, Loveland, Colorado

She was death's handmaiden.

And Sue took the job gladly. The hushed night hours lent a kinship to her caretaking. A dim lamp haloed the bed with its circle of light, almost pulsing with the patient's measured breaths. Some saw this as a deathwatch. Sue saw it as a ritual journey—as natural as all the deliveries she once assisted—and she was merely there to attend to the boarding pass. To her, it was simply a trip with God as the destination.

The thick soles of her worn, comfortable shoes padded across the room. Sue smoothed the bleached bedsheet, tucked in his thin blanket, and gently straightened the man's head to a more comfortable position. She plucked spent blossoms from a vase of daisies, tidied the hospital stand, and scooted a vinyl chair closer to the bed. The oak frame groaned as she sank her ample weight into it.

The end wasn't always peaceful. Sometimes it arrived with distress, pain, and fear, but—more often—the opposite was true. Either way, families wanted someone in attendance and, for one reason or another, many couldn't be there themselves. For some it was simply too painful; others couldn't spare the time; a few families lived too far away.

That's why Sue had replaced her cozy retirement slippers with her old nursing shoes. To tend the dying for the living. She felt comfortable volunteering to sit with terminally ill patients between the deep, holy hours of midnight and morning. She rarely slept well at home anyway. And it felt good to be useful again—especially with a patient like this one.

She and Arnold went way back. Why, they had attended the same schools, the same church, the same potluck dinners, and the same weddings and funerals in this small Iowa town. So it was only fitting that she attend his death, and Sue knew it wouldn't be long. She recognized the signs: his skin was mottled, his hands and feet discolored. And, since tonight's shift began, she'd already seen a change in his breathing.

The patient stirred slightly and moaned.

"It's okay, Arnie." Sue's strong, corded hand blanketed his, gently stroking the parchment skin.

His eyes, as pale as a work shirt that had suffered too many washings, opened and stared beyond her.

"You've had a good life, Arnie, but there's an even better one waiting." She reached over to caress his grizzled cheek. "When you're ready, Arnie, just cross over because God is waiting. It's okay. When you're ready."

And then it happened.

She felt it at almost the same time as she witnessed it: his wide-eyed look of radiant joy and then his hands reaching toward a presence. Sue glanced hopefully at the foot of the bed, all the while knowing she wouldn't see anyone there. She never could.

Then it came, an almost tangible release—as soft as the tiny last sigh that puffed from Arnie's smiling lips while his arms sank back to the bed. Expelling her own pent-up breath, Sue's trembling fingers brushed his eyelids closed.

Glancing at the clock, she noted the time then paused to feel once more the solemn sacredness in the moment. Fleeting yet perceptible. Hopeful and—hallowed. She felt privileged to behold it.

With a farewell glance toward the bed and a silent prayer of gratitude for a life well lived, Sue walked toward the door. Now it was time to tend the living for the dead. She pulled a list from her pocket with the names and telephone numbers of an entire family. Arnie's family. She had relatives to notify, a wife to comfort, children to console.

Now, she was life's handmaiden.

A "D.P." SCHOOLGIRL

by Renie Szilak Burghardt, Doniphan, Missouri

When at age fifteen I started school in my new country, the United States of America, I was classified as a Displaced Person, a "D.P." "Displaced" pretty much described both my legal status and how I felt about myself that January in 1952. My family and I had lived through World War II in our country, Hungary, followed by four years in a refugee camp. The Lord had seen us through some troubled times, and we were grateful to Him for this new chance that lay before us, but the relatively carefree life of our new country took some getting used to.

There I was, a mousy, shy, "D.P." girl with a thick accent, barely acknowledged by her beautiful American peers. For beautiful is what they were to me, those girls with their ponytails, bobby socks, and carefree, laughing ways. I longed to be just like them. But I was different; my past still haunted me.

The school I went to was an all-girls' school run by nuns. I was aware that it was a great sacrifice for my grandparents to send me there since money was still scarce in our household. I also felt lucky to have been accepted, since my English was still not up to par. One of my Hungarian friends had not been so lucky. She had been placed back into the sixth grade. Mortified, she soon quit school and got a job in a sewing factory.

When June rolled around, I was relieved to be told I would advance to the tenth grade, in spite of my poor academic performance. That knowledge meant a happier summer vacation. I spent that first summer in America working part-time at our local dime store and hanging out with Hungarian friends in my spare time.

When school began again in September, I entered the building with trepidation. Although some of the girls greeted me cheerily enough, I knew I had not turned into a swan over the summer. Then I walked into Sister Mary Ann's sophomore English class, and soon everything changed.

Sister Mary Ann had the bluest eyes, a smile that lit up the classroom, and a gentle, understanding manner. She was sensitive to my pain and began asking me about my life in front of the class so that my classmates could better understand why I seemed different from them. Upon occasion, she gently implored them to put themselves in my shoes and see how they would feel in them. My mind soon concluded that God had sent an angel into my life! Then the good sister gave us our first assignment of the new school term.

"I want you all to write an essay of at least four pages about something memorable that has happened to you. It will be due a week from today." When we left her classroom, I determined to put my heart and soul into an assignment for the first time since I'd begun to attend that school.

I wrote about being crammed, with hundreds of other hopeful refugees, on a ship taking us to our new country. I wrote about Dave, the young American who befriended me and brought me my first Coke. I wrote about my first sight of the Statue of Liberty and about being tagged for processing to the main building of Ellis Island, an enormous hall filled with throngs of bewildered people. And I realized that I liked writing.

The day after we handed in our essays, Sister Mary Ann had me read mine to the class. To my big surprise, my classmates applauded me when I finished. Then I was sent to read it throughout the school. I was astonished when I got the same reaction. I was mobbed in the hallway by girls telling me how much they liked my essay, asking me questions, paying attention to me. Suddenly, I was more than just that mousy "D.P." girl. I was being accepted as one of them.

God blessed me with Sister Mary Ann, a caring teacher. I shall always be grateful to that gentle soul in the blue-and-white habit. In my hour of need, He sent her to care for me, just as He had always done. Perhaps "D.P." really stands for "Divine Plan"?

LESSONS FROM MY ANGEL

by Susan Fahncke, Kaysville, Utah

Blue eyes. Blond hair. A smile that lights up a room. My sister. The drive to the hospital is long, too long. I am bringing her home with me. She is twenty-seven years old, and we found out five months ago that she has a brain tumor. Now they tell us that she will not make it, that the most they can hope for is to shrink the tumor as small as possible in order to buy her a little more time. They don't know my sister.

I walk into the hospital and find her in the physical therapy room. Angel's right side is paralyzed from the tumor, so they are helping her try to strengthen that side. So far, she can lift her right arm up a couple of inches. Sweat is streaming down her face at the effort. "C'mon, arm!" She grimaces at the strain. This is as close to a complaint as I have ever heard from her.

I sit back and watch her. I find myself doing this a lot these days. Trying to capture and freeze moments to file away and save for "later." She simply amazes me. In her shoes, I would be doing a lot of crying, serious complaining, and endless whining. Not her. I have never heard her, not even once, ask, "Why me?"

At home, she loves the room I have fixed up for her. We tape the countless cards to the wall where she can see them. She smiles at them. It comforts her knowing many people care. Nighttime is finally here and I am exhausted. It has been a long day of lifting and constantly helping her. But I feel good. I am taking care of my sister, and I am honored to do it. It's getting late and I get my kids to bed and help her dress and get into bed. Helping her into the bed breaks my heart. She trembles from head to toe. Her right arm dangles, dead and useless and bruised from shoulder to fingertips from constantly hitting things she can't feel with it. I swing her legs onto the bed and we smile into each other's same-color blue eyes. I hold back the tears until I get upstairs.

My husband is asleep and I am finally alone, so I let the waves of pain wash over me. Seeing her so helpless and weak and suffering is like shards of glass in my soul. I can't take it anymore. Sobbing, I begin to pray. I am no longer asking God; I am now yelling at Him, begging, pleading angrily to not let her be like this. I run out of words and just say, "Please, no," over and over, crying until I am sick. Worn out, I head downstairs, knowing I need to sleep so I can have the strength to get through another day like today.

I pause outside her room and peek in to make sure she's okay. She is awake and sees me. "You okay?" I ask for the six hundredth time today.

"I'm fine; I just can't sleep." She tells me the steroids that reduce the swelling in her brain keep her awake. I plop down in the rocking chair next to her bed and put my feet up, scrunching them under her pillow. I settle in and we begin to talk. She shocks me with what she says next.

"I know you're worried about me. I don't want you to worry. I'm really okay." She goes on to tell me how the worst is behind her, that things are getting better. She says she will get well. I look at her skeptically and wonder if the tumor has made her dense. She ignores my disbelief and continues in her efforts to comfort me. She tells me that she knows why she is sick, and that it's necessary to bring our family closer together. She doesn't mind and feels it a privilege to endure something that will effect changes in others. She tells me of the many, many blessings that have already come about because of her cancer. So many people—strangers—praying. Her faith has grown in leaps and bounds. Her life has been touched by so many people she calls her angels.

What she doesn't realize is how many people she has impacted. When she was in the hospital, she would have Mom buy dozens of roses and bring them to her. She would then take the bouquets apart and, one by one, take them to every single patient on her floor. She would also give them to the kind, wonderful nurses who took care of her. She spreads light wherever she goes. It's an awesome sight.

We talk all night, deep into the morning. Finally, as the gray turns to pinks and brilliant oranges shimmering through her window, she is tired enough to sleep. I leave her room and climb into my own bed for a couple of hours of rest. I feel lighter and more peaceful than I have in a long time. I smile and know God arranged our long talk.

The days go by and we get into the routine of things. Daily radiation and physical therapy. Countless medications. Hair falling out and the subsequent buying of hats. Cutting up her food, putting the toothpaste on her toothbrush. Even my tiny son, Noah, at two years old, helps her to get across the room by pushing on her bottom. Everyone helps and my husband is amazing. He lifts her gently out of the van and picks her up when she falls and I don't have the strength. My sister is right; this has brought out the best in everyone.

Sometimes I lose the peaceful feeling I got when we talked. Sometimes I feel numb; other times I can't stand the pain of seeing her suffer, of seeing her one good hand tremble with the stress of bringing a bite of cereal to her mouth, shaking until the cereal falls off the spoon. It still breaks my heart. Last night was one of those times.

I had fixed her shower and left the door open a crack so I could hear the water shut off—my signal to help her out and get her dressed. In the kitchen, I heard a giant *sploosh*, then a thud and a crash.

Heart pounding, I rushed into the bathroom to find her lying on her back in the tub, shower curtain on the floor and water everywhere. "Are you okay?" I shrieked yet again. She muttered that she was fine and apologized for the mess. It was then that I cracked—looking at my young, vibrant sister, lying like a stuck turtle on its back, her body a rainbow of hundreds of bruises, her head shiny and bald, thin strings of the remnants of her hair clinging wetly to her face. I helped her up and didn't let her see my tears and my body shaking with uncontrollable sobs. I would give anything, anything at all to wave a magic wand and make her strong and well again.

I got her ready and she was fine. Falling happens quite a bit. We'll get her a shower chair. She keeps saying she's fine.

A little later, we are sitting on the couch. My husband is down in his office, working. The kids are in bed, and Angel and I are sitting on the couch, just vegging in front of the TV. She looks at me very intensely and suddenly says, "Stop worrying about me."

I turn to look at her and realize I'm not hiding my feelings very well. She begins to cry and says, "I am so blessed, and I have been so well taken care of. Everything I need, I have. I *will* get well, so stop worrying so much. Get on with your life and start *living* again!"

I let a few tears escape and feel the knot in my stomach ease a bit. Her faith and her indomitable spirit are an inspiration. I decide right then and there that for her, I will do it. I will, of course, still worry and feel pain at her suffering, but I will also try harder to equal her faith. I will laugh more and live more. I smile and my face feels weird. I realize that it's been a long time since I've smiled. I do it again and she laughs. We both laugh together, and I say a silent prayer of thanks for this gift that is my sister. My Angel.

⁀ Make sure to read more great stories by Susan Fahncke in volume one of God Allows U-Turns: True Stories of Hope and Healing.

ANGEL ON EARTH

by Tamara Swinson, Tulsa, Oklahoma

Most people, especially women, roll their eyes and grin when the subject of "mother-in-law" is brought to the conversation. Wives are almost always thought to be an invasion in the lives of their sons, almost with the idea that no one is good enough for their little boy. Perhaps women don't see that mothers-in-law can be a real treasure.

My husband, Shawn, and I were both raised in loving Christian homes (regardless of the wrong path I had taken prior to my meeting my husband), and I was sure that when I met his parents, they would turn their noses up. This did not bother me terribly, because I had no intentions of being married at that time. We were just best friends. Still, the prospect that they would immediately judge me because I was pregnant (with my second child) and unmarried was definitely an issue in my mind.

The first time I met Barbara, my mother-in-law, was when Shawn's parents were in Tulsa on one of their trips from Vernon, Texas, to visit her own mother-in-law. I wore a big sweater to hide my belly, but I was sure they'd notice. They never seemed to, and even when Shawn told them, they practically shrugged. It was never a problem or up for discussion. Later, Bill, my father-in-law, told me that it never mattered to them. What mattered to them was their relationship with their son.

When I gave birth to my second daughter, and Shawn confessed his love to me, I was immediately accepted into the family. My kids called Shawn "Daddy," and they called his parents "Grandma and Grandpa." My in-laws have answered their predetermined demand of grandparenthood more devotedly and more lovingly than most grandparents do for their natural grandchildren.

I still can see my mother-in-law constantly snapping pictures. It used to drive us all crazy. My husband called her "the fastest camera loader in the West." She always got doubles without question, and I have albums full of pictures that she gave freely. There are pictures of the week she took care of little Brittany when Shawn and I went to the Bahamas for our honeymoon. There are pictures of parties at Shawn's aunt's house, with each person forced to stop at the door so she could get a shot of his or her smiling face. There were always at least twenty or thirty family members there, and there was always laughter on each holiday. There are pictures of the girls when they were small, eating cereal early in the morning, wearing their undies. This proud grandmother took pictures at all school functions that they could make it to, although later she'd be able to make it to more. She was so proud of her granddaughters, and everyone knew it. There was no shame there. It was as if these girls had been there with her in those pictures since the day of their births.

In 1995 I can remember calling my father-in-law, Bill, and saying that he was to be a grandfather, and without hesitation, he laughed. "What? Again?" And they proceeded to lavish the unborn baby with all the splendors that grandparents feel he/she should have. Naturally, I was sought after to pose for that camera. Bill and Barbara gathered up the rest of the extended family to move us into our new home in Tulsa, where we would later begin raising three healthy children.

Three years ago, my in-laws decided to move here, buy a house, and allow Shawn's grandmother, who'd had a terrible stroke, to live with them. It was a difficult transition for my in-laws, but they love Grandmother, so they made the best of it, saying good-bye to their business, their friends, and their lives in Vernon, Texas. My mother-in-law continued to be special, always giving of herself. In any way possible, I can remember them being there for us.

About one and a half years ago, my mother-in-law began acting strange. By that, I mean she wept very, very easily. She began to lose her way of speaking clearly. The words were very slow. My father-in-law took her to the doctor's office, and the doctor did about one year's worth of tests on her. He was sure that there would be a stroke found. There was not. The doctor was so stumped and frustrated, I suppose, that he concluded there was nothing wrong. My father-in-law gasped, "Nothing wrong? She can barely speak." Expectedly, then her doctor sent my in-laws to a specialist. Shortly after that, I had a terrible nightmare. I know this premonition was the Lord preparing me for what was about to happen. There was no way, in all honesty, to prepare my husband and me for any of the future news.

The phone rang, and I can remember it had been raining that morning. The fan was ticking softly in my ears as my father-in-law whispered, "They know what's wrong with Barb. . . . It's not good."

My mother-in-law is fifty-five, and she is dying. Even now as I write this, I cannot see through my tears. She has a disease called Lou Gehrig's, and it affects all of the muscles in her body. She will eventually become so weak that she will go to be with the Lord. Her body will no longer be able to breathe. Though her mind remains, and she knows exactly what is happening, she cannot tell us her pain. She can barely smile now. I cannot imagine what she is thinking when we walk through the door with three screaming kids, like always. The moments that Noah, her grandson, crawls into her lap and she is able to wrap her curled-up hands around him are fewer than I am sure she'd like. It must be heaven to her when her oldest granddaughter, Katarina, says that she wants to teach her to say "I love you" in sign language.

Then there is her little Brittany, who comes giggling in to ask if she can please have some chocolate or some jelly beans from the jar on the end table.

Still, with the help of her special seat in the van, which enables her weak body to ride in the vehicle, she insists that she has to go to lunch. She inscribes notes on paper that she has to go to the craft places she once visited without a problem. She has to watch the birds from her windows. She has to live. She has to make things like she always has. Even as I look around, I see her signature on so many things that she has lovingly painted, glued, and stitched. She can no longer walk well, but she still tries one day at a time. Her food must be blended, because even pepper on her potatoes is difficult to swallow. She chokes and breathes heavily, but she is there, in her eyes. She has lost so much weight, I hardly recognize her. Her rings have had to be sized, and her face is longer. Though she looks like a different person, she is still that same light to me.

Her caregiver, who recently lost her own husband, is so devoted to my Barbara. She comes to the house every day to make sure Barbara is getting along okay, and she assists her in making memory scrapbooks. I suppose they will be her legacy one day, when the kids are old enough to see how very much she truly loves them.

Bill works long hours as a salesman, only to come home and help her to bed. He serves her constantly in the ways that she once served him in their almost forty years of marriage. With all this family, and all her friends, she must delight in her heart that God truly loves her. I cannot understand why this is happening to someone who has had such a zest for life, but I know that it is not important that I understand it. It is important that I see life for what it is. It is so short, and it is so precious. Perhaps it is because God knows that she is ready to be cradled in His arms. There is a time when all angels must go to heaven.

LILY, THE CLOWN, RESTS TODAY

by LaRose Karr, Sterling, Colorado

Lillian, a good friend from my church, passed away. Her funeral is today. I stand looking at her and hesitate to reach out and touch her hand. I have touched others who have gone on before; this was nothing new, but something held me back. I wasn't ready to say good-bye. Instead I turned and went into the sanctuary and sat near the beautiful bouquets of fresh flowers. Among them were balloons in memory of "Lily the Clown."

I noticed one particular Mylar balloon had the sweet smiling face of a clown on it. I watched as the breeze from the air conditioner gently tossed it about and thought back on what I knew of Lily's life.

Lily wore what suited her and it was always eccentric. She would be immaculately dressed and very clean, but the outfits were always extraordinary: leopard prints, stripes, or delicate pink lace, furry hats, large hats, jeweled hats, high heels, low heels, or white high-top boots, and lots and lots of jewelry. Miss Lillian loved her jewelry.

She was known locally as "Lily the Clown" because she walked or rode in over forty parades in our town. She loved to dress up as a clown for parties and entertain people, especially children.

Lily kept historical records for our church and the community. At our church's forty-year anniversary, I was thrilled to read the many newspaper articles and clippings that she had collected and to look at albums and pictures that were taken through the years. She wrote a yearly newsletter telling everyone of all the things she had done that past year.

She sang in the choir and participated in our yearly Easter and Christmas programs, keeping up with even the youngest of the group. She was very involved in volunteer work and didn't miss a beat on most of our community activities. She even found time to keep an extensive flower garden around her home. Her love of gardening was evident in the pictures displayed at the funeral.

Lillian knew her time on earth was coming to a close. She wrote her own obituary, which chronicled the beginning with her birth in Kentucky to life in Michigan and then in Colorado. She thought it important to journal your life in words and pictures to pass on to the children and grandchildren. She picked out the songs to be sung at the funeral. At the beginning of the service was "Wind Beneath My Wings" and at the end was "I Will Always Love You."

Her grandson read a eulogy that he had written about his grandmother. He said that every square inch of her walls were covered with photos of her family. Her love of her family was evident in everything she did. He told of the time she was asked to come to a grandchild's ball game and cheer the team on. Little did they know that she would arrive with two large blue pom-poms and lead them all in a cheer. . .the entire crowd enjoying her enthusiasm.

Here was one woman who loved life to its fullest! Not a day went by that she did not do something for the community or a loved one. Whether it was her writing, gardening, singing, clowning, volunteering, or just simply listening, she was there for one and all. Our flamboyant angel, Lily, would be greatly missed.

As I stepped up to her casket and took one last look at Lillian in her pink dress and tiara on her snow-white hair, I slowly reached out and affectionately patted her hand. It was time to say good-bye.

I heard later that the funeral director drove her down the entire parade route one last time on the way to the cemetery. The final chapter of her long life of ministry and service ends appropriately, "Lily, the clown, rests today."

⌐ *Make sure to read LaRose Karr's story, "No Morning Is Just Like Another," in volume one of* God Allows U-Turns: True Stories of Hope and Healing.

CHAPTER FIVE

God's Plan

In his heart a man plans his course,
but the LORD determines his steps.
Proverbs 16:9

IN THE MIDST OF A BLESSING

by Carolyn Fox, West Bend, Wisconsin

I missed my father. This was the anniversary of his death and solitude beckoned me. Kneeling at the headstone carved with my maiden name and the names of both my parents and paternal grandparents, I whispered a prayer, left one round pebble on the headstone to mark that I'd been there, and wiped away tears with the back of my hand. The pansies and impatiens bent gently over the soft brown earth, waving a colorful good-bye as I looked back once more at the headstone. I climbed slowly into the Jeep that Dad had left me and turned on the ignition.

Looking back at the headstone one last time, I maneuvered my Jeep around the curve where Dad had taught my sister and me to back up the family car, years ago in high school. I smiled, remembering my growing frustration at the time at Dad's insistence on perfection. "Back it up again," he'd say, each time with a little more determination and a little less patience. "We can leave when you get it right." Today I wistfully mouthed a silent "Thanks, Dad," forgetting the frustration of that earlier time as I turned the corner. I had to admit to possessing good "backing up" skills after all that practice.

I came to another familiar bend in the cemetery driveway and felt an overwhelming urge to stop my Jeep. *Park here,* urged a voice inside. I got out of my Jeep and began to walk.

I was looking for another grave site—a reminder of yet another loss. Myrle. A woman who had been my adopted grandmother and whose Irish spirit reminded me often to "never give up hope or prayer." She had been solid and strong my entire life. I missed her. I needed a dose of that Irish fighting spirit today. Only a few short months ago, I had plodded futilely through the icy and snow-covered gravestones of this section of the cemetery, desperately trying to find her buried headstone. Only Dad knew exactly where it was located. *If he were here,* I thought, *he would take me to it.*

Following the intuition that was guiding my steps, I walked directly diagonally across the section of ground where I parked my Jeep, not even looking at the names on the stones. I stopped when I felt I had arrived. I was standing directly over Myrle's name. Despite the warmth of the day, I was shivering. Tears flooded my eyes as I knelt down and touched her headstone. I felt Myrle's loving presence and the return of her "Irish spirit" in my veins as I whispered a prayer of gratitude to my Creator. I sat there awhile and pictured Myrle smiling at me as I soaked up the sunshine and played with the dirt around her headstone. Green had been her favorite color. An Irish color. Myrle loved flowers. Thankful for the divine guidance that had led me to her grave site, I resolved to bring some color to share with her.

I walked slowly and deliberately back across the grass toward my car, remembering how to return to Myrle's grave in this section. As I approached, I noticed for the first time that a van had stopped and was idling just behind my Jeep. A woman sat in the driver's seat, her window rolled down and sunglasses perched atop her head over puffy eyes.

"Excuse me," she said softly. "I'm sorry to bother you. But I have to ask you a question." I approached her van hesitantly, feeling the same force that had guided me only moments ago toward Myrle's grave. I smiled at the woman.

"What does 'JD Mom' stand for?" she inquired, pointing to my license plate.

"Most people don't understand it," I replied with a grin. "I'm a lawyer and the degree they give you is a Juris Doctor—'JD'—and I have two little children, so I thought it would be clever to have a customized license plate to emphasize those two important things in my life. . . ." I stopped speaking. The woman had tears in her eyes. I continued again. "It means 'lawyer mom.' "

The woman was silent, as tears streamed down her face. When she finally began to speak to me, the sunlight cast a rainbow over the hood of her idling van.

"I want to thank you," she said softly. I looked at her, confused.

She continued. "My son Justin died on the Fourth of July. He was killed in a motorcycle accident. It's been almost four years but I still miss him so terribly. . . ." Her voice broke, but after a moment she continued. "I came to the cemetery today to visit him, and I have been praying since I woke up this morning for God to send me a sign that Justin is still with me. And I have you to thank." She paused only for an instant. Gazing intently at me, she continued, "I came around this corner and froze when I saw your license plate. You are my sign."

She paused again. "My son's name was Justin David. And I was known to all his friends as JD's mom."

I blinked back the tears and felt shivers climbing up my spine. I felt an incredible warmth enveloping me. Justin's mother was crying, but they were tears of joy. I felt a divine connection to a woman I'd never met until today. And yet I felt I had known her for a long time.

"I'm so glad I was a sign for you." I was finally able to speak. "This kind of stuff happens to me all the time. Some people call these coincidences but my pastor calls these 'God-incidences.' I'm here today because it's the anniversary of my father's death, and I haven't been able to find my grandmother's grave since she died. I believe I was divinely guided to find it," I said, pointing backward over my shoulder. "I used to walk every section of this cemetery with my dad when I was a little girl when he placed flags on the veterans' graves."

Realizing I was nervously rambling on, I stopped. "I'm so sorry you lost your son. That must be terribly difficult." My voice dropped off. We looked at each other, she and I, two complete strangers, bonded in spirit.

We continued to look at each other, completely embracing the moment of awesome connection. God had brought us together. Justin's mother spoke again. "Thank you again for being here. Thank you for being my sign."

The woman shifted her van into drive and looked back at me. "You know, don't you," she said, smiling, "that we're in the midst of a blessing?"

She reached from the van and squeezed my hands. They felt like they were on fire. There was warmth surging throughout my body. I watched her van drive slowly away, and I whispered a prayer of thanks. I stepped toward my Jeep, focusing my eyes on "JD Mom." The familiar passage I'd learned long ago in Sunday school came back to me now. "Where two or three come together in my name, there am I with them" (Matthew 18:20).

In the midst of a blessing—what better place to gather together in His name?

MY SPIRITUAL BULLETPROOF VEST

by Dr. Carol Jackson, St. Louis, Missouri

In the thirteenth chapter of the book of Romans, police officers and authoritative figures are referred to as ministers of God, ordained to keep and maintain peace. Throughout my career as a patrol officer, I have always carried this Scripture with me. I have always considered my profession to be more of a "calling" than just a career. Given some of the heart-wrenching and dangerous calls that I have handled, I have had to embrace that Scripture emotionally, physically, and psychologically to assure myself that I was where God wanted me to be.

We always pray that God will protect us from seen and unseen danger, but approximately fifteen years ago I was involved in a call that, if I had ever doubted the protection of the almighty God, I never would again.

I was on patrol during the midnight shift driving west on a main boulevard in a very affluent area of town at approximately 3:00 A.M. The officers on our department patrol solo, so I was alone. It was very quiet with hardly any traffic.

As I approached an area on the boulevard that intersected with a highway, I observed a vehicle backing away from the entrance of a highway back onto the boulevard. Even if the maneuver hadn't caught my attention, the car itself would have. It stuck out like a sore thumb in that particular neighborhood. It was a rather beat-up-looking older vehicle that was out of place in this neighborhood.

I followed the vehicle, which was occupied by four men, as it turned off the boulevard to slowly cruise down a secluded residential street. When I called in the license plate, the issue on the license number returned on a totally different vehicle than the one I was following. I did not know what I had at this point, but I had to stop the vehicle. When I initiated my emergency lights in order to stop the vehicle, everything went wild.

The car took off at a deadly speed down narrow residential streets. I found myself in a pursuit, trying to tell dispatchers what was going on. I was driving with one hand, the other hand on the radio, shouting information for what seemed like an eternity. I could hear the sirens of the backup units in the distance, but they seemed so far away that I wondered if they would get to my location before something happened. I was about to call off the pursuit when I saw some type of long weapon being thrown from the vehicle. Now I couldn't call off the pursuit due to a weapon being involved. As I informed the dispatcher of the first weapon, I saw another smaller weapon being thrown from the vehicle. I remember reaching down to feel my bulletproof vest.

When the vehicle stopped short right in front of me on a side street, I almost rammed it. Before I could move my hands from the steering wheel, the driver's door of the other vehicle flew open and the driver ran toward me with an object in his hand. Although I know it was a matter of only seconds, it seemed like an eternity as I watched him run toward me with what I realized was a small handgun. I saw him cocking the automatic weapon.

I was trapped. He was coming too fast. Even if I got my weapon out, I knew I would not be able to get a shot off before he shot me. I just looked at him as he prepared to shoot me.

I saw his eyes grow very large while he looked at me. He stood as still as a statue, holding the gun aimed directly at my head but making no move to pull the trigger. I could not even imagine what he was thinking. Was he trying to intimidate me? Was he going to shoot me? Suddenly, the suspect let out a loud scream, threw the gun, and ran for his car.

I had the advantage then. I jumped out of my car and told him to stop or I would shoot him. I ordered the other suspects out of the car, one by one, with their arms raised. The suspect who threatened to kill me would not look at me or talk to me. I was holding them at gunpoint when my backup units arrived.

I never did find out what made that man scream and run. He looked like he saw something when he was looking at me. I knew that God had allowed this suspect to see something—maybe an angel. I have supposed that an angel would have been an awesome sight. Maybe the glory of the Lord surrounded me in protection, bathing me in a light only he could see. Whatever it was he saw, the suspect didn't dare remain in my presence, let alone kill me.

I have often thought of that incident while putting on my bullet-proof vest before going to work. Yes, I continued to wear the vest. More importantly, I made sure I never left the house without the spiritual bulletproof vest that saved my life from the bullet that was meant to kill me.

1951

by Ron DiCianni, Buffalo Grove, Illinois

Nearly fifty years ago, a young mother of Italian descent walks the streets of Chicago on her way to a doctor's appointment. This is the kind of appointment that has the ability to change the course of life and the future. For reasons never fully explained, she is determined to terminate the baby inside her. Maybe it is the fear of another mouth to feed. Or the exhaustion of an already crowded home inhabited by not only her husband and child, but her mother and sister as well. Italians are well-known for keeping an extended family together. Basically, what that boils down to is that when you do something wrong, you are disciplined by more than your parents.

Everybody takes their turn. This also applies to hugs and the proverbial pulling on the cheek to show affection. Everything becomes a family affair. Possibly this new addition would be the straw that breaks the camel's back. Whatever the reason, her footsteps lead her to the place where at least one life will never be the same.

As she sits awaiting the "procedure," she is told that an injection will be needed. Consenting, she nods approval for getting on with the deed. Somewhere between the doctor filling the syringe and it reaching her arm, heaven speaks to this woman.

In her words, "I heard God tell me not to go through with this, for, 'I have a plan for this baby.' " At the insistence of the Creator, who formed that baby in the mother's womb, she boldly obeys, pushing the oncoming needle away, and walks out the door. A pivotal U-turn, as important as missing a flight that you find out eventually crashes.

Throughout the years, I heard that story over and over again, along with my fair share of cheek-pulling and kisses laced with garlic from loving relatives. You see, that was my mother who made the U-turn and gave me my life.

Mom is now nearly ninety years old and has Alzheimer's. She resides in a care center close to my home, where I visit her on occasion. The visits are more for my benefit than hers, because the disease has taken away her memory. When I call her "Mom," there's a faraway look in her eyes that tells me she would love to say, "I was hoping it was you," but a thief has stolen that ability. When the nurses say to her, "Leona, your baby is here to see you. Don't you recognize him?" she sweetly smiles and says, "No, but he's very nice."

There are days when I wish she could remind me that "God's picked you" as she so often did. There won't be any more of those days for me. But there will always be the knowledge that she loved me enough to turn the wheel of time in my direction so that I could know what I was supposed to be.

Every time I paint, I put a little of her into the work. Thanks, Mom.

SURPRISE US FOR DINNER, GOD!

by Delores Liesner, Racine, Wisconsin

"We are filled to capacity," the voice on the telephone said, "but if you believe God has told you to come, then come. I can't tell you where we'll put you, but I can almost guarantee you will not be rooming together."

We had pulled off the road and called Glen Eyrie, the Colorado headquarters of the Navigators, an evangelistic Christian organization. We had told them we were on our way to the conference at the suggestion of a mentor. The first meeting was less than twenty-four hours from then, and although we'd gotten the vacation time, packed quickly, and made arrangements for our children, we'd forgotten about registration!

Encouraged to "have faith and come on," we continued, alternating driving and sleeping until seven o'clock the following evening. "You're the couple who called from the road!" the college student at the registration table gasped. "Why, you would have had to drive all night to get here." Barely repressing yawns, we confirmed that it was exactly twenty-four hours from Wisconsin to Colorado. He quickly directed us to double doors on our left where the first meeting had just begun. "Come back after the service," he encouraged, "and I'll have your information ready."

Two hours later we returned to the table and received our separate room assignments. The only time we saw each other the rest of the week was if we got to the evening meetings at the same time or when we sat together at meals. The time flew by as we took notes, listened, and learned.

With so little time together during that week, we had plenty to talk about on the drive home.

Time after time as we talked away the miles we were amazed how the separate workshops had prepared each of us in similar ways to build up our relationship with each other and our relationship with God. I shouldn't have been surprised, then, when Ken said he felt God telling him to do something that seemingly had nothing to do with the messages or workshops.

Pulling over to the side of the road, he said he felt God wanted us to support a particular missionary. I gasped. "Me, too," I whispered in awe—"a particular amount for a certain amount of time."

"I think God was talking to both of us," he said, and then asked, "How much, for how long?" His voice blended with mine as together we stated the same amount and for the same time period! Ken took my hands in his and prayed that God would show us how we could do what He asked, and then pulled the car back onto the highway.

Once back home, we sat at the kitchen table as Ken spread the budget out before us. There was no extra money—particularly not in the amount we'd felt we were to give. We pored over and over the numbers and finally he said, "I don't know about you, but I see only one amount on that budget that equals the commitment." Silently I nodded and pointed to the line that said "food." "How can we go without food for six months?" he asked. I wondered, *Would God ask us to do that?*

However, we both felt it a miracle that God had spoken to both of us separately and decided that we needed to obey. As we prayed beside the bed that night, we told God that He would have to "surprise us" for dinner, because we weren't sure what we'd eat after the next few meals.

When the phone rang the next morning, I had to pray that my concern did not show in my voice. Though we'd not seen or heard from my oldest brother in several years, he chose that day to call and say he was thinking of me. He said that he and his family would like to stop by to visit and have lunch the next day. Then he said, "Would you mind if I brought a couple of chickens for the pot for Sunday dinner?"

Sunday? Two days of meals! I thought; what he heard was, "Mind! I should say not! Bring them on, Brother!"

The next day when the doorbell rang, I raced down the stairs, happily anticipating a reunion with my brother and his family. When I opened the door, Chris stood there staring at me with a surprised look on his face. "Oh, my goodness!" he said, slapping his forehead. "I didn't even *ask* you!"

"Ask me what?" I responded.

"If you have a freezer."

"Well, yes, we've got a freezer. . .but it's empty," I hesitantly admitted.

Any worry about my hesitant response fled as a big, silly grin spread across Chris's face and he grabbed me in a bear hug.

Laughing, he told me to open the door and point the way to the freezer. Ken, Chris, and his sons trooped past me with three huge picnic coolers and headed to the basement.

Chuckling and tossing packages into the freezer which Ken had quickly plugged in, Chris explained: "I was butchering with my father-in-law yesterday and had this big urge come over me to get you some meat and to do it right away. I don't know what made me do it, but I'm sure glad you have a freezer."

I'd just noticed that all the odd-shaped packages they'd tossed into the freezer were stark white! There wasn't a word on any of them. Noticing my glance, Chris looked sheepish and said he didn't even take time to mark the packages and offered to take them out and identify them. Ken's eyes smiled into mine as we remembered the prayer from the night before when we'd asked God to "surprise us for dinner." We told Chris the packages were fine just the way they were.

It was no surprise that there was exactly enough meat to last through the six monthly payments from our food budget that we'd pledged to the missionary. My faith was renewed day by day as I'd thaw a white package and see what was for dinner.

At the end of the six months, on the final Thursday, just before payday, I'd opened the last blank, odd-shaped white package from the freezer and did not recognize the contents. The cupboards revealed little more than a partial box of macaroni and one last jar of canned tomatoes. Flipping through the pages of a step-by-step picture cookbook, I identified the pieces of meat as "short ribs," then, glancing down to methods of cooking short ribs, I couldn't hold back the tears. "Simmer in canned tomatoes with juice," it read, "then add macaroni."

God had indeed surprised us for dinner! It was a wonderful lesson in faith that we've never forgotten, and is surely part of why we've both memorized Philippians 4:19: "My God will meet all your needs according to his glorious riches in Christ Jesus."

THE WRITE FORCE

by Brette McWhorter Sember, Clarence, New York

I am not religious. I never felt there was any kind of force directing my life. I planned my life, made my choices, and looked for results. The only part of my life that seemed to move on its own was my writing. In high school I edited the school paper and school magazine. I filled notebook after notebook with poetry and journals. There was a magnet that drew words out of my soul and onto paper.

I went to college, got married, and went to law school. Law school was what I was supposed to do. Even the birth of my first child could not keep me from my planned pathway. I graduated, passed the bar exam, and opened my own law practice. My parents were so proud of me. My father came to see my office and brought me a brass shamrock that said "May the road rise up to meet you and the wind always be at your back."

I practiced law more and more unhappily for several years. I would lie awake at night, stressed out, and my husband would ask, "What would you do if you could do anything?" I always answered him that I would write, but I knew that could never be a reality. How could I give up a law practice to write and make no money? When we decided to have a second child, we moved my office into our home so that I could handle my job and the new baby. I decided to take some time off after the birth, making no definite plans to return.

Our son was born and spent the first few days of his life in the nursery on oxygen. Although he was fully recovered in a few days, the experience had cut deeply. My children are very precious to me. I gained a new respect for the fragility of life.

I procrastinated about returning to work. I could not bear to leave my son. Conflicted and confused, I poured my feelings onto paper as I always had when I needed solace. What emerged was an essay about my desire to stay home and the pressure I felt to return to work. It occurred to me that what I had written was good. I sent it to a few magazines and one of them bought it. I was stunned. My joy lasted until I once again felt the pressure to return to my law practice.

Then I received a momentous phone call. A few years earlier I had responded to an ad that a publishing company was looking for a lawyer in my area to write self-help law books. I had never heard back. Then out of the blue, just at this pivotal moment in my life, the editor from the book company called and asked me to write a book. I accepted.

Five books later and in the middle of a successful freelance career, I look back at the moment of that phone call and know that it was more than just coincidence, or dumb luck. I can see clearly now that this was a part of a plan for my life, just not part of the plan that I made. The opportunity came to me at a moment when I could best take advantage of it and needed it most. It is clear to me that there is a higher power and that there is a God directing my life.

Like the gift my father gave me when I opened my law practice, I have found that the road has risen to meet me, in unexpected ways, and the wind that I feel always at my back is the force of God, a power I never thought I would feel in my life.

ARE YOU SITTING DOWN?

by Sandy Sheppard, Vassar, Michigan

My heart thumped excitedly as I dialed my sister's number and waited for her to pick up her phone 2,500 miles away. *Life is so unpredictable,* I reflected. When my husband, Rick, and I married twenty-one-and-a-half years ago, we had things all planned out. I'd teach school while he attended seminary; then he would pastor a church and we'd have a baby.

Some of our plans worked out rather well. I taught for five years; Rick graduated and became associate pastor of a large city church. Everything except the matter of having a baby.

I waited for my sister's phone to ring and thought of other calls and other times. The phone, an impersonal bearer of personal information, had played a large role in my life. Some calls had brought tears of sorrow; some brought tears of joy.

I tapped a pencil on the desk, and my mind replayed a call we had made more than fourteen years ago. First ring. Second ring. . ."We lost the baby." Voice subdued and sorrowful, Rick repeated the message several times to sisters and parents. For four years we had been trying. Now, for the second time in fifteen months, I had miscarried. Since childhood my goal was to be a "mommy, just like my mommy," and now I feared we would never have a child.

I had placed our name on an adoption list three years before but had heard nothing from the agency. Then, in the fall, seventeen months after my second miscarriage, the agency called. "Mrs. Sheppard, are you and your husband still interested in pursuing adoption?" After much prayer and discussion, we decided to go ahead. The home study took several months, and the following spring I received another call at work. "Mrs. Sheppard, I'm happy to tell you that you've been approved to adopt. We should have a newborn baby for you within a few months."

So close, we came so close to adopting, and then we received another call. "Rick, the bishop's cabinet has decided to appoint you to pastor a church in the southern part of the state. It's a small town about 140 miles away." Fearing the worst, we made the next call to the adoption agency and told the social worker our news. Her answer was not what we wanted to hear. "I'm sorry, but that part of the state is outside our jurisdiction. We'll have to transfer your name to another agency. The decision will be up to them, but you may have to wait at least another year. . . ."

Two miscarriages, and now this, I thought. *Our baby is close by and waiting to be born; only now he or she won't be our baby.* Another lucky couple will suddenly become parents—and we had just lost a third child.

For the past four years I had carried a business card in my purse. The card carried the name of Dr. Behrman, one of the country's best fertility specialists. His number represented our final hope, but I had never called for an appointment. As we prepared to move, I pulled out the number and decided to call and set up our first consultation.

Dr. Behrman looked at us across his massive desk, while we sat nervously waiting for his opinion. "I've reviewed your records, Mrs. Sheppard, and I believe you have a hormonal imbalance—one that is easily treated." Several tests proved the doctor's theory right, and I started on progesterone supplements. But months went by and nothing happened. I began to question God's love for me. My faith was being tested, and it was proving weak.

One day Rick gave me a tape of Ann Kiemel Anderson speaking about "God's perfect timing" in her life. Thinking of my own doubts and fears, I found myself praying, "God, forgive my impatience. Please bless the baby that is to be ours, whether by birth or adoption. Guard his or her life from the moment of conception. Please help me wait with patience instead of despair."

For the first time in years I felt at peace. I left the problem in God's hands for the next six months. In the meantime, Dr. Behrman added Clomid to my monthly regimen of progesterone supplements. At the phone's first ring, I snatched it up with trembling fingers. "Mrs. Sheppard?" Dr. Behrman's nurse sounded excited. "Your test is positive!"

I called my sister that night, ecstatic. I had waited years to make this call. Voice light and breathless, I prolonged the moment. "Are you sitting down?"

The months passed slowly. An ultrasound showed that the baby was fine. I enjoyed every kick and hiccup and took pride in my huge stomach. My water broke a few days before my due date. When I didn't go into labor, the doctor decided to perform a C-section rather than induce.

As he delivered Christine in November of 1982, he exclaimed, "The Lord was looking out for you!" Extensively wrapped up in her cord, she might have strangled during a regular delivery. As she lustily protested her arrival in the brightly lit surgical room, Rick and I cried tears of joy—and relief. She was beautiful, healthy, and had red hair like mine! Phones rang in five states that afternoon with our miraculous news.

Knowing that we wanted to have another child, our obstetrician advised us not to wait. "It might take several years," he said, "and you are thirty-three. Go ahead and try again. . . ." Christine was just learning to walk when I called my sister again. "Are you sitting down?"

I had no complications during the second pregnancy. Scott, chubby and red-haired, was born in August of 1984. Every night on my way to bed, I checked on both sleeping children and prayed beside their cribs. "Lord, I am so grateful. Thank You."

Just after Scott entered second grade, I passed my forty-second birthday, feeling that my life was at loose ends. I tried to explain my feelings to a friend at lunch one day. "My part-time job is dwindling to a few hours a week. Somehow I feel next year is going to bring big changes. . . ."

Third ring. Fourth ring. My sister finally answered, bringing me quickly out of my reflection. "Hi," I said, my tone deceptively casual. "Are you sitting down?"

Laura was born in June of 1993—six days after our twenty-second wedding anniversary—a beautiful, dimpled baby with red hair like her brother and sister.

Our plans are not always God's plans. Our timing is not always God's timing. But His ways are perfect, and His gifts are infinitely good.

A HEAVY LOAD TO CARRY

by Denise Davis Courtney, Concord, North Carolina

I have always believed that God sends certain people into our lives for us to minister to them. DJ was just such a person. God had opened my heart for this child of His.

When I met DJ, it was obvious that she was extremely overweight, but all I could see was her beautiful smile and her great personality. She answered the phone in a doctor's office and directed patients to an appointment time, or the emergency room, if necessary. She heard all kinds of stories and complaints all day long. It could be a tiresome and draining job.

We quickly became good friends, and as she began to trust me, she confided her doubts and fears. The bubbly personality disappeared as she poured out her heart to me. When I had time, I would go and eat in the small but quaint lunchroom. Some days she'd be there alone, as if she'd been waiting for me. I'd sit down and listen as she began to tell me some of the more intimate details of her life. I started to see the awesome load of guilt and shame that she had been carrying all her life, along with the weight. Those bright, sparkling eyes would give way to tears of pain and failure.

After almost a year of friendship, DJ announced that she was about to undergo a risky weight-loss surgery. It was gastric bypass surgery, commonly referred to as stomach stapling, which would enable her to lose the extra 170 pounds that her body was carrying. She openly discussed it with me, and I told her I'd pray for her.

Shortly after she told me this news, I was led away by another job venture. I said my good-byes to DJ, promising her that I'd come to see her after her surgery. Several long months went by before I went back to the physician's office to visit her. Unfortunately, DJ was not there. Six months after that, when I paid the office a visit with my own sick child, DJ was out sick.

Almost nine months had passed before I actually laid my eyes on DJ for the first time after her surgery. She had lost over 95 pounds! I could hardly believe my eyes. She was proud of her new self. I was elated and shared in her joy. I looked forward to seeing her again at a later date.

That later date turned out to be today. I was walking into the out-patient surgery center with an armload of patient films when I spotted her. She was sitting in an oversized lounge chair reading a book. She was now an average-sized woman. As I approached her, she looked up at me. I was shocked to see eyes that were bottomless wells of pain and weariness.

We talked and she told me how much weight she'd lost—165 pounds! She explained to me that she had more surgery to go, but that at the moment she was waiting for her husband, who was in surgery. As she spoke, it was all I could do not to put my arms around her.

"You've really been through a lot," I said with sympathy. Big tears poured down her face.

"Yes, I have," she said, sobbing.

"You know, God knew you needed someone right at this very minute so He sent me to you," I said. She stretched out her arms to me, and I hugged her as she unloaded some of the pain she was carrying.

"God loves you. You know that, don't you?" I asked.

"Now I do," she said with that ten-million-dollar smile. "You'll never know how much this has meant to me; you just will never know," she said.

"I'll pray for you," I said.

As I walked away, I realized that I had given hope to someone that had none. It was God's timing, not mine, that sent me to DJ over one year ago and then again today.

We never know what part we play in God's big picture. I'm just glad that He continues to use me in ways that can change lives.

FLIGHT TO FORGIVENESS

by Carmen Leal, Lake Mary, Florida

It had happened again. I had proof of my husband's infidelity. I knew he was not a Christian, but I had thought he was an honorable man. The first time it happened, I was hurt and wondered what I could do to change his philandering ways. I rationalized that if I could be a better wife, a thinner wife, a more attractive wife, he would have no reason to look elsewhere to satisfy his desires.

This time, however, I was just plain furious. I looked back over all the "I'm sorrys" and the "I'll never do it agains" and realized I could no longer trust him. My resentment grew until it was all-encompassing.

My husband's infidelity consumed me as I waited at the airport, on my way to Chicago on business. I was flying standby and nervously waiting for my name to be called for one of the coveted seats. As the crush of people converged on the gate, I assessed my odds of getting aboard, while at the same time, each thought of my husband made me fume. Though I was a Christian, I gave in to the temptation to get even. My rage got the best of me, and my mind raced even as I appeared to sit calmly in the airport terminal.

By the time my name was finally called and I took the last seat on the plane—first-class no less—I had devised a fitting plan: Have an affair and make sure he found out. It wasn't rational, but neither was I at that point. It would serve him right to feel the same betrayal and anguish I felt. So I settled into my comfortable seat and buckled in.

Glancing at the passenger in the adjacent seat, I was thrilled to note that the handsome man next to me was not wearing a wedding ring. Immediately, I began my campaign to entice him. The first-class cabin seemed suitable for this challenge and I plunged right in. I laughed and flirted and thoroughly enjoyed myself. He seemed just as eager to engage me in conversation, and we merrily flirted our way across the Pacific. That I was a married woman only added an edge to the excitement that was building within me minute by minute.

After my personal details were exhausted, I leaned over and touched his hand.

"Enough about me," I continued. "What do you do for a living?"

"I'm in the army," he replied.

"The army," I gushed. "What rank are you?"

"I'm a colonel. I'm on my way to Washington, D.C., for a conference."

I coquettishly smiled and caught his eye, convinced that he was enjoying our close quarters, and that I would be continuing on to Washington instead of deplaning in Chicago. Even as I enjoyed our banter, I gloated, visualizing the stricken look on my husband's face when he learned of my conquest. I was really going to do this. My plan was going to work!

Knowing that men can't resist the temptation to talk about themselves, I went in for the kill.

"A colonel," I exclaimed in my best Southern belle imitation. "I never knew a colonel before. What exactly do you do in the army?"

The gentleman smiled invitingly and replied without missing a beat. "I'm a Catholic priest."

I wanted to die. A priest! I had hit on a priest. I immediately feigned total immersion in my novel and remained speechless for the remainder of the eight-hour flight. For the next seven hours, I was forced to endure the uncomfortable feelings my rage had produced. Instead of enjoying my quiet time on the plane as I normally do, I was reduced to a state of near panic.

Dinner was served, the movie shown, and still I could not even glance at this impostor who dared to lounge next to me. How dare he masquerade as an available unmarried man! He should have known the effect he had on women. Worse yet, he probably did and was using his looks and personality in some perverse way. My righteous indignation continued as the miles disappeared. I felt my wrath increasing as it blotted out all thoughts of my obvious role in this predicament.

Finally, as the overhead lights were extinguished one by one, I calmed down. I thoughtfully replayed the entire humiliating scene in my head in slow motion. As I did, the man's duplicity disappeared until he became what he was—a seatmate willing to talk to me for eight hours. The horror of what I had tried to do slowly dawned on me as I took the blame and focused on my sin. And what a sin it was.

Then I remembered a Bible verse. Philippians 4:8 says: "Finally, brothers, whatever is true, whatever is noble, whatever is right, whatever is pure, whatever is lovely, whatever is admirable—if anything is excellent or praiseworthy—think about such things." What had been in my heart and my mind was the complete opposite of that verse. My outrage and misery, along with my temper, had turned me into another person.

As we drew near my destination, I was no less mortified but much more contrite. I had failed the one person in my life that mattered most of all. I could picture the anguish engraved on God's face. I knew this had been a huge crossroads in my relationship with Him, and I had taken a wrong turn. I began to pray for forgiveness, feeling that if I wouldn't forgive myself, why should He?

I forced my mind to focus on my sin and on how I had hurt God. I felt His gentle presence and knew that, even if I could not forgive myself, God could forgive me. I realized that God knew, even before I fell, that the temptation would be placed squarely in front of me. This was not the first time I had fallen, nor would it be the last—only one of the more humiliating.

I started to feel better, thankful for a God who loved me despite my actions. Then another thought entered my brain: *"If I can forgive you for your sin, you need to forgive your husband for his."* I had not been half as bad as he. I had not really done anything, while he had. My excuses continued in my mind only to trail off midway. I knew I was just as guilty as he. Until I forgave him, our marriage could not be what God had intended it to be.

Whether in marriage, or parenting, or work, or in other relationships, I can truly say that my in-flight antics marked the day I began to understand the phrase "What would Jesus do?"

Forgiveness was a nearly impossible lesson for me to learn, but learn it I did. And all because God placed a Catholic priest next to me. Could a stronger message have been sent?

Thank You, Lord!

CHAPTER SIX

Life Lessons

I will instruct you and teach you in the way you should go;
I will counsel you and watch over you.
Psalm 32:8

Whether you turn to the right or to the left,
your ears will hear a voice behind you, saying,
"This is the way; walk in it."
Isaiah 30:21

LIVE

by Susan Fahncke, Kaysville, Utah

Last week my friend Ellie asked me how I would celebrate the life of a loved one who has passed on. She is making a list of symbolic tributes to celebrate life, instead of focusing on the deep pain of losing someone we love. I know Ellie asked me this question because she is aware that my little sister is living her last days right now with a brain tumor. Angel is twenty-eight, and the bubbly, life-filled sister that I once knew is now only a vague presence in the body that is losing its battle to live. How can I give a gift, make a small gesture that symbolizes my sister?

Last year I planted a unique blue lilac tree for her, calling it my "Angel Tree." Its branches now have spring's green buds, promising blue lilacs in May. Although this was a gift for my sister that will live on, it still doesn't quite represent her. I think back over the last three decades. My little sister was my shadow, always by my side as we grew up. She copied everything from the way I dressed to the music I listened to and the boys I liked. We have had a lifetime of laughter, love, and even sisterly spats that are now frozen in the scrapbook of memories in my heart. Looking at her now, I see her pretty blue eyes have lost the sparkle that I have known forever, her body racked with pain and her mind a jumble of confusion. Yet for the last twenty-eight years, without my realizing it, my "shadow" was actually my teacher of life. She was true to her faith in God and to those she loved. She has lived life with laughter and kindness and an unending devotion to God. She truly taught me to live.

At the age of not quite three, Angel was diagnosed with leukemia. She had a 30 percent chance of survival and yet survive she did. Always a fighter, that teeny, feisty little girl beat the odds, and God granted her another twenty-five years on this earth. Twenty-five years that she used to shine for Him.

Many times over the past year, Angel has talked candidly with me about "living." She has looked me right in the eyes and told me to let go of the stress that is bringing a permanent furrow to my brow and to "live" my life. Her words. My sister reminds me repeatedly, with her words, through her example, and by the simple fact that she is staring death in the face daily, that life is precious, that every moment really does count and to live it to its fullest.

She teaches me to notice the sunshine and the clouds, to truly enjoy my children, to appreciate the goodness in other people, to be thankful for the beauty around me—to live fully in the moment. Gratitude to our heavenly Father for everything in life—*everything*—is her way of life. She even teaches me to be grateful for life's trials, as they give me an appreciation for everyday things and make me who I am.

Living is what she does best, better than anyone I know. Living is what she wants for me, in the deepest sense of the word. Letting go of anger, of pain, and of sadness is what allows life. I try to remember this each day. It is her final gift to me.

So what would be a reminder, a symbol of my little sister? Ellie's question had me thinking for several days, racking my brain for just the right celebration of Angel's life. Yesterday I hit on it, actually stumbled into it. Spending time in my favorite nursery is like spirit therapy for me. The plants, the smell of fertilizer, the sounds of the fountains, the warmth of the greenhouses all soothe my soul. I have been waiting all winter for my first trip back to J & J's nursery, and this past week has brought perfect spring weather, so my cousin and I gleefully hopped in the car and headed to our favorite nursery.

After filling my cart with the first flowers of spring, gadgets for my pond, and other things that made me feel a burst of sunshine inside, I crashed my overloaded cart into a display of garden ornaments (for the tenth time). Righting the tower of gardening goodies, I noticed a pile of painted rocks on the floor surrounding it. Each rock had inspiring words printed on it, along with pretty flowers. I pawed through the pile and turned over the one that was upside down. I gasped when I saw the single word etched into its surface. I knew it was for me.

It was the only one in the pile that had this word on it, the only one with the delicate pink flowers on its border. I looked around for my cousin, but she was off in another greenhouse. I felt hot tears sting my eyes as my fingers gently traced the one word that would forever remind me of my sister. I carefully added it to my cart and was ready to check out.

I got home and my husband helped me clean and fill the pond, the sunshine warming us as we worked. We soon had the fountain cheerfully bubbling and its soothing sound brought a smile to my face. Spring bulbs were popping through around the edge and I knew that in no time my tulips and daffodils would be wrapping the pond's border with color and life. After everything was ready, I carefully placed Angel's rock where I would see it whenever I was in the garden and every time I opened the French doors that lead out to my pond. I know that God led me to this symbol of my sister. He is always there, whether I realize it or not. He knows my heart and shows me in even "small" ways that He will take care of Angel and does not forget me.

The word emblazoned on the rock is now etched on my heart as well. Undeniably my sister, this is the perfect tribute to her. Four letters that mean everything that she stands for, everything that she has taught me as her own life ebbs away. The rock perched beside my pond will always remind me of her. The word on my rock is "Live."

⌁ Make sure to read more great stories by Susan Fahncke in volume one of God Allows U-Turns: True Stories of Hope and Healing.

A SEVERE MERCY

as told to Janice Byrd, McKinney, Texas

According to my mother, who was the disciplinarian in my home, I was a precocious boy, prone to mischief. The most severe punishment I ever got, however, was not from my mother but from my gentle father.

Many people said my dad reminded them of Jimmy Stewart. He was tall and trim with the same side-part hairstyle and boyish grin. After the movie *It's a Wonderful Life* was released in 1946, folks in our town, McKinney, Texas, teased him by calling him George Bailey. Not only was his resemblance to Jimmy Stewart uncanny, but my dad also worked at the First Savings and Loan.

I loved to walk down to the town square after school and spend time with Dad at the office. Mom didn't get home from her secretarial job until after five, so I would have at least an hour to run the adding machine, oversee a cash register closeout, or listen to some anxious patron wanting a loan. True enough, Mom had given me explicit instructions to go straight home after school, but Dad was content to keep our secret.

The trouble was I didn't always make it to the square.

I no longer remember the exact details of how it happened, but somehow a friend's yard caught fire late one afternoon after school as the two of us worked on our cooking merit badge. Mom was called at work and she was mad!

"I told you to go home after school" was all she said on our long ride home. She banished me to my room without so much as a tongue-lashing. Never before had Mom failed to administer justice when it came time to teach me a lesson. This was a first. Usually I just took my mother's corporal punishment, if not willingly, at least with a sense of relief that Dad would never have to know.

"Your father will have to deal with this," she coldly stated. I truly was repentant, but mostly I was sorry that my adored father was going to have to find out about "the accident." I secretly prayed that Mother would change her mind and storm into my room and get it over with. Alas, it was not to be.

All too soon, I heard the sound of my father's car pulling into the driveway. I heard my parents talking in the living room, and then footsteps approached my room.

We went into the bathroom to talk. Dad sat on the commode and I sat on the side of the tub. There was never a question about my guilt. I was very contrite and there was no argument about the horrible consequences of my disobedience.

"This is so bad," Dad regretfully said, "there's going to have to be a very severe punishment. Stand up, turn around, and hold onto the shower door," he directed.

As I braced myself, I heard Dad stand up and loosen his belt buckle. I heard the sound of the folded belt whizzing through the air and I anticipated the stinging blow—but felt nothing! Confused, I turned around. My gentle father's hand was poised in midair, ready once again to thrash his own leg.

"No!" I protested.

All of our past, and all of our future, hung there in that moment.

"This time, I took your punishment," Dad stammered. "You have been given mercy instead of what you deserve. We quickly forget a spanking, but we never forget what mercy feels like."

Mercy. Such as that given to us by the Lord Himself, when He died for us on Calvary's cross. Suddenly, I truly understood what mercy meant, and I would never forget it.

Though it's been close to forty years ago, I can still vividly recall my father's tear-streaked face and the disappointment in his eyes that day. I remember it most when I look into the pleading face of my own son. It is then I truly understand.

As Christ taught His children, as my father taught me, and as I strive to teach my son, may the lesson of severe and loving mercy never be lost.

CYBER WITNESS

by Cindy Appel, St. Louis, Missouri

Rubbing my burning eyes—sore from staring at the computer screen for too long, too late at night—I could hardly believe what slowly scrolled across the screen from almost an entire continent's expanse away:

"Why do you believe the way you do?"

It was totally unexpected. I was a novice at "web surfing." Recently I had stumbled upon a bulletin board system dedicated to writers and their problems. I had found it most illuminating and enjoyable. I would use it to see what new tidbits of information I could gather from others struggling to get their words into print. On this particular night I noticed an announcement on the board's home page. It said that I could "chat live" with fellow authors in "real time" in a "chat room."

Hmm, this could be interesting, I said to myself, clicking on the underlined blue print and finding myself suddenly thrust into the unusual world of cyberspace communications. The "people" there were discussing all sorts of things—some literary related and some not—using chat room jargon that I did not yet understand.

One woman asked for input on how to publish her poetry and received helpful suggestions from only a handful of the dozen or so denizens of the electronic gathering. I typed a few encouraging words and received a thankful reply. My optimism and compassion for her plight must have stood out in stark contrast from the rest of the crowd's responses. I soon discovered myself involved in a conversation with another chat room member with more serious undertones: "I am a loner. I don't feel as if I will ever be anything but lonely. . . ."

I was surprised by the plaintive plea for help. The faceless world of cyberspace contains "real" people after all—individuals who feel alone and unloved. In the anonymous realm of the electronic age, I had found a human being who desperately needed to know the love of the Lord.

In simple terms, I shared my Christian faith across the World Wide

Web with this one searching person. This person whose face, name, and heart can be known only by God. It wasn't a simple task. There were others who interjected their comments into the discussion—sometimes helpful, sometimes frivolous, and sometimes quite cynical. I kept right on typing. I gave my testimony to the power and love of Christ as I had seen throughout my life and in others' lives.

The hour grew later, my eyes wearier, and my hands tired. Soon my "cyber friend" and I were forced to call it a night. I could only pray that the seed that I had planted might take root and grow, eventually to blossom into faith within the life of this one individual.

My pastor has exhorted our congregation many times to always be prepared to give witness, because all Christians are witnesses to the glory of our risen Lord. For some reason, I had never imagined that my faith would be questioned or challenged in anything other than a face-to-face exchange. I would have immediate feedback—no twenty-second lags between mainframe computers on the Internet, no mistaking the impact of my words since I could visually gauge the other's reaction.

Certainly, typed words on a computer screen couldn't have the same effect on a person as the spoken word—could they? Perhaps they can. As the twenty-first century dawns upon us, Christians should stand ready to follow Peter's instructions. He told those early believers to "always be prepared to give an answer" no matter when, where, or how the answer is needed.

As you sit at your terminal and "talk" with your friends, loved ones, or even strangers, remember to "be prepared."

Jesus Christ is our Lord and Savior for all time and of all ages. He abides with us even today—even in the cold complexity of the computer-dominated domain in which many of us reside. Perhaps because of that the warmth of His love and forgiveness is needed now more than ever.

⌐ Make sure to read Cindy Appel's story, "The Nativity Scene at Easter,"
in volume one of God Allows U-Turns: True Stories of Hope and
Healing.

SEARCHING FOR SOLUTIONS

by Pastor Aaron D. Lewis, Manchester, Connecticut

It was a bitter cold morning, about 6:30 A.M. I was driving my two youngest children from the downtown Hartford area back home after dropping off their mom, Tiwanna, at the hospital where she worked. The ride usually took about ten to fifteen minutes, but the weather this morning was terrible, and the trip seemed to take forever.

When I finally crawled to the entrance of my street, the snow was at least eight inches thick. I realized that I couldn't drive all the way into my driveway without getting out and shoveling a path. I thought that I would just leave the little ones in the car as I grabbed the shovel in the garage. It was, after all, only about five feet away and it would only take a couple of seconds to grab the shovel, shovel a quick path around the car, and drive into the garage. And if I left the engine running, the kids wouldn't get cold. Seemed like a good idea at the time.

Within seconds of my grabbing the shovel, my two year old, Israel, unstrapped himself and was jumping all around the car. When I went to open the car door, I also found that Israel had locked the automatic door locks. I panicked; I lost it; I totally freaked out. Nightmarish possibilities, all of which concluded with two small caskets, whirled through my head. No one had told me that Israel was capable of unstrapping himself, but how could I have been so stupid? If anything happened to those two small children, it would be all my fault.

I began to plead with Israel to unlock the door. Unlocking the car door was something that I knew he could do. He was a veritable expert at locking and unlocking the car door. It was his favorite pastime while riding in the car. But Israel decided to add something new to his repertoire that day. It is called amnesia. No matter what I chose to do or say, it seemed like Israel just couldn't seem to remember how to unlock the door.

I asked nicely, "Israel, open the door for Daddy."

He said no just as nicely.

I screamed, "Israel, Daddy's going to give you a spanking if you don't open the door now."

He yelled back, "No, no, no." And then he turned up the heat to its highest setting. I was afraid that his sister, Madonna, would be ill from sweating. Then he decided to turn on the radio, crank the volume up, and pretend to be a rock star strumming his guitar to an audience of thousands. When he became bored with that, he turned on the windshield wipers, the blinkers, and the signal lights. Poor little Madonna adjusted to her chaotic surroundings as if this is how life should be. At this point, the ordeal had gone on for more than a half hour.

Maybe if I just get the extra set of car keys, I can open up the car, I thought. But I was afraid to leave the children unattended, fearing that Israel would put the car in gear during his antics. *On the other hand,* I thought, *if I find the keys this nightmare will be over.* I decided to take my chances and ran into the house. I went through every drawer, every cabinet, and every nook and cranny. Do you think I could find the second set of keys?

Now I was beginning to panic. I was afraid to ask assistance from a neighbor. He'd probably think I was the biggest jerk of a dad that any kid could have. Even more fear gripped me when I thought about calling the police. They would surely report this incident to the Department of Child and Family Services and take all five of my precious children away from me. I'd never see my kids again. My wife would surely divorce me. It would probably be in the headlines, PASTOR AND HIGHLY ACCLAIMED AUTHOR AARON LEWIS SENTENCED TO LIFE IN PRISON FOR THE WILLFUL ACT OF CHILD NEGLECT AND MANSLAUGHTER. For the rest of my life, I would have a bona fide prison ministry. I felt as if I had no more choices. Until. . .

I took a deep breath, then I said this simple prayer: "Father, in the name of the Lord, help me to find an answer to this problem that I am facing. Amen." Suddenly, I heard within me the voice of God saying, *"The key is within you."* I thought to myself, *What could this mean? The key is within me?* Then it dawned on me.

For the past forty-five minutes, I had allowed fear to overtake me. It literally sabotaged my ability to think and create a simple solution, rendering me useless. I looked inside the house for an answer. I could not find the keys. Pleading didn't work. Intimidation didn't work, either. The answer was neatly tucked away in the place that I refused to consider. The answer was to look to God for guidance.

Fear always suggests the lie that your situation is so intense that there is absolutely nothing you can do about it. Fear in and of itself is one of the great sins of the soul that wars against God. Fear always fights our faith in God, our faith toward God, and God's faith within us. Throughout life there will always be challenging situations, but if we realize that the answers to our problems lie with God, we will conquer all of our battles.

I was finally able to convince little Israel to unlock the door. You may ask how I convinced him to open the door. Well, it wasn't with threats and intimidation. Neither did I have to impose a future punishment on little Israel. After praying the simple prayer and hearing God's voice concerning the matter, I simply made a deal with Israel. "Israel, if you open the door for Daddy, Daddy will give you a piece of candy. Will you do that for Daddy?" I asked.

Israel said, "Yeah, Dad." And, he unlocked the door.

My answer wasn't in the keys; it wasn't in imposing fear; neither was it in standing and doing nothing. The answer was then, and will always be, neatly tucked in the same place. With God.

THE DAY I LOST MY DAD'S FISHING HAT

by Jon Alessandro, Grapevine, Texas

Splash! The water was cold and murky. My dad's favorite fishing hat went sailing off my head as I scrambled and kicked, trying to keep my head above the water. I knew I was about to drown, but all I could think about was my dad's fishing hat.

As a rule, my dad did not spend an exorbitant amount of time with me as I grew up, but there were those rare moments when we braved life's storms together. On one occasion, when I was about eight years old, we went out with his buddy, Ed, and fished for trout at one of Dad's favorite fishing places somewhere along a cold stream in Wyoming. On our first and last fishing trip, my dad let me wear his favorite fishing hat. Thinking back, the hat was really rather ugly. It was an orange color with brown splatters all around the brim. Those splatters were probably stains, but I wasn't sure. My dad's last words to me that morning were, "Don't lose my hat!" I was proud and felt like a real fisherman. After all, it was the hat that made the man. It didn't matter if you knew how to fish or not. If you had a fishing hat, you were a real fisherman.

We arrived at the fishing area early that Saturday morning and set up a small day camp. Ed prepared a hearty breakfast for everyone using one of those Coleman stoves he placed on the truck's tailgate. Following breakfast, we gathered our gear and split up. Each man went his own way, searching for the perfect fishing spot. I climbed on a rock and surveyed my kingdom. I hopped a little stream and wandered into the valley, searching for a good place to settle in and fish. I poked around here and there and even tossed in a line now and again. There is no feeling quite like the smell of fresh, clean air and the babble of a brook beside you. I wasn't having much luck fishing, so I decided to venture farther out. Before I knew it, I was bogged down in ankle-deep muck. I tried to gracefully wade through all that mire carrying my fishing pole and gear, but eventually I was covered in this awful-smelling gunk. I decided to head back since it was starting to get a little late.

I ended up on the opposite side of the creek from where I actually needed to be. I originally crossed a small section of the stream that was easy enough to hop over. I ended up beside a fast-moving section of the creek that was five or six feet wide. By this time I was muddy and tired, and I didn't feel like continuing on over to the smaller area of the stream. Besides, the other side of the creek didn't look to be that far away, so I decided to simply jump across. I backed up as far as I could, and with all of the strength I could muster, I jumped. Smack in the middle of the creek. At eight years old, I had little experience swimming so I panicked, screaming and thrashing about in the water.

Dad's favorite fishing hat was the first to go. I remember seeing it out of the corner of my eye floating in the water, the brim filling with water as it was steadily taken downstream. All of my gear disappeared, too. I yelled, "Help! I can't swim!"

Ed heard my desperate cry and called out, "Where are you?"

I went under and remember being quite amazed at how cold and deep this creek really was. I managed to break through to the surface and somehow grabbed hold of some of the weeds growing on the bank. I held on as the water swirled about me. I felt very heavy and called out, "Help! I can't hold on!"

Ed called back, "Hold on! I'm coming!" I felt like I was going to sink back under the water. I gasped and choked and grabbed at more weeds, trying to find a better grip. As I pulled on the weeds, they began to give way. I snatched another handful and pulled. I heard the woods around me crash and crunch as Ed made his way toward my location. I remember feeling comforted at the sound of his steps coming toward me.

"I can't find you; keep talking," Ed screamed, almost panicking. I struggled at the bank of the creek and began slipping under the water. In a last desperate attempt, I pulled on the handful of weeds I had grasped in my hands. I noticed my body surfaced a little so I pulled at the weeds some more. Hand over hand, I began to pull myself out of the creek. As I rolled up onto the bank, I called out, "Never mind; I'm okay now."

I rested on the bank, cold, humiliated, and shaken. Then it dawned on me. My dad's favorite fishing hat was gone. I knew then I should have drowned. I did not want to face my dad's anger—not here, not now. I got up and started to make my way toward Ed. We finally ran into each other, and I could tell he was a little upset at not being able to find me.

Calmly, he brought me back to camp and we waited for the inevitable. It seemed to be an eternity for me, but my dad showed up a few minutes later, oblivious as to what I had just been through. Ed didn't say anything as we packed up the truck to head back home. As my dad climbed into the cab, I said, "Dad, I lost your hat." I saw his face begin to turn all kinds of different shades. He started to lecture me on the meaning of responsibility and trust. He made it quite clear that he was very disappointed with me. He continued his diatribe as he put his hand on my shoulder, and then he suddenly stopped. He looked at me curiously and noticed how damp my clothes were.

"What happened?"

Ed found his opportunity and broke in, explaining how I had fallen into the creek. My dad's face went from bright red to a sickening pallor. "You, you could have drowned!" With that revelation he looked at me and said sheepishly, "I'm sorry, Son." He didn't say anything more, but I could tell he felt really bad about having just yelled at me about a silly old hat.

Dad and I laugh about that day now. Every now and again, I'll ask Dad if he remembers the day I lost his favorite fishing hat. He sarcastically remarks, "Yes, and I still think you should have held on to it." Sometimes I wonder if he doesn't mean that, but I really know better. I know the love for a silly hat is worth far less than the love for your child. Jesus said in Matthew 6:26, "Look at the birds of the air; they do not sow or reap or store away in barns, and yet your heavenly Father feeds them. Are you not much more valuable than they?"

My dad said he may have lost a hat that day, but he realized he could have lost something much more valuable: me. I think about this when my son or daughter accidentally stains the carpet with grape juice or loses that special toy I bought them for the umpteenth time. I can look at them and say in the midst of a great big bear hug, "I love you anyway. Did I ever tell you about the day I lost my dad's fishing hat?"

FALL THERAPY

by Ginger Broslat, Ocala, Florida

Fall therapy. . .it's an interesting concept, and a course all Christians should take.

As a young child diagnosed with a form of muscular dystrophy, it was obvious I would have some falls in my lifetime. After one corrective surgery, I was taken to physical therapy. Tony was a big guy who was my physical therapist. Looking back now, I don't know if he was really that big or if he just appeared that way to a seven-year-old child. Tony was fun. He laughed a lot and was determined we were going to have a good time, and we did. When I first met Tony, I was still in the hospital after surgery. He took me through all the proper procedures for using crutches. The fun facts of exactly how you balance and go, and how you really don't want to go down steps with your leg down and crutches up—your face doesn't appreciate it very much once it hits the bottom of the steps. Part of that therapy was what you would expect: a series of exercises intended to strengthen what muscles were there and encourage balance. But the most interesting part of my physical therapy came later. It was a session called "fall therapy."

Part of Tony's job wasn't to teach me to walk but to teach me to fall. This may sound negative and pessimistic. Why discourage a child by telling her she's going to fall a lot? Why be so depressing and negative? Well, the answer is obvious: It was for my protection. By learning how to relax my body once I anticipated a fall, I was able to prevent injury. I guess the fact that in thousands of falls I have never broken a bone is testimony to the effectiveness of Tony's lessons. However, the fact that I dislocated my elbows at least eight times is testimony that my God protected those bones, even when I didn't heed the proper procedures of fall therapy. You see, the trick to falling properly is to do just that. . .fall. Don't fight it; don't make a big deal about it; in the words of Nike, "Just Do It." Letting the fall occur without reaching out to save myself protects my other parts. When I feel my knees buckle and know I am about to fall, I am supposed to relax, pull my arms to my chest—almost in a fetal position—and go down gracefully. This process many times makes the falls look quite interesting. My sister used to lovingly tease me that I was the only person she ever knew who could fall in slow motion.

The times when I have dislocated my elbows were when I reached out to brace the fall. It's a natural reaction. Most people do it. For me, the power of the fall when my body is fighting the fall is greater than the joints can stand. The arm stuck out in protection makes the sacrifice. The elbow twists around from the normal position in the socket to take the jolt. The result is a lot of pain, and people around me with grossed-out looks on their faces as they look at my arm. . .but it's not broken! The advantage to this happening so many times is that now it's much easier to set back in place. The joint is loosened and recovers much easier than it used to. Whether a dislocation occurs or not, usually the best thing to do is just sit for a minute to recover.

Then, when I do get up, there is more security for the walk ahead.

How similar my physical falls are to my spiritual falls! When I stumble on my walk with Christ because of sin in my life, instead of allowing my knees to buckle and take the fall, I reach out in pride to save myself. I think, *No one will know,* or, *I can fix this,* only to see the elbow take the hit.

It's then that I realize my only hope is to accept the sacrifice that was already made on my behalf. It's then that I see the disjointed, but not broken, body of Christ as He hung on a cross for the sins that I would commit one day. It's only when I sit with my spirit in prayer that I can recover and have the strength to face the walk ahead.

Yes, just as doctors knew a little girl with muscular dystrophy would need to know how to fall, our heavenly Father knew we would all need Someone to take the first fall for us. Christ was willing to leave the grandeur and splendor of heaven to be the sacrificial joint in our lives. The more times we turn to that sacrifice, the easier it becomes.

No, falling is not fun. But we work on our fall therapy. We go into a humble fetal position of the heart and stop reaching out in pride to save ourselves. That sacrifice was already made. We can experience strengthening renewal as we wait quietly to recover. It is when we are willing to go down with the fall "gracefully" that God can pick us up to walk on a brighter journey down a new road of spiritual healing.

SWEET AS STRAWBERRIES

by Carol Russell, Fort Scott, Kansas

"What are they doing?" I asked as Bob and I drove up the lane of my in-laws' farm. Dad drove the tractor slowly through the garden, pulling the large wooden farm wagon, and Mom shoveled something out of it.

"They are putting chicken manure on the strawberries," Bob said.

"How disgusting!" I declared. Bob laughed at me as he got out of the car.

Bob and I waved at them, then sat on the back porch steps while they finished their task. Laurie Ann, our two year old, began playing with the cats that had wandered up from the barn. I watched Bob's folks as they worked and thought about how little I knew about the farm and growing things. I was a city girl. Every time we came to the farm, I learned something new.

"Hi, you two," Dad said as he came across the yard. "Bob, I'm glad you're here. I need you to look at that tractor. I think I have a problem."

As Dad and Bob walked off, Mom bent down and stole a kiss from her granddaughter. Pulling off her gloves and sitting next to me on the steps, she sighed. "That's hard on old backs."

"I don't see how you do it," I said. "I just can't imagine standing in that wagon, shoveling that stuff."

"Well, it isn't my favorite job and it certainly isn't the nicest, but all jobs can't be nice and smell good. It's still an important part of growing things. If we want good sturdy plants and want them to produce the best fruit, then we have to care for them.

"It starts with planting. Then we must weed and water them. Then they have to be nourished. That includes putting fertilizer on them. It will make the largest and sweetest berries."

"Thanks, but I think I'll just use sugar on my strawberries."

Mom laughed and said, "It's work, but the fruit we have in the end is worth it. You two go on in the house. I have to put away a few things and then I'll be in."

Later, as Mom was placing glasses of milk on the table, she asked her next question: "Well, how are things going?" This sent me into a long discourse of my trials and tribulations.

"That old wringer washer is broken again. We need an automatic, but the money just isn't there. I'm not sure it will last through another baby. I guess Bob will just have to fix it again," I said. Mom sliced two large pieces of bread from her homemade loaf. She began to toast the bread.

"The cost of Laurie's medicine went up again. Every time I have that prescription refilled, the cost goes up." She set the plate of toast on the table and walked to the refrigerator.

I lifted Laurie, put her into the high chair, and continued my complaining. "They changed Bob's hours at work. He is still early morning man at the station, but now he has two hours in the morning when he comes home and then has to go back. It sure has messed up our schedule." Mom took out a bowl of strawberry preserves and placed it on the table. We said grace and then began to enjoy our snack.

"I know what the Bible says," I continued. "I know what Matthew 6 says. God tells us that He watches the sparrows and cares for the lilies of the field. I know He loves and cares for us and that we shouldn't worry about tomorrow and about 'things.' It's hard, Mom. The harder we try, the harder it gets."

Thoughtfully, Mom placed a spoonful of preserves on the corner of her toast. "Maybe you and Bob are God's fruit," she said. "Maybe God is just putting fertilizer on His strawberries."

I never looked at strawberries—or trials—the same again.

THE SOUP LADLE

by Claudia C. Breland, Maple Valley, Washington

Sometimes when I'm standing at the kitchen sink doing dishes, I'll glance up at the curtain rod where I've hung a stainless steel soup ladle. It looks odd up there, hanging down from its curved handle, but I've put it there because it's an heirloom, part of our family history. It's also a vivid reminder of the things in life we can survive.

My husband, Richard, often tells the story that occurred when he was only two. After being away all weekend at a gospel singing convention, he and his family headed home to Gulfport, Mississippi. They pulled up in the driveway late that evening to find their house fully engulfed in flames. Everything they owned was destroyed. The only thing left was a stainless steel soup ladle, used as a water dipper, that was hanging on the back porch.

The marks of the fire are evident even from a distance. The bowl of the ladle is marked with charred black spots and pitted by the intense heat of the fire. The fire did not melt the stainless steel—its basic shape remains unchanged, perfectly usable. You can still read the manufacturer's name and the date (1927) clearly on the handle. The outward scars it bears, however, show witness to what it's been through.

It's the same way with each of us. In our past, there may be events or relationships that have marked us for life. The death of a parent, alcoholism, infidelity, catastrophic illness, the loss of a child, deep depression—these are all things that have a profound effect on our lives. When we turn to Jesus, we may be healed, but the marks of our past are still there.

No matter how hard we may wish those scars away, they are part of what makes us who we are. In spite of (sometimes because of) those scars, we are still perfectly usable in God's kingdom. As it says in Job 23:10, "When he has tested me, I will come forth as gold." Or even, in some cases, as a stainless steel soup ladle.

⌐ Make sure to read Claudia Breland's story, "A December Story," in volume one of God Allows U-Turns: True Stories of Hope and Healing.

THE VERNAL POOL

by Judi Braddy, Elk Grove, California

Our new home sits directly across the street from a vernal pool. What, you will surely ask, is a vernal pool? To be honest, I wasn't sure, either. I had to look it up. It is not a body of water as the name suggests, but rather an area reserved and protected for whatever animal and plant life lives and grows there.

Trusting that the surrounding neighborhood would offer the same amenities to its "people life," we bought the house. Mostly, though, I loved looking out the window at the open space. We moved in at the end of November.

It wasn't until late January that I was finally able to look up from my decorating magazines long enough to examine what lay immediately beyond the front door. What met my view was a vast lumpy field full of rangy brown grass encompassed by a dark chain-link fence. At that moment, I pondered whether we had made the wisest choice of location. As for animal life, all I ever saw were birds—most of them little brown birds that blended into the overall color scheme so that you didn't see them so much as hear them. Occasionally, a lone brown hawk circled the field, looking, I imagined, for little brown mice. In other words, everything at that moment, looked. . .well. . .brown. Add to that the lonely whistle of the train cutting across the far side of the field and the winter rain producing a wet hay smell, and you have a rather bleak picture.

That was when I looked up the word "vernal" in the dictionary. The definition stated simply, "of, relating to, or occurring in the spring." Spring being a few months away yet, I went back to the activities of my busy household.

My son, daughter-in-law, and grandson, Liam, had come from Oregon to live with us a few months prior to the move to facilitate my son's completion of a teaching degree. Just as we were getting used to having an active four year old in the house, we were all surprised to learn that a new baby was expected in the spring.

It was the worst timing in the world, and we were all in an initial state of shock. The adjustment was hardest, perhaps, for my son, whose immediate goals seemed in jeopardy facing the responsibility of a growing family. He was just beginning to chart a promising course after some very difficult years.

Eventually we settled into the wait, although the tension of adjustment was evident. Spring seemed like a long way off on all accounts.

Sometime in February, Grampa and Liam started the routine of walking our two dogs in the field-that-will-be-a-park. One day Liam burst through the door with exciting news. "Gramma, we saw *four* rabbits!" The great rabbit-counting adventure began. The brown, lumpy field had become a wild safari seen through the eyes of a four year old.

The late spring rains began, the large white egrets came, and my daughter-in-law took on the mysterious beauty of a lady-in-waiting. My son worked longer hours, studied late into the night, and looked very tired. Their marriage definitely showed signs of stress.

Life in our household and the vernal pool was changing. The

question still remained whether either would be for the better.

One night I couldn't sleep and got up to do what moms do best—pray and worry. Needing solitude, I stepped out onto the front porch and was met with the surprisingly loud *brik-brik-brik* of frogs coming from the vernal pool. I could not see them, but obviously they were there—the sound of life coming from the darkness. And I thought of the heartbeat of my unborn grandchild.

I have lived long enough to witness the cycle of many seasons—some very difficult—and to finally understand how necessary and integral they are to each other. Even the bleak times must be celebrated in the hope of what is to come.

Pondering that, a lesson from the vernal pool began to reveal itself: We can't always regulate or predict nature, but if we can lovingly protect it and give it a chance, it will grow and thrive.

Suddenly I understood that God had brought my son and family to live with us through such a season. He makes no mistakes. This was another opportunity to apply our faith and prove Him faithful.

On the April day that tiny, beautiful Olivia Roseanne came home from the hospital with her mom and dad, I sat at the top of the stairs looking out the transom window at the vernal pool.

By now it was a lush green carpet with serendipitous stripes of color—wildflowers of yellow and purple and orange and white. Life in the vernal pool—and our home—had come full circle. I had seen the look on my son's face as his new daughter made her way into the world and watched now as he sat on the couch holding the tiny pink-wrapped bundle in his strong arms. I thought of Ecclesiastes 3:1: "There is a time for everything, and a season for every activity under heaven." And I remembered the words of a favorite old song: He makes all things beautiful in His time.

Thank You, Lord, for life, seasons, and the lesson of faith from the vernal pool.

GETTING OUT OF GOD'S WAY

by Barbara Curtis, Petaluma, California

Christine's shriek whipped into the room, slicing into my phone call midsentence.

"*Barbara!* Your car's rolling down the hill!"

Throwing down the receiver, I spun and raced down the hall. As if something had picked me up, shaken and booted me into a more focused dimension, I could see only the door at the end of the hall, hear only the pulse surging in my ears.

Seconds slowed and separated, like drops from a leaky faucet. Grabbing the only emergency cord I could, I begged, "Oh, God, dear God, please let the car be empty."

Moments ago, I had been leaving Christine's office, my toddler in my arms, my oldest son by my side. At the door we had taken extra time for Jonathan to wave bye-bye. When the phone rang, Christine had turned back inside. The parking lot gravel was crunching under my feet when she appeared again at the door to say my husband was on the phone.

"Honey, will you put him in his car seat? I'll be right back." I turned to Joshua, eleven, who was everyone's right-hand man. Christine had asked him to come to physical therapy today to distract Jonathan from the discomfort and tedium of his workout.

"Sure, Mom," Joshua said. I put his brother into his arms. At three, Jonathan was still too wobbly to negotiate the rocky parking lot safely. Down's syndrome meant his physical as well as his mental development was delayed. But for his family, his cute little face spelled courage and perseverance.

Why had my husband called that day? Neither of us can remember. He only recalls my cry of dismay and the phone clattering on the floor. Then my screams.

"No! Oh, no! Oh, God, please, no!"

The car wasn't empty. Through the windshield, I could see the top of Jonathan's blond head framed by his car seat. He was being carried backward down the sloping driveway toward the two-lane road below. On the other side of the road was a thirty-foot drop to the San Francisco Bay.

"Oh, Lord, not here, not now," I pleaded. Moments from Jonathan's brief but difficult life flashed through my memory. I could hear the beeps of the monitors in the ICU, see the tangle of cords and wires from the limp body, feel the tug on my stomach when the doctors prepared us for the worst. So many times we had been through these things, with so many people praying for our special little boy. And, one by one, God had healed him of his frailties. For the past year he had been so healthy we had actually begun to relax.

Could God really choose to take him now, after all He'd seen us through?

Not if my son Joshua could help it. Horrified, I saw him behind the car, straining his ninety-five pounds against the ton of metal grinding him backward. Running awkwardly in reverse as the car picked up speed, he was on the verge of being crushed any second. I couldn't lose two sons! "Joshua, let go! Get away from the car!" I screamed. Christine was screaming, too. Even as we pleaded with him, I understood my son's heart. He always took responsibility. Everything within him would rage against giving up the battle to save his brother.

I screamed again, "Joshua! Obey me! Let go!"

At last, he jumped away from the car. As Joshua let go, Christine and I stopped screaming. The quiet was eerie. The moment hung poised like the last drop of water from the faucet. The car seemed to hesitate, the rear wheels to shift. Now the car was moving at an angle toward the edge of the driveway, losing momentum, grinding to a halt. Almost gracefully, it came to rest against an old and faithful-looking tree.

Bolting for the car, flinging open the door, I found Jonathan unhurt but bewildered—he had never been in a moving car all by himself before! Catching sight of Joshua right behind me, he grinned and stretched his arms wide—his way of saying "Life—what an adventure!"

I've been behind a rolling car. I've tried to pit my puny weight against circumstances that were way too big for me to handle. Perhaps that's why I understood Joshua's reaction all too well.

"Mom, all I could think of was that I couldn't let him die," Joshua told me later.

"All I could think of. . ." That's me all over, willing to sacrifice everything for some good purpose. And ever overestimating my indispensability. Even if I know I need God's help, don't I often think He needs mine as well? Don't I often act as though God can accomplish the supernatural only if I stay involved?

Maybe sometimes He is just waiting for me to get out of the way and let Him take care of things before I get myself hurt. Maybe He'd like to do something truly miraculous, something I'd always remember—something I couldn't take credit for myself. Maybe He'd like me to be more like Jonathan, just going along for the ride, a little worried, perhaps, but remembering I'm in good hands and ready for the rescue.

I hadn't put my car in park. That little bit of carelessness almost cost me two sons. But God chose instead to teach me a lesson about His mercy and His might. He gave me a picture I will never forget—one son trying to avert disaster, letting go in desperation, and being saved. The second powerless and utterly dependent on God's own outcome.

Because Jonathan is who he is, he might always keep that sweet simplicity. And I will ever be learning from his triumphant trust as he stretches out his arms and smiles. "Life—what an adventure!"

CHAPTER SEVEN

Faith and Forgiveness

We live by faith, not by sight.
2 Corinthians 5:7

*"And when you stand praying, if you hold anything against anyone,
forgive him, so that your Father in heaven may forgive you your sins."*
Mark 11:25

I'M TRYING TO TELL THEM, ROY

by Pastor John Roberts, Sterling, Colorado

The day I met him in April 1995, he had just seen the doctor and discovered he had cancer. One of his friends heard the news and asked me to go with him for a visit. After some introductions, we had a wonderful time of prayer.

I didn't find out until later that, just after our visit, he had poured down the drain the quart of vodka he'd bought on the way home from the doctor's office.

I was surprised to learn that he would have considered that, so he told me about his drinking days.

"Were you an alcoholic?" I asked.

"No. 'Alcoholic' is too nice a term. I was just a drunk," he replied. "And I was so upset about the cancer, I thought about getting drunk again. Thank God you two came by just in time for me to return to my senses."

I knew right away I was going to like this guy.

A few weeks later, the surgery took place. Afterward, the doctor came out and told us more bad news. The cancer had spread too far for surgery to do any good. Instead of removing a tumor, the surgeon had simply closed him back up.

"Six months, maybe more," the doctors told him. "Make the most of it."

That, of course, was an unacceptable prognosis. He determined to "fight the good fight. . .and keep the faith" (see 2 Timothy 4:7). He did the faith thing.

Call the church leaders.

Ask for prayer.

Deepen his trust.

Find more ways to serve the Lord.

For almost six years, he looked to God for solutions to a problem for which medicine offered little or no hope. In the process, we who came to know and love him received a wide assortment of blessings.

Mostly we learned what real-world faith is about. Two more times he heard the same prognosis: "You only have a short time." So, two more times he called for prayer. And, two more times God extended his life.

Finally, a couple of weeks ago, he realized that he had, indeed, "finished the race." With his family present, he looked around the room, reminded them to follow Jesus, and then asked to be alone with his wife.

The words he spoke to her, which I now repeat with her permission, reveal a loving, faith-filled heart.

"I've loved you for years, and you're my best friend," he told her. "But this is more than I can handle. So, may I have your permission. . . ." He paused.

"My permission for what?" she asked.

"Your permission to go to heaven," he said. "I want to stay, but I can't."

So, with her permission, a few hours later he went to heaven, joyously hoping not only to see Jesus, but to see his friends and family there as well. The last thing he said to me was, "Tell them all how to get to heaven, because I want to see them there."

I'm trying, Roy. I'm trying.

⌁ *Make sure to read more great stories from Pastor John Roberts in volume one of* God Allows U-Turns: True Stories of Hope and Healing.

FORGIVENESS

by Lucy Sennett, Leland, Mississippi

While a classroom teacher, I was the victim of a young teenager out of control. I suffered a fractured shoulder and a number of other injuries.

The teen was expelled for the remainder of the school year. His return the next year was conditional on his receiving professional help.

It wasn't until the last day of school the following year that our paths crossed again. While absorbed in grading my last stack of exams, I realized that I was not alone in the room. Looking up from my papers, I found myself gazing into the eyes that had haunted many a sleepless night. I had no escape and could find no words.

Then he took a deep breath and nervously said, "Will you forgive me for what I did to you? Please, it's really important to me that you forgive me."

During my years as a teacher, I had heard "I'm sorry" hundreds of times, for everything from uncompleted homework to cutting class. I had never heard a request for forgiveness. Not like this.

Forgive? Oh, yes. I hadn't realized how much I needed to forgive until asked by this truly repentant young man.

My life was forever changed by that request on that afternoon. I will always remember the joy and peace we both felt at that moment. There is no doubt. Forgiveness is important to everyone involved. First Kings 8:30 (KJV) states: "And when thou hearest, forgive."

It truly makes all the difference in the world.

GOD OPENS WINDOWS

by Cyd A. Donaldson, St. Ann, Missouri

My life has been full of God opening and closing windows. During the summer of 1985, the first of many opened. I met a man at a time when I had decided that a love relationship was not in my future. I had been divorced for five years, gone back to college, graduated, and was in the midst of trying to find a job. I had gone to a convention in Indianapolis, and the second person I met was Ron. The minute I shook his hand, I knew that this was the man God intended for me to marry. I knew there would be problems, for he was a person of color and I was not. My parents would not accept it, nor would many of my friends. I started to pray, "Lord, Thy will be done. Please help me to accept it, if not understand it."

At the same time, however, another window closed. Not long after my parents found out about my involvement with Ron, they decided to spend their Christmases, which had always been a time of family and celebration, in Texas. My prayer at that time was "Lord, lead me where You need me to be, and please help me to overcome my own bitterness about my parents' attitudes."

After seven years together, Ron and I were married in 1992. The son of a minister, Ron felt we needed to state our commitment to each other in front of God. His father performed the wedding, and his family was present.

During all this time, my parents referred to my husband as many things but never as my husband. It took them over twelve years to even acknowledge him by using his name. They never came to our home. They never invited both of us to dinner or family gatherings. I was always welcome but never with him. That was a window that remained closed.

I continued to keep in contact with them, trying to have a "normal" relationship. And I prayed, "Lord, give me tolerance for the influences under which they grew up and patience to cope with them for ignoring a part of my life that was incredibly important. Most of all, Lord, please help me find a resolution to the problem, whatever it is and no matter how it happened." My mantra was "Lord, in Your time, not mine. Your will be done."

The opportunity for that window to be opened came in late September of 1999, when I was hospitalized for blood clots. When my mother called, the question of whether or not she and my father needed to come was raised. My immediate response was, "Yes, but, Mom, my husband is here, and I don't want any of us to be uncomfortable." They arrived two hours later.

The next few weeks were an emotional roller coaster, with memorable moments of God at work. I watched through a drug-induced haze as my mother brought in meat pies and apple dumplings for the entire hospital ward because, she said, that was what Ron wanted her to make.

Thank You, God, for her saying his name and looking at him.

The Lord was hard at work as my husband, tired and worried, sat in a chair after my second surgery, snapping at anyone who said anything. My mother, being a universal "mom," walked over and said, "Son, you are tired and you need to go home. We are here. Go home, sleep, and come back later. It will be all right." My husband looked at her, shook his head in acquiescence, picked up his stuff, and left.

Thank You, God, for giving my parents a son-in-law who can love and forgive.

I had yet another prayer answered the morning when my father and Ron left my hospital room together so that Mom and Sharon could bathe me. When Dad and Ron returned forty-five minutes later, they were laughing. They had been discussing improvements to the house that Ron and I were buying. My husband's father was not "handy" around the house, but my father is, and Dad was tickled by some of Ron's ideas of how to go about things.

Thank You, God, for giving my father another son to help and teach.

In late October of 1999, my parents invited both of us to dinner at their house. My mother and Ron found that they had art in common, which has deepened their relationship. My father and Ron often talk about home improvement and how to do it.

My prayer now is "Thank You, God, for the lessons I have learned through the people and situations You have given me to deal with in my life. Help me to continue to follow the path You have set for me, knowing that at times I will not understand the master plan or where it leads. Give me the strength to continue no matter how difficult it is.

Thank You for teaching my family to 'love one another.' And, Lord, thank You for the family that You have given back to me and the joy they bring me."

↶

RISING FROM THE DEAD

by Dianne Smith, Fremont, California
* Names have been changed at the author's request.

The doorbell rang at one o'clock in the morning and Ann groggily rose to answer it. *Who could that be at this hour of night?* she wondered. Her ten-year-old son was sound asleep in the small apartment they'd recently moved to, and she hoped he wouldn't wake up. She was a single mother and Blake was her whole world.

She peered through the peephole in her door and was surprised to see the maintenance man of the apartment complex. When she opened the door to let him in, the man grabbed her, put a knife to her throat, and yanked her outside.

"Don't fight me or I'll kill you," he rasped.

Paralyzed with fear, Ann was dragged to a barren field nearby. When she was found, she was barely alive. She had been brutally raped, stabbed, and left for dead. She was whisked away to the hospital in an ambulance, and her family was notified of her situation. Her pastor was also told, and the next Sunday he stood before the hushed congregation to tell them what had happened. Ann was one of their Sunday school teachers.

Lying in bed, Ann felt broken, humiliated, and worthless. Where had God been when she needed Him? Didn't He care? Didn't anyone care?

Then one of the most remarkable experiences of her life occurred. The people from her church would not allow her trauma to be buried. They did not let her wounds fester in her soul. Instead, they enveloped her with an overwhelming compassion. Their ardent prayers rose to heaven. A generous fund was created to pay for her medical bills, and care was provided for her son, Blake. On a daily basis, she was showered with attention. No need went unmet. As soon as she was able to see visitors, her room was flooded with supporters. They told her she was still a beautiful person and that they needed her among them. She was loved, no matter what, and God would heal her broken body from the inside out. She was slowly, miraculously overcoming an experience that most women could never surmount.

A few months later, she was able to rejoin the congregation. With visible scars on her face and neck, her serene demeanor amazed those with whom she spoke. A peace no one but God could manufacture was unmistakably reflected in her eyes.

Ann had a life to live and people to serve. She wasn't going to be deterred by evil, not even the most unspeakable evil. Christ, the Great Physician, had used His people to bring her back from the depths, and she knew that ultimate healing resided with Him.

⌒ Make sure to read Dianne Smith's story, "Remember the Cross," in volume one of God Allows U-Turns: True Stories of Hope and Healing.

DEAR MR. B.

by Merrie Maurer, Russels Point, Ohio

My sister died as a result of injuries she received in a head-on collision with a drunk driver. It was a Saturday afternoon and he was on her side of the road coming over a hill when the impact occurred. My sister was a truly good person who left behind a husband and five children, including a fourteen year old who's mentally and physically handicapped, as well as siblings who loved and needed her more than words can ever say.

I have always believed in God, and He has gotten me through some bad times. However, this time I blamed Him for letting my sister die. For ten years I blamed Him and the drunk driver for making my life so empty. One morning I awoke to realize that my life was empty because I was missing my relationship with God. I was an empty shell. I got down on my knees and prayed like never before, asking God to please forgive me. I knew He had, but I knew that I also had to forgive the drunk driver and, somehow, with God's love and help, I did. The following is the letter I wrote to him.

Dear Mr. B.:

We have seen each other a few times. I'm not sure if you will recognize my name or if you would even recognize my face if we should ever meet again. I am not sure if you have ever thought about me, but I have thought of you often.

Pat was my sister. She died as a result of your driving while drunk. The day she died, a big part of me died, too. Mr. B., I have lived with depression, hate, and loneliness ever since that day almost ten years ago. I have allowed these feelings to eat me alive, turn me into a near alcoholic myself, although I never drink and drive, and keep me from fully living my life.

I have cried and hated more in these ten years than anyone can imagine. The tragedy of losing my sister turned me into a person that I didn't like. Ten years is enough time to wallow in hate. My sister was a good and forgiving person who would have forgiven you a long time ago. It took me longer, but I do forgive you. I have to, so that I can let go of that horrible day and begin to live again.

Mr. B., I can no longer hate you. I hate what happened, but we can't change the past. None of us are perfect; we all make mistakes. I know that you didn't set out that day to intentionally hurt or kill someone. It just happened. Maybe it was supposed to be that way. We have all learned a great deal from it. I loved my sister so very much and I will always miss her and regret that she isn't here. I will still have bad days, but I will no longer blame you for them.

Please forgive me for hating you all these years. Let's both move on with our lives and never look back with hate again. Mr. B., I wish for you a life of happiness, love, laughter, and many blessings. Take good care of yourself and, if you haven't yet, forgive yourself, too, and live life to the fullest. My sister would want it that way as I do now.

May God always bless you and your family.
Merrie Root

The day I wrote that letter I was free. My healing had begun and in time my emptiness would be a thing of the past. For the first time in ten long years, my heart and soul were at peace. And I know that my sister, in her heavenly home, rejoiced along with me.

DON'T HOLD A GRUDGE

by Joe Seay, Greenbrier, Arkansas

Our church team was excited about our first practice on this beautiful spring day. I was the player-coach and shared their enthusiasm. As the players arrived, I suggested they start the practice session at the same position they played last season.

Jack, who played second base last year, didn't show up. I assigned a rookie to play his position. We enjoyed throwing the ball around and then started a practice game. During the second inning of the practice game, Jack showed up. He walked over to second base and told the rookie that he would take over now. The rookie, a younger man excited about getting to play, refused to leave.

Jack walked over to me and said, "I've played second base for three years. Are you replacing me?"

"No," I explained, "but you were not here, so I asked the new guy to play second for awhile."

"I'm here now and ready to take over," he said in a determined manner.

As coach, I made the decision to leave the rookie at second for awhile. I told Jack he could resume his position a little later in the game. It seemed like a logical plan since Jack arrived late and I had already asked the rookie to play second. Jack's feelings were hurt, and he demanded that I put him in the game at second base immediately.

I assured him that I would put him at second base after a couple of innings, but he became angry and shouted at me, "Just kick me off the team because I'm a few minutes late!" We glared at each other, then he walked off in a huff. "I've had it! I quit!" he shouted back at me.

Jack and I had been good friends for a long time. I was disappointed over this incident, but I assumed it would blow over and be forgotten in a few days. I was wrong. It didn't. Jack avoided me at church. His ego was wounded, but so was mine. It seemed to me the fault was on his side, not mine, since he was the one who was late and then started the trouble.

As the days went by, nothing changed. It seemed that our friendship was over. I could live with that if it was the way he wanted it. *It's his problem,* I thought, *not mine.* A few days later I read in my Bible that if we do not forgive people who offend us, God will not forgive us. The words pricked my conscience and I read it again and thought of Jack. Reading further, I found that God expects us to forgive many, many times. I thought of Jack again.

The next Sunday at church, I saw Jack coming down the hall toward me. He saw me about the same time and looked away. Stepping directly in front of him, I said, "Jack, I want to apologize to you for the way I acted at softball practice. Will you forgive me?" I offered him my hand. He looked at me without a smile and ignored my hand.

People were watching us. Jack still refused to respond. *Oh, well. I tried. Now it's up to him.* Then someone seemed to whisper in my ear, *"How many times should we forgive others?"* And the answer was very clear: *"Seventy times seven."* I breathed a quick prayer and tried again. "Please forgive me. I want to be your friend again."

Jack pushed my hand away. . .then smiled and gave me a big hug. He said, "It's okay, Joe."

We were friends again and it felt good. No hard feelings. No guilty conscience. Soon Jack was playing second base again. He was his old self. Our team had a good record that year. It looked like we would make the play-offs.

A few days before the play-offs were to start, I received a call from Jack's wife. He had a terrible headache and had to miss a game. The next day they put him in the hospital for tests. The doctors discovered a major blood vessel that was inoperable had burst in his head. Jack was bleeding to death.

I saw Jack one more time. He was lying in his hospital bed, dazed and weak. "Joe," he said in a squeaky whisper, "hold my position for me. I'll be there in time for the play-offs." I assured him that his position on the team was secure, and we shared one last smile.

Our team didn't make the play-offs that year, after all, and Jack never made it back to play. He is now playing on a much bigger and better team, and I know he's a great team player. I'm so glad that Jack and I forgave each other and that we didn't wait too long. Jack was one of my best friends when he was alive, and I thank God he was still one of my best friends when he died.

CHAPTER EIGHT

Prayer

Therefore I tell you, whatever you ask for in prayer,
believe that you have received it,
and it will be yours.
Mark 11:24

GO FISH!

by Linda Parker, Windermere, Florida

I was a young mother with two beautiful daughters and one out-of-the-picture ex-husband. And while the first two completely made up for the latter, I also faced the challenge of being the mom, the dad, the bread-winner, the plumber, the painter, the gardener, and the auto mechanic.

So, in recurring intervals, when my two beautiful daughters got that longing look in their beautiful eyes, I experienced all the pangs of failed parenthood. A child should have a pet. A pet means companion-ship, responsibility, and that special bonding.

Fish were always my solution—a compromise, my default position, and the backup plan. We couldn't afford a dog or a cat.

Plus, my plate was already full. How could I manage to be respon-sible for one more living creature on this earth? Trust me—fish were the best I could do. But when a little girl really wants a white kitten so badly that she names her fish "Fluffy," that fish carries extraordinary responsibility as a pet.

Early one unremarkable Saturday morning after Fluffy had been swimming in circles in a glass bowl on the kitchen counter for many months, I noticed he wasn't looking his glowing best. His usual deep maroon color was gray-tinged and he lingered near the bottom of the bowl. *Uh-oh,* I thought, dreading the presumed inevitable.

I changed the water in his small container. I carefully replaced the seashells and plastic mermaids that Fluffy's young decorators had lov-ingly added to his abode. "Come on, Fluff," I coaxed. "Carrie adores you." Fluffy, as usual, was noncommittal.

I heard two sets of bare tramping feet come down the stairs. I knew from experience that before they got the cereal box, even before they came to look for me, seven-year-old Carrie would go to the counter and check on Fluffy, and little sister, Amanda, like a faithful sidekick, would be right behind.

Three, two, one, I counted silently. "Mooom!" Carrie called out from the kitchen. "Mom, something is wrong with Fluffy!" Her voice quivered.

"Well, maybe he'll be all right," I reassured. "I changed his water," I added, as if that might have promoted a miracle cure.

As the morning passed, it seemed apparent that Fluffy was passing, too. By late afternoon his color was entirely gray. His usual rounded form seemed strangely flattened. *Can a fish be dehydrated?* I wondered.

Carrie and Amanda checked on their patient frequently. As the worst seemed unavoidable, I tried to prepare them. "You know, Fluffy has been with us a long time, in fish years."

"And he is going to be with us until we are old, isn't he, Mommy?" Amanda contributed cheerfully.

"Well, Honey, pets like fish and turtles don't always live as long as people."

"Mommy, there are Lapagos turtles that live forever. I saw it on TV. And there are catfish that are as old as you!" Amanda continued, emphasizing the word "old" a bit more than I liked. Amanda was such a bright, helpful child.

"Oh, Sweetie, all I am saying is that it may be time for Fluffy to go to live in heaven. We know he'll be so happy and healthy there."

As if on cue, Fluffy took a turn for the worse. He now floated diagonally, almost at the surface of the water. His gills appeared motionless. I had to admit that Fluff had never charmed me quite as he had Carrie and Amanda. Now that he looked like a canned sardine after the canning, I felt quite sorry for the little guy.

"You know, girls, maybe the kind thing would be to go ahead and take Fluffy out of his bowl. He's dying; he looks terrible. I think he is almost gone and we don't want to see him suffer."

Tears began to roll silently down Amanda's pudgy cheeks. Carrie was very quiet, and then she spoke. "No, Mom, let's not bury him yet."

"But, Carrie, he's. . . ," I wanted to say gross but fumbled for a kinder word. "He's miserable."

"No," said Carrie, "let's give him a little more time."

That afternoon Carrie was very low-key. By bedtime, poor old Fluffy was floating sideways on top of the water. His splendid red color was gone. He gave no sign of life.

"Girls," I began, "I think it is time to. . ."

"No, Mom!" said Carrie authoritatively. "Fluffy is going to be fine." Her tone was insistent.

"Honey," I spoke gently, "Fluffy has gone to heaven. Let's get a nice little box and we can bury him under the big tree in the backyard."

"Mom, Fluffy is going to get well," my faithful daughter insisted once again.

"Carrie, I am sorry, but I think Fluffy is dead."

Amanda looked first at me, then her big sister. For a change, she was speechless. I looked at Carrie's silently pleading face and, against all logical judgment, I said, "Okay, Sweetie, we'll leave Fluffy in his bowl until morning."

I did not have to face my morning alarm clock. Carrie's excited voice woke me, just before daylight. "Mom, come see Fluffy!" she shouted. *Oh, dear,* I thought, rubbing my eyes and fumbling for my slippers. Fluffy's bowl had been my last stop just before bedtime. His gray, lifeless body had floated on its side on the surface of the water.

"Carrie," I stopped my sentence. Words weren't forming in my brain, much less my mouth. In his little bowl, our fish, Fluffy, was swimming—and swimming vigorously! His color was deep red and his shape was firm and plump again. I couldn't think what to say. If Carrie had not been a seven year old in flannel pajamas, I would have believed that she had been to the pet shop and purchased a replacement Fluffy.

"What happened?" I asked as Carrie and Amanda jumped about and giggled.

"I prayed," Carrie answered matter-of-factly.

"What did you say in your prayer?" I asked incredulously, as I held Fluffy's bowl up to the light, still not accepting what I was seeing.

Carrie's look, as she was already getting out her cereal bowl, reflected what a dumb grown-up question she thought I was asking.

"Mom, I just prayed for God to make Fluffy better!"

"Well, God certainly listened to your prayer, Carrie."

"Sure, Mom, that's what He does," she responded, quite matter-of-fact.

After several days I gave up checking on Fluffy in his bowl every few minutes, as if I anticipated at any time to discover him floating, colorless, on the surface of the water again. Good old Fluff lived another two happy and healthy years with us. When he finally died, Carrie and Amanda buried him sadly, but with acceptance. They wrote "Fluffy" on a small board and placed it over his grave. I added the name "Lazarus."

Fluffy-Lazarus lived his small life *large*. His recovery and Carrie's uncomplicated faith became a symbol in our family of what the power of prayer, fortified by sincere conviction, can accomplish. In the years to follow, my father faced serious surgeries with confidence because Carrie and Amanda had said prayers for his healing. My best friend laughed over Fluffy's resurrection but leaned on it as an example that faith would lead her through the painful events of her divorce.

Many times since that day, the story of Fluffy has reassured me that even my smallest problems are worthy of prayer. My now-teenage daughters, our three cats, and I have gotten through the years strengthened by the knowledge that the sparrow, the number of hairs on our heads, yes, even the little fishes are watched over and valued, too.

POWDERFUL PRAYERS

by Mildred Blankenship, Union City, Georgia

A large family is a blessing, even if at times it seems the work will never end and the money will never stretch far enough. We had four children, one girl and three boys, and the one thing I always had plenty of was dirty laundry! Two of my boys lived to play outdoors, enjoying every game to the fullest and making sure they brought back plenty of the outside on their clothes. My youngest son, Robert, enjoyed playing when he could, but having been born with a heart defect, he couldn't be part of all his brothers' games.

Because Robert was so ill, it was impossible for me to work outside the home. I added a little income to our family by keeping a friend's two children during the day, but that earned me only ten dollars a week. The money was small, but it did help buy staples like milk and bread. It also helped pay the bus fare back and forth to the hospital with Robert, since we didn't have a car. But there were no frills, and at times even money for the much-needed laundry detergent was hard to come by. It was during one of these lean times that God proved to me how very true to His word He can be.

Before leaving for the grocery store, I checked my laundry detergent only to find it nearly gone. Daily washing was a necessity at our house, and it didn't take much calculating to discover that my detergent would be gone within a week. I've always loved the Lord and taken Him at His word. That's how I lived with Robert's illness and coped with the many hospital stays that were completely out of my control.

Being a woman who had learned the reality of prayer, I decided to apply it to my weekly shopping. Knowing that I wouldn't be able to budget cleaning supplies back into my buying until the beginning of the next month, I decided I needed some divine assistance. I quietly and simply told Jesus that I was depending on Him to let the soap powder last until I could afford to buy more. I then thanked Him in advance for what He was going to do.

That Saturday afternoon, as I put the few items I could afford into my shopping cart, I had to fight the impulse to get the laundry detergent and leave something else off my list. After all, I really needed to keep the children's clothes clean for school. But I quickly decided to stand firm and allow God to help me with this part of my family needs.

Sunday passed, then Monday morning rolled around. I was busy cleaning the kitchen after the children left for school, when I heard something outside my back door. I went to see if someone was there, and to my delight found a full-sized box of a new laundry detergent hanging in a plastic bag on my doorknob! The noise had been someone delivering a product sample to my home—but not just any product—a laundry detergent! I was immediately thrilled and relieved that God had answered my prayer so quickly. I thanked Him, put the detergent away, and continued to clean my house.

When I reached the front of the house, I was still basking in God's love for the small things in our life. I decided to take my joy outside and sweep the front porch. As I opened the front door to go out, there, to my total amazement, was another full-sized box of the same laundry powder! By this time, I was overwhelmed by God's generosity. He had provided even more than I had hoped for. I continued to sweep the front porch, but my mind was on greater things. Imagine, my heavenly Father loved me enough to help me keep my children's clothes clean!

There was a spring in my step as I continued my household duties. The mail had been delivered by now, so I ran down to our mailbox to pick it up. I almost did a double take when I spied the now-familiar plastic bag hanging on the mailbox. Here was box number three of the same soap! By now I was beginning to praise the Lord and laugh at the same time. This wasn't possible, yet it was happening. Now I had three full-sized boxes of detergent, when only several hours earlier I had barely enough to get through the day.

I gathered my latest box of detergent and headed back up the stairs that led to my house when I happened to notice something hanging on my basement door. You guessed it: another box of detergent! I had never had that many washing products at one time in all my life.

So many times we find God trustworthy in the large areas of our lives but fail to take Him at His word concerning the day-to-day events. He is the God who wants to meet all our needs. Whether it's something as monumental as a visit to the hospital with a very sick child or as practical as having detergent delivered to the door. . .He truly cares. For our part, all we need do is believe Him when He says, "Ask and ye shall receive. . . ."

Since that day I've held the firm belief that God not only does the miraculous, but He knows the value of a clean pair of jeans!

LICENSE PLATES FROM HEAVEN

by Sally John, Coal Valley, Illinois

"Mom!" eight-year-old Christopher called from the living room. "Watch this!"

Grinning to herself, Sally tossed the sponge into the pail, hopped off the stepladder, and hurried toward her son's excited voice. Scrubbing kitchen cupboards could wait; Sally knew these special childhood moments could not.

Just as she turned the corner, a G.I. Joe figure floated from the second-story landing, his miniature parachute billowing, and tumbled at her feet. "Cool," she said, as she scooped the doll up and climbed the staircase.

"What's your sister up to?"

Towheaded Christopher laughed. "Unpacking."

She laughed with him. Three-year-old Elizabeth made a "home" wherever she was, whether it was in the car, a motel room, or this empty town house. It didn't matter that the rental contract wasn't even signed yet or that they were only spending a few hours here in order to clean. Elizabeth was a "nester," and it made everyone smile.

Sally found her chubby-cheeked daughter in one of the bedrooms, busily organizing her treasures on a low closet shelf.

"Hi, Sweetie. Do you like this room?"

Elizabeth nodded. "Chris-ta-fa said I could have this one." She knelt on the floor and dug into her backpack.

"I'll be in the kitchen if you need something," Sally said, knowing full well the words wouldn't break through her tot's concentration. The children's excitement was infectious. Even scrubbing sounded like fun. Downstairs, her husband, Tim, and friend, Dave, were walking around the living room, eyes on the carpet, pressing their toes here and there.

"We've got a problem," Tim said. "The carpet is soaking wet in spots. There's probably a broken water pipe."

"Which means?" she asked.

"Ripping up carpet, tearing out the flooring, digging up the front yard."

She stared at them. The situation was incomprehensible. "I'm going to scrub." In the kitchen she climbed back onto the stepladder and plunged her hands into the pail of now-cool sudsy water. She squeezed the sponge and began vigorously scouring inside a cupboard. The effort didn't alleviate her frustrations.

"Be anxious for nothing." The words from Philippians 4:6 (NKJV) came to mind.

"How?" she complained to God. "How am I supposed to stop being anxious when one thing after another happens?"

Two years ago her husband had started a business. Eighteen months later they were out of money and sold their Illinois house. Bill and Jane, a pastor friend and his wife, invited them to settle in San Diego, California. They arrived six months ago, having decided to start over. In time, their household goods were shipped out and put in a storage unit. For eight weeks, Bill, Jane, and their sons shared their home with them. After that, Tim and Sally house-sat for a family that was living overseas for four months. Now, the time was up and that family was due home in a week. This rental town house had seemed perfect.

Rental housing was scarce. They had investigated every condo, town house, apartment, and house available in the area. This place had been the only option within their budget, and now something had gone terribly wrong with the plumbing.

After talking with the town house owner about the plumbing problem, it was evident they didn't have a place to move into in time. Plans had to be changed yet again.

The next morning they searched the newspaper again. A new listing had been added. Although the cost was more than they wanted to pay, they went to see the place. It was a roomy two-story house, light and airy. They instantly fell in love with it. There was even plenty of space for guests. The owners were eager to rent out their home because they were moving in two days. The timing was perfect, but the price was frightening. And there were other people interested in renting or even buying the house.

Tim and Sally went to the park to pray. They reminded each other once again of Philippians 4:6–7 (NKJV), the verses that had sustained them throughout the past two-year ordeal. "Be anxious for nothing, but in everything by prayer and supplication, with thanksgiving, let your requests be made known to God; and the peace of God, which surpasses all understanding, will guard your hearts and minds through Christ Jesus." Then they thanked Him and they asked Him for the house and the means to pay for it. And although their stomachs churned, they left it there in His hands.

Later Tim talked with the owners. They wanted his family to rent their house! Then he talked with his boss, who offered him enough money to pay for the rent.

Two days later Sally walked through her new front door and felt a distinct impression of the question, *"What if you have to give this one up, too?"* Was it anxiety chipping away at the pleasure of at last finding a home? By now she recognized anxiety for what it was: an opportunity to talk to God. "Father," she said, "if You want to move me somewhere else, it's okay by me. Thy will be done." Friends helped them unload their long-packed things from the storage unit and move into the house. It was a celebration not just of having their own place, but also of God's faithfulness.

A short time later, new California license plates for their car arrived in the mail. Tim opened the package and burst into laughter, and then he became solemnly pensive. . .staring at the plates in amazement. He wordlessly showed them to Sally, who was soon giggling and crying with him.

It seemed the Creator of the universe had just given them a wondrous gift in the form of royal blue license plates. Randomly designated letters and numbers issued by the state? They didn't think so.

Imprinted with gold numbers and letters their new plates read: PHL467.

GROWING PAINS

by Suzy Ryan, Oceanside, California

Dressed in crisp clothes, the line of freshly scrubbed kindergarten kids stood proudly with their bulging backpacks hanging from their small shoulders. Only their nervous smiles and darting eyes revealed their fear of the first day of school. I fought back tears, squeezing one last hug from my five-year-old son, Keegan, before his teacher whisked him to his classroom.

I stumbled to the car, wondering how he could already be starting school. Finally, it was time to pick him up. I arrived early, noticing his sigh of relief after spotting me in the crowd of anxious parents. Before heading home, I found out that Keegan cried during lunch. He had clutched his small cooler, refusing to eat.

Day after day, this pattern continued until I thought I could not bear it another moment. I asked him if he wanted to take a special stuffed animal to class.

"I only want you, Mom," he quietly replied. We cut a small piece of his "special blanket" and carefully placed it in the pocket of his shorts.

"It's our secret," I explained. "Whenever you're homesick, reach down in your pocket and your blanket will remind you of my love."

"All right, Mom, just make sure you pray for me not to feel sad tomorrow."

As I dropped Keegan off the next morning, I fought the urge to yank him from school and take him home. I hovered outside the closed classroom door, silently praying. *Lord, take care of my little boy. I trust You to hold his hand and guide him since I am relinquishing control of my firstborn.* I could feel a peace blanket me. *Help him to grow independent from me. And give me the courage to let him go—let him grow. Replace the panic in my spirit with the joy of knowing I can trust You completely with the baby You knew even before I did.* After my prayer, I walked to my car, relaxing for the first time in weeks.

Three short weeks later, I watched as my little boy sprinted to class with his new friends. My confident, exuberant son forgot to say goodbye. I brushed away a tear.

He is maturing. We are both growing up. "To every thing there is a season," the Bible says (Ecclesiastes 3:1 KJV). This was the season for maturing.

GETHSEMANE

by Carol McAdoo Rehme, Loveland, Colorado

Is this my Gethsemane, Father?

I rubbed at the small of my back and gazed out the barred window of the waiting room to the deepening dusk outside. Headlights flickered as cars filed from the parking lot like fireflies in formation.

I felt as bleak and gray and cold as the darkening night.

A sigh shoved a path from my knotted stomach to my throat. It snagged on the jagged lump lodged there and erupted in a jerky whimper.

How long had I been on my own personal "midnight watch"? Hours. No—days. Did it even matter anymore? A single phone call—the phone call every parent secretly both awaits and dreads—had disrupted our family's lives, altered our course. Perhaps forever.

At times throughout the day, I had managed to hold Kyle but never my own tears. Even now they slipped down my cheeks, a mirrored reflection of the persistent rain pelting the glass windowpanes in front of me.

It had been a long day—bedside—in the Trauma Unit. After thrilling everyone with his initial but sporadic moments of awareness earlier in the week, Kyle—victim of a hit-and-run drunk driver—now lapsed into unresponsiveness.

Absolute. Total. Complete.

Instead, a wild, aggressive agitation replaced his once promising breaths of lucidity. I felt cheated somehow, like a child promised a coveted gift only to have it snatched away.

How dare You let my hope grow and then trample it like this?

For eleven hours that day I had hovered over my firstborn son. Suctioning paste-thick mucus from dangerously full lungs. Encouraging him futilely while deep, painful coughs racked his weakened body. Sponging his brow over and over and over again only to watch sweat beads pop out like measles. Quieting his long, flailing arms and legs that tangled the bedding and threatened the life-giving tubes.

Wasn't it enough to deal with the combined traumas of blood clots, brain hemorrhages, broken bones, high fevers, and pneumonias? His problems read like a medical book index. Now, still comatose, Kyle was a danger to himself. Already his persistent thrashing had disturbed an IV and dislodged a catheter.

Someone ordered restraints for Kyle's "own safety."

I stood by helplessly, watching when a nurse—armed with two white corded belts—encircled my son's ankles and fettered him to the computer board at the foot of the bed. She stuffed the limp fingers of each hand into mounded mitts, as plump as boxing gloves, that she manacled to the side rails.

There he lay. Constrained by shackles. Tethered by tubing. Strapped to his bed. And still he twisted and writhed.

He's my son, God, a human being! He isn't an animal. Must he be harnessed like one?

My unsaid words shoved roughly against my thoughts. I bit the inside of my lip and swallowed the rusty taste of blood.

Each glance into the cement faces of the nurses and doctors screamed out reality. I knew I was standing at the lip of death's yawning chasm. Death—cold, clammy, and chilling. I sensed it; I smelled it; I shivered with it. Jacketed in fear, I had fled Kyle's room and raced down the long hall.

Now I staggered under the burden that bowed my shoulders. The pain of a deathwatch. Icy and dark, like the night shadows prowling the empty waiting room.

I am exhausted and as weary as the watchers at the tomb, heavenly Father. How much more can You ask of me?

Death scenes, detailed and descriptive, flashed in erratic sequencing behind my eyelids. I massaged my temples to erase the grisly images that thrummed through my mind. My stomach quivered and clenched in protest against the weighted anguish that plummeted from my heart to settle there.

Pressing my tearstained cheek against the fogged window, I prayed.

I prayed for enough strength to bear this trial.

I prayed for enough courage to see it through.

I prayed for enough faith to believe that. . .

For enough faith to. . .

Oh, Father, this is too hard to manage, too heavy to carry, too much to ask of any mother.

Let this cup pass from me!

Please.

I prayed for—faith enough.

BUILDING BLOCKS

by Margaret Shauers, Great Bend, Kansas

It seems a long time ago since I started teaching my first church school class and met Johnny. Today I count my experience with him as one of my richest.

Johnny's behavior caused my predecessor to stop teaching the class in the middle of the year. His behavior was also the reason I often wondered if I should follow her example.

Johnny ran into the street when we went for a hike. He pushed other children, pulled girls' hair, yelled, screamed, and even occasionally bit. Many of the words that came from Johnny's mouth were far from appropriate for a church school classroom. Johnny was a four-year-old handful.

The one thing he liked to do was play with the building blocks. While building, he actually quit yelling. Sometimes, if the others let him be the boss, Johnny allowed them to help him. There was only one remaining problem. Once Johnny began to build, he didn't want to stop.

"Won't put up the blocks!" he would insist sullenly when I announced that it was time to put the toys away and move to the worship center. That simple phrase brought us back to the yelling, screaming, and cursing.

I never did solve the problem of Johnny through any wisdom of my own. The only contribution I can claim is prayer. With Johnny around, I found many opportunities to pray—and these prayers were answered through Johnny.

One week, I decided to pick up the blocks for Johnny. We were wasting too much time arguing.

"No, Teacher, no!" Johnny screamed, grabbing the end of the first block I picked up from the large "house" outline he had strung across the floor. "Johnny just built his house. No, Teacher, no!" he cried.

Then, stubbornly, Johnny added, "Johnny will stay in his house. Johnny will hear the story from here."

Without consciously thinking, I put the block back in place. "Okay," I said. "If you can't come with us to the worship center, we'll come to you." And we all went to "Johnny's house."

Johnny's face reflected surprise, doubt, and a bit of the selfishness he always showed over the blocks. But there was another emotion, too. That was pride of ownership. And it won out that day. Solemnly, Johnny showed the other children to the "door" of his house. Being Johnny, he was not tolerant of those who tried to walk over a "wall." For the first time since I began teaching the class, however, Johnny wasn't pouting or causing trouble.

Having our story in "Johnny's house" became routine. Because he wanted to have the most impressive house possible, Johnny began to grow more lenient toward the other builders. Instead of announcing, "Johnny's going to build a house," he began to urge the others on. "Hurry," he'd say. "Let's build the house for our story." As he learned that working together was fun, Johnny began to participate more freely and peacefully in other activities.

This change was gradual. There were still many Sundays when I wondered why I had taken the class. But the magic of Johnny's house never failed to make him happy. Each Sunday as I watched him listening to the Bible story, I knew that I would not resign from teaching that class.

As I said, those early church school lessons often seem long past, but recently I began to teach again. Johnny, now a long-legged teenager and the office helper of the day, popped into my classroom just as story time drew near.

He glanced curiously at the children scurrying to put away cars and dolls. Then his eyes fell on several long lines of blocks, placed end to end to form the outline of a house.

"The house!" he exclaimed. "You still use it."

"Of course we still use it," I said, warmed by the glowing smile on his face. I couldn't help but compare this friendly young man to the sullen, angry four year old I had first known.

I should have visited in Johnny's home in the days when he was a four year old. If I had, I would have learned that Johnny received little or no attention there. He had an infant sister and an ailing mother. There wasn't much time left for Johnny.

The only thing I did have enough sense to do, back then, was to ask for God's help. God helped me give Johnny the sense of importance he so desperately needed, He helped an angry young boy find peace, and He helped this humble teacher understand the true power of prayer.

CHAPTER NINE

New Direction U-Turn

Therefore, if anyone is in Christ, he is a new creation;
the old has gone, the new has come!
2 Corinthians 5:17

SMILEY

by Karen Garrison, Steubenville, Ohio

Lily Sturgeon changed my life. She was eighty-seven years old when I first met her, and I was a prima donna at the self-centered age of seventeen. She was a resident at the convalescent home I'd been volunteering at to better my final Health Assistant grade.

For weeks I had grumbled to my boyfriend about having to tend to people "for free." "After all," I told him, "every penny could've gone toward our 'after-graduation' celebration in New York." He heartily agreed.

And even worse, I soon realized, were the bright yellow uniforms my classmates and I were required to wear. On our first day at the geriatric center, the registered nurses took one look at our sunshiny apparel and nicknamed us "The Yellow Birds."

During my scheduled days, I complained to other yellow birds about how changing bedpans and soiled linen and spoon-feeding pureed foods to mumbling mouths were not things any teenager should have to do.

A tedious month passed, then I met Lily. I was given a tray of food and sent to her room. Her bright blue eyes appraised me as I entered, and I soon became very aware of the kindness behind them.

After a few minutes of talking with her, I realized why I hadn't noticed Lily before, even though I had been past her room numerous times. Lily, unlike so many of the other residents, was soft-spoken and undemanding. From my first day at the geriatric center, I had learned the staff had their favorite patients. Usually, the favorites were ones that stuck out in some characteristic way. From joke-tellers to singers, the louder and more rambunctious the patient, the more attention they received.

Something inside of me immediately liked Lily and, strangely, I even began to enjoy our talks during my visits to her room. It didn't take long to realize that Lily's genuine kindness stemmed from her relationship with God.

"Come here." She smiled to me one rainy afternoon. "Sit down. I have something to show you." She lifted a small photo album and began to turn the pages. "This was my Albert. See him there? Such a handsome man." Her voice softened even more as she pointed to a pretty little girl sitting on top of a fence. "And that was our darling Emmy when she was eight years old."

A drop of wetness splattered on the plastic cover and I quickly turned to Lily. Her eyes were filled with tears. "What is it?" I whispered, covering her hand with my own.

She didn't answer right away, but as she turned the pages I noticed that Emmy was not in any other photographs. "She died from cancer that year," Lily told me. "She'd been in and out of hospitals most of her life, but that year Jesus took her home."

"I'm so sorry," I said, disturbed that God would take away this beautiful woman's daughter. "I don't understand why He let her die. You're such a true follower of His," I said.

"It's okay," she smiled slightly, meeting my eyes. "God has a plan for every life, Karen. We need to open our hearts to Him regardless if we understand His ways or not. Only then can we find true peace." She turned to the last page. Inside the worn album was one more picture of a middle-aged Lily standing on tiptoes and kissing a clown's cheek.

"That's my Albert," she laughed, recalling happy memories. "After Emmy died, we decided to do something to help the children at the hospitals. We'd been so disturbed by the dismal surroundings while Emmy was hospitalized." Lily went on to explain how Albert decided to become "Smiley the Clown."

"Emmy was always smiling," she recalled. "Even in the worst of times. So I scraped together what fabric I could find and sewed this costume for Albert." She clasped her hands in joy. "The children loved it! Every weekend, we'd volunteer at the hospitals to bring smiles and gifts to the children."

"But you were poor; how'd you manage that?" I asked in amazement.

"Well," she said and grinned, meeting my eyes, "smiles are free and the gifts weren't anything fancy."

She shut the album and leaned back against her pillows. "Sometimes the local bakers would donate goodies, or when we were really hurting for money, we'd take a litter of pups from our farm. The children loved petting them. After Albert died, I noticed how faded and worn-out the costume actually was, and so I rented one and dressed as Smiley until about ten years ago, when I had my first heart attack."

When I left Lily's room that day, I couldn't think of anything but how generous she and Albert had been to children who weren't their own.

Graduation day neared and on my last day of volunteer services at the ward, I hurried to Lily's room. She was asleep, curled into a fetal position from stomach discomfort. I stroked her brow, worrying about who would care for her the way I did. Lily hadn't any other surviving family members, and most of the staff neglected her except for her basic needs, which were met with polite abruptness. At times I wanted to shout Lily's virtues to them, but she'd stop me, reminding me that the good things she'd done in life were done without thoughts of self.

"Besides," she would say, "doesn't the good Lord tell us to store our treasures in heaven and not on this earth?"

Lily must've sensed my inner torment above her bed that day as she opened her eyes and touched my hand. "What is it, Dear?" she asked, her voice concerned and laced with pain.

"I'll be back in two weeks," I told her, explaining about my high school graduation. "And then I'll visit you every day. I promise."

She sighed and squeezed my fingers. "I can't wait for you to tell me all about it."

Two weeks later to the day, I rushed back to the center, bubbly with excitement and anxious to share with Lily the news of my graduation events. With a bouquet of lilies in my hand, I stepped into her clean, neat, unoccupied room. The bed was made and as I searched for an answer to Lily's whereabouts, my heart already knew the answer. I threw the flowers on the bed and wept.

A nurse gently touched my shoulder. "Were you one of the yellow birds?" she asked. "Is your name Karen?" I nodded and she handed me a gift-wrapped box. "Lily wanted you to have this. We've had it since she died because we didn't know how to get in touch with you."

It was her photo album. Written on the inside cover was the Scripture Jeremiah 29:11: " 'For I know the plans I have for you,' declares the Lord, 'plans to prosper you and not to harm you, plans to give you hope and a future.' " I clutched it to my chest and departed.

Three weeks later my horrified boyfriend stood before me. "You can't be serious," he said, starting to pace back and forth. "You look ridiculous." We were in my bedroom and as I tried to view myself in the mirror, he blocked my reflection. "You can't be serious," he repeated. "How in the world did you pay for that thing anyway?"

"With my graduation money."

"Your what?" he exclaimed, shaking his head. "You spent the money we were going to New York with on that?"

"Yep," I replied, stringing on my rubber nose. "Life is more about giving than receiving."

"This is just great," he muttered, helping me tie the back of the costume. "And what am I supposed to tell someone when they ask me my girlfriend's name? That it's Bozo?"

I looked at my watch. I had better hurry if I wanted to make it on time to the children's hospital. "Nope," I answered, kissing him quickly on the cheek.

"Tell them it's Smiley. Smiley the Clown!"

I DON'T REALLY WANT TO HURT MY CHILD

by Kathy Collard Miller, Placentia, California

Darcy's training pants were wet again. Again!

Marching over to my two-year-old daughter, I directed her into the bathroom. As I struggled to pull down the soaking pants, I felt a rush of frustration and a sense of failure.

"Darcy, you're supposed to come in the bathroom and go in the potty chair. Why can't you learn?" I continued to berate her. As I began spanking her with my hand, my tension and tiredness found an outlet. Spanking changed to hitting. Darcy's uncontrollable screaming brought me back to reason. Seeing the red blister on her bottom, I dropped to my knees.

"How can I act this way?" I sobbed. "I love Jesus. I don't really want to hurt my child. Oh, God, please help me."

The rest of that day I held my anger in check. The next day started out pleasantly. I watched my happy daughter. But as the day progressed and pressures closed in on me, I became impatient. I looked forward to a few moments of peace while Darcy and two-month-old Mark took their naps.

Telling Darcy to play quietly in her room, I rocked Mark to sleep. Just as I laid him carefully into his crib, Darcy burst into the room shouting, "Mommy, I want to color."

Mark woke up crying. I grabbed Darcy by the shoulders, shook her, and screamed, "Shut up! Shut up! I want him to go to sleep!"

Both Darcy and Mark cried as I shoved Darcy aside, rushed out of the bedroom, and walked through the house, banging walls and slamming doors. Only after I kicked a kitchen cupboard and dented it did my anger subside.

As the weeks turned into months, my anger habit worsened. At times I grew so violent that I hit my toddler in the head. Other times I kicked her or slapped her face.

As a Christian for ten years, I was ashamed. "Oh, God," I prayed over and over again, "please take away my anger." Yet no matter how much I prayed, I could not control my anger when Darcy didn't perform according to my desires. I turned into a screaming mother, wondering whether I might kill Darcy in one of my next rages. In time, I had to be honest with myself—I was abusing her.

"Oh, God, no, I'm a child abuser! Help me!"

I was afraid to tell Larry, my husband. As a policeman, he arrested people for the very things I was doing. I certainly couldn't tell my friends. What would they think of me? I led a Bible study. I was looked up to as a strong Christian woman. But inside I was screaming for help.

Convinced God no longer loved me and had given up on me, I concluded suicide was the only answer. Then I wouldn't hurt Darcy anymore. But the thought sprang into my mind, *If people hear a Christian like me committed suicide, what will they think of Jesus?* I couldn't bear the thought that Jesus' name would be maligned, even if I wasn't acting much like a Christian.

With suicide no longer an option, I didn't have any hope. God didn't answer my prayers for an instantaneous deliverance from my anger, so I thought He must not care. I was in a pit of despair and depression.

One day I shared briefly with a neighbor friend about my anger. She didn't condemn me like another friend had when I'd tried to share my pain. She even indicated she felt angry toward her children, too. "Oh, Lord, maybe there's hope for me after all," I cried out when I left her house that day.

From that point on, God seemed to break through my despair and, little by little, revealed the underlying causes and the solutions for my anger. And there were many. I had to learn how to identify my anger before it became destructive. I forced myself to believe God wanted to forgive me. Reading books about disciplining children effectively, I became more consistent in responding calmly to Darcy's disobedience. She became better behaved.

I also copied verses like Ephesians 4:31 and Proverbs 10:12 onto cards, placing them in various locations throughout the house. As I took Darcy into the bathroom, I would be reminded that "Hatred stirreth up strifes: but love covereth all sins" (Proverbs 10:12 KJV). These verses helped to break my cycle of anger.

Eventually I had the courage to share my problem with my Bible study group. James 5:16 (TLB) admonishes us to "admit your faults to one another and pray for each other so that you may be healed." They prayed for me and their prayers indeed had "wonderful results."

Through a difficult process of growth over a year, God's Holy Spirit empowered me to be the loving, patient mother to Darcy that I wanted to be. I learned many principles during that time that I now share in the parenting books I've written like *When Counting to Ten Isn't Enough* (Harold Shaw Publishers). I also teach parenting seminars. . .imagine!

I'm thankful to the Lord for healing the relationship between Darcy and me. A beautiful twenty-four year old, Darcy has forgiven me for the way I treated her. We share a close relationship and have written a book together called *Staying Friends with Your Kids* (Harold Shaw Publishers).

Although I wondered during that unhappy time of my life whether God could ever forgive me for the horrible things I'd done, I know now that He has. As Psalm 40:1–2 says, He pulled me up out of my pit of destruction and set me on the solid rock of Jesus. With God, we can turn around—even from being a child abuser.

MAMA SCHWARZENEGGAR

by Mary Pierce, Eau Claire, Wisconsin

My five-foot-four-inch, 110-pound mother started lifting weights a couple years ago just before her eighty-fourth birthday. "You're Mama Schwarzeneggar," our family teased.

"But I'm not Austrian," she protested.

A few years earlier, when her third husband was in the nursing home, she trekked over a mile in each direction—uphill both ways, she bragged—several times a week to visit him. She bought a treadmill so she could stay in shape on the off days.

"The old people like it when I visit. I don't want to let them down," she explained.

Mama chooses to look on the bright side.

"And when you can't see the bright side, get a flashlight," she advises.

Her doctor explained on a recent visit that her hip pain was caused by a groove worn into the bone.

"I'm groovy at last!" she reported, certain she'd rather wear out than rust out.

She started the weights because she needed "a little more strength."

"More strength?" I said.

Three times a widow and a single working mother at times, she's known hardship. She's coped. She's gone without. She took in ironing to supplement our father's handyman earnings. Wooden broom handles across two dining room chairs held rows of white, blue, and yellow oxford cotton shirts with button-down collars. She stood for hours pressing perfect pleats in the backs of the shirts, for boys I thought were rich, spoiled brats.

Mama said, "When you see them at school, remember they wouldn't be half as good-looking if their shirts weren't so nicely ironed!"

I hear the hiss of steam and smell starch, and I remember conversations around the ironing board and the scratch of her callused palms as she stroked my cheeks. She was there. She was strength, shelter, and wisdom.

She invented the dill pickle test for mumps, designed to flush out malingerers suffering "schoolitis." "I have the mumps. It hurts right here," I complained the day of the spelling bee finals in sixth grade, pointing to a spot under my chin near my ear.

"Only one way to know for sure," she said. She opened the dill pickles and handed me one. "Hold this in your mouth."

I hated pickles but did as instructed. The sour sting shocked my jaw. "Ouch!" I yelped, sure she'd send me straight back to bed.

"Good!" Mama said. "If you had the mumps, it wouldn't hurt." I went to school. When I came home crying over my spelling defeat, she was there to comfort me.

She still comforts me. I called, interrupting Martha Stewart time, to complain about my hectic life. She listened and then said quietly, "But you love that. You get bored when things go too smoothly." A mother's gift—a reminder of who I really am, from the person who has known me longer than anyone else on earth.

Mama always credited her strength of spirit to her Finnish *sisu*—a sheer force of will that guts life out. She never read the Bible, prayed, or went to church. Sisu was enough.

Godly parents are a powerful blessing in a child's life. Christian heritage is a precious gift. But even without that heritage, God was at work in our circumstances, bringing all four of Mama's children into His family through the years. Mama remained an agnostic, just not sure whether there was a God or not.

At the age of eighty-five, she changed her mind.

We watched God draw her closer and closer. When a wise pastor explained how she could open her heart to God, she chose to do so. After they prayed together, she said, "Everything is different now. I felt empty before. I'm not empty anymore."

And she prays. Just as Mama was leaving our home at the end of a recent visit, our puppy ran away, disappearing into the woods behind our house. I fumed about this rebellious pup who bolts at every opportunity. I imagined the worst. Mama, familiar with the ways of the prodigal, looked me in the eye and asked, "Where's your faith?"

My faith? Swift and sure conviction swept over me. This little woman was suddenly a spiritual giant towering over me. Where was my faith? "I'll pray about this," she said, patting my arm, lifting my burden with her touch. My mother was going to pray. Everything would be all right.

Within five minutes of her departure, the dog was back in the house, happily wolfing her dinner. When I passed along the good news later on the phone, Mama said, "Boy, He works fast! I talked to Him just as we left your driveway!" As I hung up, the words to an old Southern gospel song came to mind. "When Mama prayed, heaven paid attention. . . ."

Mama looked for eighty-five years and never found anything in this world to fill the emptiness that only God can fill. She's taught us this latest, best lesson—that it's never too late to change your mind or to accept God's invitation to be His child.

And when Mama Schwarzeneggar did that, she lifted us all.

DO NOT BE AFRAID, LITTLE FLOCK

by Michael Adair Gibbs, Fincastle, Virginia

The driver of a dented and rusting four-door sedan switched his headlights off as he turned from the illuminated street into the parking area of a small apartment complex. He exited the vehicle and turned his jacket collar against the blustery February cold. A witness would later describe the man as middle-aged and "unkempt." He fumbled in the dark until he located a particular apartment door. Roused from sleep, the lady of the house, who was the unkempt man's estranged wife, answered his knock. Upon realizing the danger, she attempted unsuccessfully to close the door. Her daughter now entered the front room, having been alarmed by the noise. Once inside, the intruder retrieved a .38 caliber revolver from his jacket pocket and shot his wife and stepchild. As he left the apartment, the aforementioned witness telephoned the police, providing them with the vehicle description and tag number.

My recollection of that night has not dimmed in twenty-eight years.

As a rookie state trooper patrolling a major highway thirty miles from the shooting scene, I was responsible for covering two rural counties from midnight until 8:00 A.M. I scribbled the out-of-state tag number as the dispatcher gave it to me.

My voice was calm and professional as I responded over the radio.

"Ten-four, Central. I'll head south on Route 8. If he's headed back to his home state, that's the most logical route."

I spotted the car at an ill-lit drive-in restaurant situated in a sparsely populated area of the county. The restaurant was closed. The driver was out of the car, inside a telephone booth adjacent to the parking lot. I drove by and then turned onto a dirt road that ran behind the drive-in. Before leaving the cruiser, I advised Headquarters of the situation. My increasing anxiety was revealed in the slight tremble present in my few words.

"Unit 908 to Central. I'm out of the car twelve miles south of the interstate. I need backup."

After a short delay, the dispatcher replied.

"Nine-zero-eight, the closest available unit is off duty. He has been advised. ETA is forty minutes."

So there it was. This was my show, and mine alone. I ran through the drive-in's snow-covered back lot and positioned myself at the corner of the building before taking another look at the phone booth. He was still there. The light inside the booth revealed that his left hand held the telephone receiver, and his right hand was inside his jacket pocket.

At that moment, the fear set in: the kind of cold, intense personal fear that you feel deep in your chest. I had to take an armed felon who had already shot two people. I had to do it alone and I had to do it right. But the fear would not let go. I had no doubt this man would attempt to shoot me as soon as he knew my purpose. The temptation to back away from my responsibility was great. On that night, I had not as yet met Christ. I knew nothing of His protecting love. I knew fear, loneliness, and duty. I walked to within twenty feet of the booth before the man turned, and our eyes locked.

During my encounter with the criminal in the telephone booth, I was truly alone. I did not know Jesus. I could have died there on the cold pavement, having never received perfect love. Fortunately, the cold eyes of the criminal did not see the fear that lay in my bosom like a stone. He only saw the uniform and my unholstered revolver as I maintained a steady pace toward him. The arrest was effected without incident. I can now see clearly how God had been with me in every aspect of that arrest.

Ten months later, in a little country church near my home, I heard the pastor's words as he read from Hebrews 13:5–6: "Because God has said, 'Never will I leave you; never will I forsake you.' So we say with confidence, 'The Lord is my helper; I will not be afraid. What can man do to me?' "

Initially, I did not recognize the depth of that promise. I could not even see the reality of my own need. But God was patient. The offer was made again and again, as I continued to face the daily trials that are so much a part of a police officer's life. In the hum of my tires across the endless miles of a lonely predawn interstate, the words were audible. Above the electronic scream of my siren as I sped to each new emergency, His whispers touched my thoughts.

"Never will I leave you; never will I forsake you."

Over time, my heart became flooded with a hope I had not known was absent. I became aware of a great void in my existence. In that surrender, I met the Savior. He gave me His strength, free of charge. My views of life and death were changed forevermore. I cannot say that I have not since experienced fear. I have. Fear's basic function is to guide us out of harm's way. I have been afraid of ridicule, loss of respect, and of innermost secrets being revealed. I have been the victim of extreme fear that came in sickening waves of foreboding during the pending loss of a loved one. I have known fear during dangerous situations that arise in my job. The difference for me now is that the initial fear is soon replaced with a peace that can only come from the knowledge that God is in control. I know now that God is love—perfect love.

First John 4:18 taught me, "There is no fear in love. But perfect love drives out fear, because fear has to do with punishment. The one who fears is not made perfect in love."

I still patrol by that little drive-in on occasion where duty was done. I still carry the same bright badge. But now there's more than duty behind it. Now I hold God's love. As I gaze at the spot where gunmetal once gleamed through the subdued shadows of trepidation, I offer thanks to Him for loving me and for preserving my mortal life long enough for me to find salvation, and the resulting freedom from fear.

" 'Do not be afraid, little flock, for your Father has been pleased to give you the kingdom' " (Luke 12:32).

THE ARROGANT NUCLEAR SCIENTIST

as told to Dr. Muriel Larson, Greenville, South Carolina

Even though I had always gone to church with my family, I was an agnostic. A nuclear scientist, I prided myself on my knowledge and accomplishments. As a student of the Bible, which I considered a marvelous history book with beautiful poetry, I prided myself on being able to destroy the faith of others in God's Word.

All my life I had been interested in science. Every nuclear power plant in the United States, as well as many around the world, had benefited from the processes I had developed for the protection of nuclear plants against earthquakes and flooding. *Who needs a god?* I reasoned. If I had a god, it was my work or myself.

When my company transferred me to Massachusetts, my family and I started attending the first church that had ever made me feel uncomfortable. There the minister preached that all are sinners, that

Jesus Christ had died for our sins, and that in order for us to be saved from eternal damnation, we had to trust Christ as our Savior. The pastor's altar call every Sunday bothered me, too. They wouldn't let anyone join that church unless he was what they called "born again."

About six weeks after we started attending, Jean and our children went forward when the altar call was given.

She changed immediately. Always before, my wife had looked up to me as Number One in her life. But now Christ was first. Where before she would meekly do everything I said, now she began saying, "Honey, I don't think that's what Jesus would want us to do."

"Jesus! That's all you can think of," I exclaimed, "as if He were God or something!"

"He is," she said with a smile.

Jean took a course on Christian womanhood. She became sweeter than ever. Instead of meeting me head-on when she didn't agree with what I wanted to do, she lovingly talked me out of my ideas. Knowing how I prided myself on my biblical knowledge, she began to ask me questions about the Bible. Flattered, I started digging to get the answers for her.

"I'm praying for you, Honey," she often said. "I know I'm going to heaven someday, and heaven won't be heaven for me if you're not there."

"There is no heaven or hell," I declared authoritatively. I had so much to learn. God was going to teach me that I wasn't as self-sufficient and all-knowing as I thought. He decided to use my health.

A few weeks before a scheduled trip to Asia, I began to hemorrhage. Tests revealed diverticulosis and a lesion on my colon. The doctor operated and found it necessary to remove eighteen inches of my colon because of malignancy. After the surgery, thinking I was still asleep, the surgeon talked to Jean outside my room.

"Mrs. Faid," he said, "I have to tell you very bluntly we have found many, many more cancerous growths in your husband that we weren't able to remove. I'm afraid he hasn't much of a chance. We're going to run some tests, and in five days we'll know the definite answer."

Jean called her brother Jim in Baltimore, who had connections with hundreds of Christians who believed in the power of prayer. They all went to prayer for this self-sufficient agnostic who scoffed at their personal God, their Jesus Christ.

Five days later, when the pathology report came back, it revealed that those lesions, which the doctor had been sure were cancerous, were not. I began to wonder if maybe there was some truth in what these Christians had been telling me.

When I got home, I read every Christian book I could get my hands on. I discovered, to my surprise, that a lot of intelligent, successful people believed what I had always considered fantasy.

Then I attended a men's prayer breakfast where I heard testimony revealing God's power in a man's life. The Holy Spirit began working on my heart, and that week I finally acknowledged God.

The following Sunday, Jean took the children to Sunday school. I planned to join them for church. I got dressed, and as I walked through the family room, it suddenly seemed as if the Lord were actually speaking to me as He did to Saul on the Damascus road! And suddenly I could no longer deny that Jesus Christ was who He said He was, the Son of God. I saw and acknowledged that I was the sinner He loved and had died for. I felt God's Spirit fill my whole being with His love as I humbly yielded to Him in awed amazement. I was no longer in control, and it was okay.

When Jean came home, she found a brand-new husband. I was no longer the arrogant scientist, but a lowly follower of Jesus Christ. "Everything's going to be all right, Honey," I exclaimed. "Whatever happens, we'll have peace and joy with the Lord in this house!"

Thus Christ became Number One not only with my wife, but with me, too. As a member of the American Nuclear Society, I had written several technical papers as well as articles for various scientific magazines. Since I've come to the Lord, I have used my scientific knowledge as well as my knowledge of God's Word to write books to prove the existence of God and the truth of His Word. And I praise God every day for His loving grace.

TRASH TO TREASURE

by Jennifer Smith-Morris, Valdosta, Georgia

In July 1990 I was barely twenty years old. I had a boyfriend, one of many, although this one seemed to be a little more caring than the previous ones. I had just flunked my sophomore year of college, where I drank, smoked, and racked up credit card debt, and was home for the summer to work and do more of the same. Then one afternoon I found out I was pregnant.

Numbly, I drove to a river and, while watching the current, took an honest look at myself. It was not a fruitful inventory. I swore habitually. I screamed when I was angry. I was angry most of the time. I wore black leather and torn jeans and spent most of my waking hours drunk or hungover, wild and uncontrollable. Just the sight of me so horrified my boyfriend's judgmental mother that every time we left for a date, she called after us, "Remember, God's watching!"

Frankly, I didn't care; God wasn't anywhere in my life. As far as I was concerned, my boyfriend's mother was just like that obnoxious Christian at work who'd given me a New Testament and a tract about being saved. I thought they were both well-meaning but misguided simpletons.

By twenty I had come to the belief that people invented religion out of a heartfelt need for comfort. And my heart, tough and shriveled after years of unstable living, certainly didn't need comfort. Life was what I made of it, and I was going to make mine "fun." Somehow "fun" became synonymous with illegal, dangerous, self-destructive, foolish, or immoral behavior. Never mind that after so much "fun" I felt like a mildewed dishrag. Never mind the emptiness I was trying so hard to run from; never mind the hurt my running caused. I didn't eat three meals most days. I took diet pills to avoid feeling hungry. I tried almost any drug that was offered to me, hoping I'd find one that blotted out how horrible I felt. The longer I treated myself like a piece of trash, the easier it was to believe that's what I was.

That day by the river I saw myself for what I was: immature and thoroughly selfish. I was regularly kicked out of my parents' house and slept in my car. It had always been my policy to live an unhealthy life (because "ya gotta die of something"), but in spite of my utter lack of qualifications, I was now responsible for someone.

I realized that a twenty-year-old kid who behaves the way I did is not the same as a twenty-year-old mother doing those things. The word "mother" conjured up many images for me: It meant a sun-filled kitchen, an apron, helping with homework (the mother I someday wanted to be); it also meant tiptoeing around before school, being afraid to ask favors or advice, and the words "resent" and "victimized" (images of my mother). That July afternoon I was nowhere near the former and rebelling painfully against the latter. What in the world was God thinking, saddling me with this responsibility when I couldn't even take care of myself? Me? A mother?

Gradually, I came to see my life for what it was as well. It wasn't fun or carefree. Rather, I was spiraling in a toilet bowl of self-destruction, nearly sucked into the sewer time and again. My boyfriend's gentle acceptance slowed it somewhat, but deep down I didn't feel worthy of his love or even God's. I'd slept with all kinds of people, done all kinds of drugs, woke up in squalor I didn't even know existed until I was in the middle of it. I was tired of living, certain that life had very little to offer someone like me. But soon I would be sharing my life with a baby. From that moment on, I began to see myself through my baby's eyes. I was struggling to make sense of my own childhood; what would this child grow up to see in me? What was there to respect, to esteem, to be proud of?

I immediately stopped putting harmful things into my body. I retired my motorcycle jacket and the jeans with the torn-out seat. Most importantly, on August 8, thanks to my Christian coworker, I accepted Christ as my Savior and dedicated my life to the Lord.

The next few months were a blur. My boyfriend and I were married, we moved, and our son, Brady, was born in January 1991, two months early. I had my first practice in prayer next to Brady's incubator, begging for his life. As time went on, I was determined to live a life my son would find admirable. I applied to the university and was accepted. I came to see my judgmental mother-in-law as a rock of faith, a mentor as I developed a living faith. She encouraged us, supported us, and prayed for us. My husband and I both attended college full time, organizing our schedules so one of us was always with the baby. Sometimes we met on campus with Brady bundled in the stroller, handing him off between classes. Brady was two when I graduated, having finished my senior year on a full academic scholarship. Along the way, I found some gifts God had given me; they were like new discoveries.

By our first anniversary, I was completely different from the girl my husband had met and fallen in love with. I didn't dress the same, talk the same, or act the same as the old Jennifer. Instead of blaring hard rock and cussing, I was spending food stamps at the grocery store. As is his nature, my husband welcomed and supported the changes I made, but it was difficult for both of us at times. I learned that marriage was yet another area of my life to lift up to God, and we worked hard to establish a solid relationship that began under unusually stressful conditions.

Brady turned ten this past January. He is in the fourth grade, earning straight As. His hobby is rocket building. His father and I will celebrate our eleventh anniversary in September 2001, and Brady now has a little brother and sister, too. The Morris family's number-one goal is to glorify God, and the five of us love the Lord. I tell my children things I grew up missing: that God has created them for a purpose, that they are worth more than a trunkful of gold and diamonds to Him, and that He'll never stop loving them, no matter what. It's hard for me to tell them this without tears in my eyes, because I know, better than many people, how far God can bring a willing heart. I know that there is no mountain of slimy sin too tall for God to forgive, and I am proof that any life is too precious to waste.

One day when I explain to Brady the circumstances of his birth, I will also explain that it was God's unearned and arguably misplaced trust in me that motivated me to become who I am now; that is, a woman of faith. I hope he will see what a life-changing blessing he was to me. God gave me this child to show me that His love is not something to be earned, not something anyone is ever good enough for. It is always there, and I had simply to turn to Him, claim it, and begin healing. It was this gesture, this gift sent in a receiving blanket, that motivated me to dedicate my life to God. I have been grateful ever since.

FROM THE POOLROOM TO THE PULPIT

by Johnny Hunt, as told to Gloria Cassity Stargel, Gainesville, Florida

I was a seventeen-year-old ne'er-do-well that summer of the ugly car. A high school dropout, teenage alcoholic, and habitual gambler, I was living my "lofty" life's goal—managing the local poolroom. I'd hung out there ever since I was able to come up with a forged ID the year I turned fourteen.

My first car was a beat-up thirteen-year-old Chevrolet. That car was *so ugly* I dared not be seen in it. It was so bad I asked my friend Dave to drive me home every day after work.

One day Dave said, "I'm kind of in a hurry today, John. Do you mind if I let you off at Carolina Beach Road? You could cut right through to your apartments." I told him I didn't mind, so he let me off, and I began walking toward home.

Just as I was about to cut through to the apartments—at 319 Bordeaux Avenue—I spotted a cute little girl about five feet two inches tall outside her house, twirling a baton. The closer I got, the prettier she looked.

The next day, I decided it was silly for Dave to go so far out of his way just to take me home! "Why don't you just let me off at Bordeaux Avenue?"

From then on, he dropped me off at Bordeaux Avenue and I walked by that house. I wasn't even a Christian yet, but I remember praying, *If there is a God in heaven, please let her be out there!* And sure enough, every day she would be outside, twirling her baton.

That cute little five-foot-two baton twirler named Janet became my bride six months later. And what I didn't know at the time was that every day when she was outside twirling her baton, she was really waiting for me to walk by!

It's a wonder Janet ever got her parents' permission to marry me because of my bad habits. And sure enough, our marriage hit serious snags right away.

My downward spiral had started early. My mom worked two jobs to provide for me and my four brothers and sisters. As the youngest, growing up with little adult supervision, I found it easy to get into trouble.

The government housing project where we lived had a community center, and on weekend evenings all the older guys would go up to the dance. I thought, *Boy, they are so cool!* My buddies and I began slipping into the bushes behind the building where they hid their whiskey; and at the age of eleven, I experienced what it meant to be drunk. By thirteen, I was an alcoholic.

At fourteen, I found a driver's license, used it illegally to "prove" I was sixteen, and became a regular, hanging out at the poolroom.

Every morning, Mom gave me lunch money for school. I'd walk straight to the poolroom and ask: "How long can I play for ninety cents?" For five years of my life, I played pool—sometimes for as long as eight hours a day. All the while—a cigarette dangling from my lips— I drank, cursed, and gambled—for large sums of money.

The first thing I did when I actually *turned* sixteen was to get my own driver's license. The second thing was quit school. Right away the poolroom owner hired me as manager, which meant I spent most of my days *and* evenings there.

My lifestyle flirted with self-destruction. One night, in a borrowed car, I drove some buddies to a drive-in. Drinking heavily, we got into a scuffle that didn't go our way. I went home with one of my friends and got a shotgun, then headed back to the drive-in with every intention of killing the guy who I felt had done me wrong.

On the way there, I ran off the right side of the road. When I jerked the wheel back, the car went into a spin across the median. When we finally stopped, the car was upside down, facing the traffic. I was hanging out of the car, having been dragged down the road.

That escapade netted me a trip to the hospital, a night in jail, and a very angry owner of the car I had totaled.

After Jan and I married, I *tried* to do better, even worked an extra part-time job at a hardware store. But I always slipped back into my old ways.

Now Janet began talking about our need for church. About every two months, on Saturday night she would ask me, "Can we go to church tomorrow?"

"Well," I would say, "let's wait and see in the morning." But in the morning, I would act like I was so tired I couldn't get out of bed.

Then N. W. Pridgen began coming by the hardware store. Mr. Pridgen never left without saying, "You know, Johnny, I wish you would come to church with me sometime." And I always made some excuse.

Mr. Pridgen's message began to change. One day he said, "Johnny, do you know an old boy that hangs around the poolroom by the name of Dan Tritt?"

"Yeah, I know Dan."

"Did you hear what happened to him last week?"

"No, I haven't seen him lately."

"Well," he said, "Dan got saved and Jesus changed his life."

Now, I had never read a Bible verse and didn't know what it meant to get "saved." I thought people simply decided whether or not to be religious, and I had chosen not to be.

But let me tell you about Dan. At a Saturday night party, Dan had stood out in front of the poolroom, shaking his fist at the sky and saying, "If there's a God in heaven, strike me dead!" And now I was hearing that Dan was going to church and that God had changed his life!

Week after week N. W. Pridgen came in, often with a report that Jesus had changed the life of yet another "good ole boy." And always he said, "Well, you know what I'm going to ask you, don't you?" And I sure did. I had heard it so many times it sounded like a recording on Dial-A-Devotion!

Finally, I told my wife, "If you're going to keep hounding me about church, let's just get up and go to the little church down the street where N. W. Pridgen goes."

After attending for several weeks, I began to feel pretty good about myself. Nothing had changed in the way I lived, but after all, I was in church now.

Then something began to happen to me. I would go to church and everything was fine so long as the sermon was being preached or somebody was singing. But then the preacher would say: "We're going to stand together and sing an invitation hymn." And I would begin to weep.

It embarrassed me, a big shot who hung around the poolroom—*crying!* While the others bowed their heads in prayer, I'd ease out a handkerchief and erase those tears.

One cold Sunday morning in January, my wife and I were sitting in church, close to the back as usual, when they began to sing:

"Just as I am without one plea,
And that Thou bidst me come to Thee. . .
O Lamb of God, I come!"

This time Jan caught me—weeping. "Are you all right?" she asked.

"Yes, I'm fine."

"Well, then, why are you crying?"

I just told her to "shut up." I didn't know what was happening to me or how to answer her.

Then the preacher, just before the closing prayer, said, "There's a young man here, and God's dealing with him. Let's just pray that God will bring him back and save him tonight."

After lunch that day, I didn't go to the drag strip where on Sunday afternoons I usually raced my red '67 GTO. I told Janet, "Why don't we hang around the house and go back to church tonight?"

Janet could hardly believe it. "You want to go back to church *tonight?*"

"Yeah, you know the preacher was talking about me this morning."

"Oh, Johnny, he wasn't talking about you! There were three hundred people in that church."

I knew better. "Janet, you know I've tried to clean up my act but failed." She nodded *yes*. "Well, if Jesus Christ can change my life, He's welcome to it."

"It's true, Johnny. He *can* change your life, make you a *new person*—that's why they sometimes call being saved, being born again."

Janet added, "Johnny, there's something I never shared with you. Before we started dating, I accepted Jesus and was saved."

"*You're saved?*" I was impressed. "Well, then, since you're saved, I want you to do me a favor. I want to go to church tonight, and when the invitation is given, I want you to go down and tell that preacher that *I* want to be saved!"

"No!"

"Come on! You know how timid and shy I am! I am not going to walk that aisle in front of all those people. I just can't do it. I'm too scared! Just go on down and tell him."

"No, *you've* got to go tell him yourself."

It came time to leave for church. "Listen, Janet, why don't we go down *together* and you tell him I want to get saved?"

"No, Johnny, this is something you'll have to do on your own."

"Okay," I said, taking a deep breath, "I'm gonna do it. But Janet," I cautioned, "if Jesus doesn't change my life, I'll be the same old me tomorrow—I'll still be cussin' and drinking just like always. So I don't want you to bug me—"

I sat there during that whole service, my mind consumed by the fact that when the invitation was given, I would be going forward to trust my life to Jesus Christ. When the singing started, I said, "Now, Jan?"

She said, "Now."

I went down front and told the preacher: "I want to give my heart and life to Jesus."

And that night, January 7, 1973, *Jesus changed my life!*

Word spread around town. "Have you heard about Johnny? He's got religion and now he can't drink and gamble anymore."

To which I explained, "No, I didn't get religion. I got *saved!* Jesus Christ changed my life! I don't drink and gamble anymore because I don't *want to.* Jesus changed my 'want tos.' "

I went to all my old haunts, sharing the good news. Telling people that what Jesus did for me, He would do for them. When I told the poolroom owner, he and his wife both got saved. Next day, he hung a sign on the front door—"Gone Out of Business."

At the saloon, the manager, Roy Burch, was playing with a cap pistol. I said, "Roy, I just want to tell you the reason I haven't been coming down on weekends. Jesus changed my life! And, Roy, I don't drink anymore; I don't cuss anymore; I quit smoking—He's just changed my life. Man, I'm living for Jesus!" And as I was sharing my experience with him, Roy laid that little toy pistol against his cheek and caught the tears that were falling from his eyes into the barrel of the gun.

Everywhere I went, I told people that Jesus had changed my life. One day a skeptic, knowing my sordid past, asked: "Well, Johnny, what are you going to do now that you're saved and going to heaven?"

The answer came easy. "Take as many people with me as I can."

Now, twenty-eight years later, my mission remains the same. I continue to tell everyone who will listen, "If Jesus could get me from the poolroom to the pulpit, He can change *your* life, too! Jesus is in the life-changing business!"

All the while my heart is adding, *Thank You, Lord, for rescuing this wayward son. Thank You for that ugly car, that pretty girl, and for Mr. Pridgen.*

IN MY WEAKNESS HE IS STRONG

by Amy Beres, Collegeville, Pennsylvania

My love for alcohol began in the fall of 1987, as a naive college freshman. Coming from a fairly sheltered and conservative environment, I went from having to follow a certain moral code to "Here's the key to your room!" This newfound freedom was something I wanted in the worst way but had no idea how to handle. "Friends" introduced me to alcohol.

I liked what alcohol did to me. It had the power to transform me into an extrovert. My inhibitions suddenly vanished. I felt confident, well-liked, and accepted. No longer did I worry about what people thought of me. I said what was on my mind and people seemed to really enjoy it. "You're hysterical!" they would often say amidst gales of laughter.

But what happened to me as a result of my drinking was far from hysterical. After a night of peach schnapps and very little orange juice, I fell victim to the violent act of rape. Physically, I survived, but mentally, I was numb. I didn't know who to turn to. Telling my parents wasn't an option.

An experience like that should have been enough to sober me up, but it did just the opposite. Alcohol became my source of deliverance. It was the only thing I could turn to and not be judged. I drank myself into oblivion every night that I could, in my futile attempts to kill the pain. I contemplated suicide on many occasions and even tried it once, but to no avail.

I moved back home and got a job as a waitress. I succeeded in concealing my alcoholism from everyone. Once I could, I left home and found myself an apartment. I became friends with people who introduced me to the joys of smoking marijuana. Getting high was my new reason to exist. I loved the way it relaxed me and rendered me unable to think about my sorrows and my problems.

Every night was a big party. Many nights, I drove completely under the influence. Then I met a man I thought was going to fulfill all my needs and fix all my scars. I told him right away about the things that I had been through and, strangely, he didn't seem to mind. He loved and accepted me for who I was. Yet I still continued to drink heavily. It was now a huge part of who I had become.

We married and a year later we had our first child. I was still drinking. I had my second son two years after the birth of my first. I was totally unprepared for the responsibility of raising two children. One was generally calm and good-natured, but the other was a different story. He would often cry and cry, and nothing would soothe him.

My husband and I fought constantly. I cried often and was angry all the time. I felt helpless and out of control. I was soon put on anti-depressants, which stabilized my feelings but left me feeling numb and unable to concentrate. I drank when I could after I was sure the kids were asleep.

Less than a year later, I was pregnant again. During all three of my pregnancies, I managed to stop drinking for the sake of my unborn children, but I thought about it and dreamed about it often. When my daughter was born, I decided that she would be bottle-fed so that I could immediately indulge in a couple of glasses of wine!

My husband started a new job working twelve- to fifteen-hour days, six days a week. With him working all the time, I had virtually no relief. This was not my dream of how family life was supposed to be. I could no longer drink as much as I wanted because my children needed me. I drank only when my husband was home "to pick up the slack." I suffered from depression, insomnia; and anxious thoughts often filled my head. My heart was filled with anger, bitterness, and resentment; and it grew deeper with each passing day. I didn't know how to get rid of it nor did I think I ever could.

One day I came across a pamphlet about a Bible study that met at a nearby church once a week, and child care was provided! The Bible study part sounded rather boring to me, but the prospect of sitting around and drinking coffee while the kids were being cared for sounded like a dream!

I decided to go. The only thing I expected to get out of it was two hours of sipping coffee and time away from the kids. But it turned out to be so much more.

The women I met there were accepting, loving, and nonjudgmental. Never before had I experienced an atmosphere that was so encouraging and supportive. While sipping coffee and munching on tasty breakfast items, I began to study passages of the New International Version of the Bible. A cigarette-smoking, alcoholic mother of three, with a mouth like a sailor, started to actually read the Bible and see what was in it for me.

A "spiritual awakening" began to take place in my life. I realized that alcohol had ruled my life for over ten years. I had bought into the lies and deception that drinking cures all stress and discomforts in life. Thankfully, through the course of this Bible study, I came to a belief that God was the only One who could restore me. I asked God to forgive my past and made a heartfelt and genuine decision to step out in faith and turn my will and life over to His care.

Almost immediately He lifted the tremendous load of guilt and pain from my shoulders and replaced it with a deep sense of lasting peace, joy, and contentment. He gave me an entirely new perspective and attitude. He enabled me to stop drinking and smoking at the same time, which for me was truly a miracle! He showed me the answers to many things that I had spent most of my life searching for. He led me to discover AA and the joy of fellowship with others who share similar struggles and adversities.

I have now been sober for well over a year, thanks to God and AA. I know that I will never be perfect, and circumstances in life aren't always going to be enjoyable. There are days when I seriously entertain thoughts of drinking. At those times, I commit myself to prayer and meditation of Scripture verses. I humbly admit to God that I am weak and that I desperately need His strength and His guidance to carry me through. God continues to uphold and sustain me.

I am convinced that faith and perseverance is the key to conquering my addictions. If I persevere and have faith, God will hold true to

His promises and carry me through. Each day the battle will be won and I will have run the race with God by my side.

My entire life stretches before me anew, and I need only take one day at a time to live it.

FROM BUDDHA TO CHRIST

by Nelum Himali Haththella, Sri Lanka

My name is Nelum Haththella and I am twenty-one years of age. I live in Sri Lanka and come from a Buddhist background. I want to tell you my story. I want to share my U-turn toward Christ with you.

I was a typical Buddhist, attending all religious events, going to *dewala* (the place of idol worship to other gods). Even though I had heard of Jesus Christ, I never believed in Him and was constantly criticizing Him whenever a friend mentioned anything about Christianity. My personal encounter with Him was in April 1999.

Since I can remember, I had made a firm decision that I would not change my religion for any reason. My resolve did not weaken even when I fell in love with a man who was a Christian. When we became engaged, we made a decision. That is, I would go to church with him and he would come to the temple with me. When we had children, they would go to both houses of worship until they were old enough to choose the religion they wanted to follow.

After our engagement, I started going to the temple more often than before, hoping that my fiancé would be touched by it. He helped me dutifully in just about everything. . .except worship of the gods or Buddha. When I asked him why he wouldn't do that (because I sang with him in church), his reply was that he would never bow down to any other god but his God.

My first reaction was that, *Well, I have a god, too.* But then he said, "My God is a living God. Yours isn't."

It was then I understood the difference. It was then I realized that all my life I had been worshipping a god, or rather a person, who was already dead and couldn't do anything for me. He couldn't so much as hear me. And if I had a personal need, I had to run to another god like Kataragama or Vishnu.

Then I met my fiancé's mother, who had converted from Buddhism to Christianity. She helped me to realize what it meant to have a living God. And along with the number of testimonies I heard, I received the most precious gift on earth from his mother—the Holy Bible. I had many questions which his mother answered patiently.

When I accepted the Lord as my personal Savior on May 30, 1999, my life was forever changed. My old religion could not compare.

My mentor from church helped me immensely in understanding the Word of God. It was such a wonderful time. That was when I was nourished in Christianity. It is a process one must go through if you have not known Christ before. Once I knew and felt that I was truly born again, I took water baptism as a step of obedience on November 14.

I want to tell you that our God is an amazing God. Sometimes we may feel as if God has forgotten us, but He is watching each and every move we make. He knows what's in our hearts. And He never tests us beyond our limits. Our God is more of a friend, and that's why He is our "personal" Savior. Our God never lets go. Believe in Him, love Him, obey Him, and fear Him. I am so happy with the almighty Father and Jesus Christ, who is so attentive to all my needs. He is there for me the instant I cry out to Him and I am so proud to serve Him.

Being a Christian, I live with hope for tomorrow. I know that I will not just die and turn into sand, but my Savior will come for me to take me home to heaven. That is perhaps one of the most joyous aspects of my new life. . .that I will dwell in the house of the Lord forever.

BURNING BUSHES

by Wendy Dunham, Brockport, New York

Several days ago I was looking through my hope chest. I came across a letter tucked inside a yellowed envelope that I had written as a child. On the front of the envelope was written, To God. As I opened it, I was overwhelmed by God's goodness to me. Now, twenty-four years later, I still have the childlike faith that burned in my heart when I wrote this letter:

> *Dear God,*
> *I feel so confused, but I'm glad I can talk to You. I don't know what to do about my dad; he doesn't believe in You. I'm sorry, God. I wish he did. He says the stories from the Bible aren't true and that there's no way they could have happened. Like the story about Jonah and the whale; he said it is a fable because no one could live in a whale for three days. And he said that Moses didn't lift his rod and separate the Red Sea, because the laws of physics make it impossible. He's heard about the burning bush, but he says that if it were on fire, it would have been burned up, and that I should know bushes don't talk! What should I do? I love You, God, and I believe the Bible is true. But what about my dad? I always thought he knew everything, but now I'm not so sure. Can You help?*
> *Love, Wendy*

At the time I wrote that letter, my mother was a "silent" believer. She felt "being quiet" about her faith would help keep peace in our home. Several days had passed before I discovered my mother had found the letter and written a response:

Dear Wendy,

I found your letter; please forgive me—I couldn't help but read it. I hope you understand. I'm sorry about your dad. I wish he believed, too. I know how confusing all of this must be for you. You see, sometimes adults reason too much with their minds, and not enough with their hearts. Your dad reasons with his mind. He has chosen his disbelief, but don't let that change yours. Be strong in your faith, and continue to seek God. You have been saved by faith, a gift God has given you. If you look in your Bible, at Mark 10:15, you will read: "I tell you the truth, anyone who will not receive the kingdom of God like a little child will never enter it." And yes, Wendy, burning bushes do talk!

Love, Mom

Now, late in life, my dad has come to know the Lord with a child-like faith. Bible "fables" have become facts. Jonah is no longer a fictitious character but a real man whom God had a plan for. The Red Sea no longer represents the laws of physics but a miraculous passageway for the Israelites. And as for burning bushes, just the other day I over-heard him reading to his grandchildren: "And when Moses saw the flames and realized the bush did not burn up, he went over to see it. Then God called to him from within the bush, 'Moses! Moses!' And Moses said, 'Here I am.' 'Do not come any closer,' God said. 'Take off your sandals, for the place you are standing is holy ground. . . .' "

Joy filled my heart as I heard my father share his childlike faith with my own children. God is still a God of miracles! "Though you have not seen him, you love him; and even though you do not see him now, you believe in him and are filled with an inexpressible and glorious joy" (1 Peter 1:8).

MY FIRST EASTER AS A CHRISTIAN

by Meriam (last name withheld), Kiawah Island, South Carolina

I arose before sunrise here in the Great Smoky Mountains of North Carolina where sunrises are miracles in themselves. Leaving my husband, Jack, asleep, I put on a heavy robe and slippers, knowing it would be cold outside since it was just April.

At almost sixty years old, I am trying to understand how I, as a Jew, will live the rest of my life as a saved soul, a Christian. I almost felt sorry for the born-to-the-fold Christians who take so much of their faith for granted. There was a feeling within me of sadness for Christians who have become complacent about what Jesus really did for them and how it should, but often doesn't, affect their entire worldview and behavior for the rest of their lives.

I went outside on the deck facing our view and knelt down on a wooden bench to pray. I found myself imagining Jesus' life from Passover to Resurrection, trying to place myself in the picture as it had happened. In my mind and heart, I walked with Him as He dragged His cross and as He bled from thorny cuts and had the nails driven into His hands and feet. I tried to "feel" the pain, as well as the joy. My mind kept saying, *He is risen,* and I automatically began reciting the Lord's Prayer. Never before had I felt such fulfillment.

I stood absolutely motionless for forty-five minutes, praying to God that I might share Christ's experience in some way. The sky slowly lightened as the sun rose over the peaks, and the cold penetrated my muscles and bones. When I determined, as the sun crept over the mountaintops in a huge reddened sphere, that my devotions and prayers were complete, I found I couldn't move.

Without my realizing it, the cold had so chilled my muscles and ligaments and bones that it practically paralyzed me. It was excruciatingly painful to walk even two steps. I managed, over my shock at not being able to move, to slowly turn toward the door into the living room, thinking, *If I feel this way, I can only vaguely imagine what Jesus had to have felt.* It was then I realized that a prayer had been answered. I had asked God to let me know what Jesus felt, and to a lesser degree, He did exactly that. What a blessing!

Inside, after a hot shower and coffee, I found an Easter card from Jack, wishing me for the first time a "blessed" Easter. He had never used the word "blessed" before. It was a special moment.

Also, today, Easter Sunday in the year 2000, after I'd completed my prayers, my shower, and had my coffee, the first hummingbird arrived to draw from my feeder. I adore hummingbirds. When we arrived here in the mountains, one of the first things I did was set up my hummingbird feeders on the back deck, happily anticipating the frisky hummers buzzing and feeding. Until this morning, no hummingbirds were to be seen. Now I can see a number of them crazily chasing each other in a whirly, kamikaze frenzy of feeding! Just another little gift from God.

While God shapes our lives with major events, He appears every single day in the smaller events, which we miss if we are not looking for them. A cold, foggy day in the mountains. Stiff joints. A spectacular sunrise. Hummingbirds.

God is good.

TEACHING WITH CLASS

by Dr. Debra D. Peppers, St. Louis, Missouri

"From Hall of Shame to Hall of Fame" read a recent headline when I received the honor of being one of only five teachers inducted into the National Teachers Hall of Fame. Who would ever have imagined that an overweight, rebellious high school dropout in the late 1960s would become Teacher of the Year? It certainly wasn't something my parents, my teachers, or even I would have thought possible.

At sixteen, I was confused and angry with low self-esteem. I was extremely overweight, and as my grades began to plummet, I gave up trying to compete with my older sister, Donna. She was head cheerleader, prom queen, and valedictorian of her senior class; she was everything I wanted to be but wasn't. It was much easier to get attention by being the class clown; and the only honor I received in high school was being voted "Wittiest." Eventually, however, I became more pathetic than funny when I began drinking, hanging out with the wrong crowd, and eventually running away from home.

My mom and dad were hardworking middle-class parents who did all they could to provide a good home. They had raised me in a good Christian home and made sure I was in church every week. But like many teens today, I gave in to the temptations of the world and turned my back on all that my parents taught me. As a prodigal daughter returning home after numerous times of running away, I was always welcomed home by my parents who continued to pray for me. They also did everything they could to get me help. They had been at school with my teachers numerous times, had taken me to doctors, counselors, and always "bailed me out" of trouble or jail whenever they could. The last time that I ran away they couldn't find me for weeks as I stayed anyplace I could find. It didn't take me long to realize that the freedom for which I had longed was full of empty promises. With nowhere to live, no money, and none of the "glamorous lifestyle" I had anticipated, once again the prodigal child found her way home. And once again my family welcomed me back with open arms. This time, however, my parents' unconditional love set the much-needed boundaries I had lacked. I had to agree to their rules as I reluctantly returned to school.

The first day back was as miserable as I had anticipated. I heard all the names as my peers jeered, "Hey, Fatso!" or "The jailbird is back!" I probably would have run away again had it not been for a familiar voice from the end of the hall. Mrs. Alma Sitton, who let us fondly call her

"Miss Alma," had been one teacher who had always treated me with respect and dignity. However, she was tough on all of us and immersed us in literature, grammar, and speaking. Ignoring the taunts of my classmates, I dutifully trudged down the hall as Miss Alma called to me from a distance. As expected, she ushered me into her warm, familiar classroom, near the table of missed assignments. I said nothing as I rolled my eyes, bit my tongue, and waited for a lecture to accompany the piles of missed homework. But what came next was so totally unexpected.

Miss Alma glanced down the hall and, after making sure no one was near, she turned toward me with her back to the table and did the most paradoxical, most unbelievable thing that a teacher had ever done to me. She quietly closed the door, put her purplish ditto-streaked hands on my shoulders, looked me straight in the eyes, down to my soul, and then put her arms around me! As she hugged me, softly in my ear Miss Alma whispered, "Debbie, God is going to do something great in your life if you'll let Him. And I'm here for you, too."

I vaguely remember the piles of papers she began explaining, but I will never forget her loving smile and the words of encouragement. That ten-second gift of hope and my love for Miss Alma has lasted thirty years. I don't remember the stacks of missed assignments, but I do remember that day that Miss Alma became my "hero." I know now that I had seen the love of Jesus Christ personified in "Miss Alma."

I began to watch everything Miss Alma did. I saw her compassion and love for all of her students—especially those of us who were "extra needy." I went to her often for advice, for help, or for a hug. I took every class Miss Alma taught and joined every extracurricular activity she sponsored.

It may have been a surprise to my entire hometown that I of all people would become a high school teacher of English, speech, and drama—just as Miss Alma had been. But it was no surprise to me—or Miss Alma. Twenty years later in 1988, I had lost 100 pounds, married, and was teaching in St. Louis when I was selected as Teacher of the Year. I was compelled to return to my hometown and thank the one who had so inspired me. Miss Alma, now retired, was serving at her church social—fish and loaves of bread! How appropriate! As Jesus had fed the thousands so long ago, I envisioned the thousands Miss Alma had "fed" through the years. I knew that I was blessed to have been one of them.

As I approached her, I was immediately transported back to that same insecure, anxious teenager, unable to speak. Once again I was enveloped in that warm, encouraging hug. "Oh, Debbie! Look at you! You've lost a hundred pounds! And I heard you have become a teacher— I am so proud of you." I wanted to tell her what an inspiration she had been, how much I thanked her for not only saving my life but also for inspiring me to be all that I had watched her model. I wanted to tell her how I had trusted Jesus Christ as my personal Savior and how I now share the same love and hugs with my students—as she had with me so many years before. But I was too choked up to say much of anything at the time.

Now that I have traveled throughout the United States as a member of the National Teachers Hall of Fame, speaking to thousands of schools, businesses, and churches, I have always included the inspiring story of Miss Alma. As a radio and television talk show host, I have interviewed everyone from the president of the United States to prisoners on death row. But last spring was one of the highlights of my life. I was invited to speak at Miss Alma's church.

I knew I would sob as I told the "Miss Alma" story and would finally have the opportunity to publicly thank her for being such a role model, such an encourager, and the very reason I became a teacher. I learned from her that kids don't care how much you know until they know how much you care. I also found out there are so many ways— even in a public school—to share your faith and model the love of Jesus Christ, as Miss Alma did. I couldn't wait to feel her arms around me one more time and to tell her that I have passed on that hug and encouragement to over ten thousand other "Debbies," who also needed to be reminded that "God has great plans for their lives." I couldn't wait to tell her that many of my former "troubled" students had also turned their lives around, and many had become Christian teachers. One of the greatest compliments I have ever received is hearing the words, "Mrs. Peppers, you are my Miss Alma. Thank you for showing me the love of Christ."

I could scarcely make it through my presentation before we both tearfully and joyously hugged, took pictures, and reminisced about "old times." As I finally had the opportunity to thank her for being the one who welcomed me back so lovingly after I had run away and gotten into such trouble, she gasped in astonishment!

"Why, Debbie," Miss Alma whispered, "I only remember you as such a good student!" Miss Alma had seen me through the eyes of faith and loved me with the love of Christ.

I have kept in touch with Miss Alma and was invited last summer to speak at the graduation ceremony in her hometown. My parents, who are now in their late seventies and travel all over the world to hear their "prodigal daughter" tell *their* story, drove Miss Alma to the ceremony where I was speaking. As I had shared my past with thousands of my own students through the years, I shared with this graduating class how Miss Alma and my loving parents had literally saved my life when I wasn't even sure I wanted to be saved! I reminded them that God gives second, third, and "hundredth" chances so that one day we will be the encourager to someone in need.

After the service, I saw a line of former students waiting to hug the beautiful ninety-year-old lady who had such an influence on so many. I watched parents of "troubled" kids flock to my parents for hope and encouragement to deal with their own children. There are some who won't know until eternity all the lives they have touched, but I have made sure that Miss Alma and my own parents certainly know! There is no doubt that one day soon they will hear our Savior say, "Well done, My good and faithful servant!"

As I have hosted a daily three-hour radio program for the past five years, called "Talk from the Heart, with Dr. Peppers," I have learned there are as many hurting and needy adults as there are children. I also know that the same faithful Savior that paid the price for all two thousand years ago on Calvary can still heal, restore marriages, and return prodigal sons and daughters. I am so grateful for all the faithful prayer warriors and seed-sowers in my life through the years—my parents, my husband, my family, former Sunday school teachers, my friends, my church family, and, of course, Miss Alma.

At my recent high school class reunion, I was voted "Most Changed." Indeed, God allows U-turns!

JUST A REGULAR OLD LADY

by Lucinda Secrest McDowell, Wethersfield, Connecticut

By the time I became a mother at age thirty-one, I had already experienced ten years of an exciting career in journalism and ministry. I was grateful to God for not only helping me to discover my gifts and passion, but also for using me to encourage others on their journey of faith.

But marriage, motherhood, and a move from San Francisco to Seattle definitely changed my life!

Soon after my marriage, I adopted Justin (age nine and born with mental retardation), Timothy (age seven and just finishing up first grade), and Fiona (age four, who was only one when her mother died). I was delighted to embrace this new season of at-home motherhood, but I was definitely on a high learning curve!

The only thing in my life that hadn't changed was God. Everything I was doing I didn't know how to do, and everything I did know how to do was only a distant memory in a faraway world.

What a challenging time of reevaluating my own sense of identity. Who was I now that my audience was three little ones rather than a congregation of a thousand? And writing grocery lists wasn't exactly keeping me in tune with the publishing world.

But God was clearly helping me to understand grace—His great gift of love for me that I didn't deserve and could never earn, no matter how much I "accomplished" for Him.

And a little child led the way.

One day when he was in fifth grade, my oldest son and I sat on the floor in the living room doing a puzzle. I asked him, "Justin, what do you want to be when you grow up?"

He quickly answered, "A professional basketball player," and then turned the tables.

"Mom, when you were my age what did you want to be?"

I knew exactly what to say. In fifth grade I had read a biography on Marie Curie and even though I knew no female doctors at the time, my hopes were high. "Justin, when I was in fifth grade I wanted more than anything to grow up to be a doctor."

To which he immediately replied in his innocent and candid way, "And look what you became—just a regular old lady!"

Inside I cringed and wanted to cry out defensively, "Excuse me! A regular old lady? I'll have you know that I have a master's degree and have published articles and traveled around the world twice before I was thirty and. . ."

But of course I didn't.

Not only would none of that have been impressive to him at all, but what he wanted and needed from me was to be a "regular old lady," the one who was always there when his bus dropped him off from school, who cheered for him in Special Olympics, made oatmeal cookies, and read with him each evening.

In this *kairos* moment, God showed me how unimportant my accumulated credentials were for where He had placed me. And slowly I began to joyfully embrace my new priority of nurturing and teaching and training my children.

By saying "yes" to motherhood, I inevitably had to say "no" to some other really tempting opportunities. But today, eighteen years later, when I look at the fine young men and woman Justin, Tim, and Fiona have become and the fine young lady their little sister Maggie is growing into, I know that, in God's economy, being "just a regular old lady" may be in fact my greatest achievement of all.

CHAPTER TEN

Thankfulness

Be joyful always; pray continually; give thanks in all circumstances,
for this is God's will for you in Christ Jesus.
1 Thessalonians 5:16–18

MY "GREAT" AUNT

by Marjee K. Berry-Wellman, Clarion, Iowa

Aunt Cora smelled delicious wearing Evening in Paris perfume that came in a beautiful blue bottle. Her skin was translucent and wrinkled but felt like rose petals. When I cuddled on her comfortable lap in our creaky, wooden rocker, stroking her soft, ancient arm, I wondered how long I would have to wait before my skin felt like velvet and my straight brown hair would have soft, snow-white curls. I loved the softness of Aunt Cora.

Despite my grumbling and groaning about waking up so early, Aunt Cora took me to church with her whenever I slept over on a Saturday night. The only thing that kept Aunt Cora from attending church was a bad health day. She told me God was everywhere and not just at church. I looked behind the sofa and chairs and even under the rug for God, and the only time I was certain I saw God was when I looked into Aunt Cora's eyes. I would say, "There He is!" and she would hug me and plant kisses on my cheeks. I loved the way God sparkled.

Most folks thought dollar bills were important, but Aunt Cora knew the best things in life came from dimes. She always had dimes handy to buy me a treat from the ice cream man. She had dimes for bottles of cola on a hot summer day. She gave me dimes to give to the Lord in the offering plate as it was passed my way, and, in turn, she put dimes in my glass piggy bank, which sat proudly upon her wooden dressing table. Aunt Cora sure knew the worth of a dime and the blessing of giving—and receiving.

In the summertime, every Thursday evening Aunt Cora and I had a date that I looked forward to all week long. Hand in hand, we would march to a park bench in front of the Sterling, Illinois, Central Park bandstand with two boxes of Cracker Jacks. We never knew what prize we would get, but no matter how special her prize was, Aunt Cora always found it in her heart to give it to me. Aunt Cora not only knew how to love, but she knew how to share.

Then I would sit, leaning against her comfy frame, as we watched daylight completely disappear, and the Sterling Chamber Orchestra would begin to fill the evening air with the beautiful sounds of Bach, Chopin, Mendelssohn, and Tchaikovsky. Aunt Cora gave me the blessing of music and taught me what beauty there was in the world around me.

Aunt Cora loved to pray. She thanked God for our food. She prayed for me when I was sick, and I got well. She even prayed for me when I wasn't near her. I could always count on God to answer Aunt Cora's prayers.

A beautiful picture of the only baby Aunt Cora ever had hung above her bed in an oval, bubble-glass frame. Aunt Cora's baby girl died as an infant. Aunt Cora missed Goldie Bell very much. Whenever Aunt Cora told me that someday she would be reunited with her daughter in heaven and with Uncle Artie, who died of pneumonia, I could see the yearning in her face. But I didn't want to have anything to do with the notion that someday she might die. I told her that I needed her with me for always. But Aunt Cora taught me that we would be together forever in heaven.

Life took me in a direction very far away from Aunt Cora physically but never far from the remembrances of her. I visited her often in my mind and, as often as time and finances would allow, in person.

One day my phone rang. It was my sister, Cath, calling me long distance, and she was crying. She said Aunt Cora had died. The greatest aunt that ever lived had left this world. I was very sad that Aunt Cora was gone because I would miss her—and yet part of me was also happy for her because I knew she was once again with her baby Goldie Bell and Uncle Artie.

Sometimes when I'm remembering her, like today, I can still smell the scent of her Evening in Paris perfume, and I can hear her jolly laughter and feel her soft, loving arms around me and feel her prayers being answered. Some things never change. Even at forty-five years of age, I still wish I could snuggle on her lap and rock-a-bye in our old, creaky, wooden rocker, eating Dilly Bars and Cracker Jacks and laughing until we cried.

I hope you can read this from heaven, Aunt Cora. I love you more than ever. Thank you for all the splendid times we had together—for taking the time to teach me right from wrong, for sharing your dimes and being a living testimony of sacrificial love, for showing me the power of prayer, for demonstrating what forgiveness is. Thank you for always making me feel safe, for giving me the gift of laughter, for sharing with me your love of music, your Cracker Jacks prizes, and, most of all, thank you for letting me see God in your eyes. I miss you so much, Aunt Cora, but, someday, we will meet again.

Your loving great-niece,
Marjee

THE THANKFUL CHAIR

by Bob Perks, Shaverton, Pennsylvania

It was the year following the flood. I was working for the Commission on Economic Opportunity where my job was interviewing low-income families to assess their needs. I was relieved that this house was the last stop for me. Thanksgiving Day was the next day, and, quite frankly, my heart was not in doing these surveys. I just wanted to start my holiday early. Tomorrow, like millions of other families, we would be snuggled around the table filling ourselves to capacity.

This home hadn't actually been in the flood area—it just looked like it had been a part of the destruction. The front porch steps were missing, replaced by a few cinder blocks and planks. There were several broken windows and part of the foundation had caved in, exposing the basement to the weather. That particular day it was in the upper thirties with a heavy wind blowing snow from the west. The house was bitterly cold.

Several times the young children ran through the kitchen playing and laughing. Noticing they were barefoot on the cold linoleum floor, I thoughtlessly said to one of the youngest girls, "You should go put your socks and shoes on before you get sick."

She asked, "Mommy, did this man bring me some shoes I can wear?"

"No, Sissy. He didn't. Go put on a pair of mine. He's right. You need something on your feet." I was embarrassed for having put her in that position.

"Well, I'm finished here. Thank you for your time. I hope you have a wonderful—" I didn't know what to say. How could they possibly have a wonderful anything?

I hadn't even thought about what this family was looking forward to. I just figured they would be taken care of by some organization or church. I looked around for some sign of a charitable box of goodies but saw nothing.

"Look, I'm sorry. I know there must not be much to be thankful for these days," I said nervously.

"Well, you certainly are wrong about that! I have so much to be thankful for I wouldn't know where to begin," she said. I wouldn't have known, either. I couldn't find a thing that she could include.

Rising to her feet, she walked into the middle of the living room and stood there. "My dear," she said, "I know this doesn't look like much, but I am truly blessed for all of this.

"See that chair? All in all, how much do you think that chair is worth in dollars?" she asked rhetorically. "Nothing. It's probably worthless even to a junk dealer. But I wouldn't trade it for anything. I sat in that chair and waited for months when my son was in the Vietnam War. It was my Worry Chair. I sat in that chair, prayed, and gave thanks when the good Lord brought him safely home to me. When they announced that John F. Kennedy was dead, I wept in that chair. When my daughter told me she was going to college because she got a full scholarship, I was sitting there and it became my Joyful Chair. It was also in that chair that I sat, slept, and cried when my father came home here to die."

Crossing the room, she pointed to a photograph on the wall. "You see this man? He's my husband, the man who has loved me for all these years. He's at work now. He doesn't make much but he works hard for it. He paid for that chair in sweat. There isn't enough money in all the world for the true value of love.

"Those kids out in the yard. Do you hear them? They're laughing as they are playing with all the other kids in the neighborhood. How much would you pay to find something to laugh about when things aren't so good?"

Then, walking closer to where I was seated, she looked down at me and asked quietly, "Should I go on?"

"No," I said, picking up my briefcase. "And thank you."

"Oh, one more thing," she said, sitting down in her chair. "I call this my Thankful Chair. Tomorrow when we gather round the table to share whatever meal God will provide—and He always provides—I will be thankful that He had sent you here to talk to me," she said, smiling.

"I already am," I replied. On my way home, I reflected on all she had said to me, and I realized that they didn't need me or any person. They had their faith and grateful hearts. On the contrary, I needed them. To count my blessings. To be truly thankful.

MOVING DAY

by Brenda Sprayue, Chandler, Arizona

It took nearly a week to drive all of our possessions and our two children across the country from Chicago to Phoenix for my husband's new job. It had been an exhausting trip, and we were nearly out of both money and energy. But the worst was ahead of us.

The day we moved into our new home happened to fall on Thanksgiving Day. All of our family and friends lived in the Midwest, so the four of us unloaded the truck ourselves. It was no small job. My four-year-old son pulled smaller things in his wagon, and my eight-year-old daughter carried a steady supply of lighter boxes. It bothered me to have to ask them to work with us, especially on a holiday. We had been working since early morning without a break. We were getting slower and slower.

"You doing okay?" my husband would ask regularly as we struggled up the steps with the couch or a mattress.

"I'm fine. You?"

"Yep."

Other than that, conversation was nonexistent. Even though no one said so, I could tell we were all starting to feel sorry for ourselves. We were stuck doing all this backbreaking work on a day that families are supposed to be feasting and playing together. We weren't feeling very grateful as we started our new life.

At 2:30 in the afternoon, we still hadn't stopped for lunch, but no one was complaining about being hungry. I think we all just wanted to get the job finished. I had just started to wonder where we could go to get something to eat on Thanksgiving Day. I was also praying to myself, *Father, I believe You brought us here safely, and You will also take care of us.* I set down the box of books I was carrying, sighed, and headed back to the truck for more.

That's when I saw a man walking up the sidewalk. "Time for a break," he said, smiling. He introduced himself as our neighbor. "You folks need to come on over and get some lunch. We just finished eating and we have so many leftovers. Everything's on the table waiting for you."

My husband and I hesitated, but the kids started cheering. Seeing we needed a little more convincing, he said, "I just moved here myself a couple months ago, from Georgia. I know exactly what you're going through. While we've been cooking, we've been watching you work. To be honest, you folks are starting to drag a little, and you all need to come get some nourishment. These kids need to eat!"

He was right. We followed him to his home and were met by his daughters, two babies, and a few other relatives. We lost our shyness the minute we smelled the food. Sliced turkey with all the trimmings was laid out on the table.

The amazing thing is, it didn't end there. We had been back to work for a couple of hours when he showed up again. "Okay, folks, we're having dessert now. You need to come over for some pie," our neighbor said. We felt we had imposed enough, but he insisted.

One good meal with a huge helping of kindness can really change your perspective! We suddenly felt as if our Father had gathered us, His well-loved children, into His arms for comfort. We thanked our Comforter for whispering in our neighbor's ear the words that caused him to open his heart and his home to us.

A few weeks later I tried to express in a card what our neighbor's kindness meant to us. The cookies I baked just didn't seem like thanks enough. Then it dawned on me that feeling as if my thanks were inadequate was perhaps the beginnings of true gratitude, the kind that humbles you. It stirs in you a desire to give to others from your place of blessing, to attempt to make someone else feel what you have felt.

My neighbor's act of generosity, a beautiful reminder of God's faithfulness, changed the way I look at those around me. As I start my new life here, I want to keep that giving spirit alive by being more aware of people who might also be in need of some nourishment—for body *and* soul.

THE GIVER

by Jeanne Zornes, Wenatchee, Washington

He wasn't someone who'd climb the executive ladder, this man I'll call "Ralph." He ran the shipping department of a small company where I worked one year. Built like a bear, his searching eyes almost hidden behind thick-lensed glasses, he put in his hours in a sunless room piled with boxes. Then, his day done, he'd catch a bus home.

I already knew Ralph was a Christian. Somehow he learned I played the violin. Maybe the subject came up in the company's attic lunchroom, as we sat at cast-off tangerine café tables and visited over peanut butter sandwiches and vacuum bottles of soup.

"My daughter wants to learn violin," he said. "There's one we could buy but we don't have enough money for it." When he named the price he could afford, I knew it would buy only a no-frills student violin.

I played a student violin, too. I loved playing violin and studied it through college. Though music didn't become a vocation, I still played in small orchestras, at church, at meetings, even for my grandmother in a nursing home. I knew the positive dimension music brought to my life. I wanted that for Ralph's family.

But Ralph's problem with stretching a paycheck was also mine. Single and thirty years old, I'd just finished two years as a missionary and used up my savings to attend a year of Bible college. Now I was saving for graduate school. What could I do, when I didn't earn much above minimum wage?

When Thanksgiving came, I sensed giddiness among other employees as the finance officer passed out checks. I opened my pay envelope and found my employer's Christmas bonus.

Give it to Ralph, an insistent inner voice said.

But, Lord, I hardly know him, I protested. *You know how much I need to save for college. Every bit helps.*

Give it to Ralph.

God had been working in my heart over the past few years. Living on so little had caused me to pay closer attention to Scriptures that talked about the poor. I had come to understand that God didn't see me as "poor" but rather as one through whom He could bless another.

I was surprised at the joy that replaced my anxiety as I wrote a check equal to the bonus and put it in a card I left on Ralph's workbench. "Please use this toward your daughter's violin," my note said.

A few months later Ralph's family invited me for dinner and a "concert." Three excited children clung to me as I entered their little home with its tired furniture. His wife, her hands knobbed with arthritis, served chicken on mismatched plates. His oldest daughter provided the after-dinner concert on her little violin, playing "Twinkle, Twinkle, Little Star."

I never missed that money. I still had enough for graduate school and for other times God prompted me to give to someone in need. "Cast your bread upon the waters," says Ecclesiastes 11:1. I could only cast crumbs on a vast ocean, but each time I did, I experienced quiet joy in simply obeying God.

Twenty years passed. I married and we had two children. I passed on my love of music by enrolling both children in the school orchestra program. I listened proudly as they learned to play on used violins, advancing from "Twinkle, Twinkle, Little Star" to Bach and Beethoven. My husband's salary as a teacher wasn't extravagant, but it was sufficient for our needs. God allowed me to supplement our income with an at-home business involving a computer. But after ten years that computer was outdated.

The hope of replacing my computer was ended when a drunk driver plowed into our car as we returned home from a weekend away. My husband's last-second swerve to the ditch spared us a head-on collision and possibly our lives, but the side impact shot glass across our son's face, breaking teeth and pocking his face with wounds. Insurance wouldn't cover all the medical expenses. The next months were a challenge.

A year later I took my son in for his final plastic surgery to minimize his scars. The appointment meant not being able to see a Christian friend who was in town on business. I'd helped him a couple years earlier with a project that had proven very successful for him.

The next day, my husband insisted on taking me out to lunch. Eating out wasn't a high-priority budget item for us, but he had a two-for-one coupon.

"You've made some great friends in your work," my husband remarked as we poked chopsticks into our stir-fry. His remark veiled a secret to which I was not privy. "Let's stop by a computer store on the way home," my husband said as we paid for the meal.

"Let's not," I said. "I can't buy one."

I steamed as he pulled me into a local computer store and started browsing. Still ignoring my pleas to go home, my husband went to find a salesman. Both of them smiled at me.

"A friend of yours was here yesterday," the salesman said, showing me the friend's business card. And then pointing to a pile of boxes, he said, "He bought this for you. You're supposed to take it home and enjoy it."

I started shaking and crying as my husband revealed how this friend had called while I was at the hospital with our son. My friend said he was obeying a nudge from God by buying a computer system for me. I couldn't believe that someone would do this for me. I cried all the way home.

As I started unpacking the computer and figuring out all its plug-ins, the last part of the verse from Ecclesiastes came back to me: "Cast your bread upon the waters, for after many days you will find it again."

I had never expected to see that "bread" again, but "after many days" God, the greatest giver of all, had chosen to wash it back ashore in the shape of a computer. I smiled as I thanked Him.

GIVING CHRISTMAS

by Robert Diacheysn Jr., Sanford, Florida

It was October 1990. My wife, Sharon, had just given birth to our second child (we now have five), and I had broken two toes in a work-related accident. What could be better than being out on medical leave with a two year old, a newborn, and a postpartum wife? Now, workman's compensation only paid 70 percent of my income, and with the addition of another mouth, it soon became clear that this year we were going to have a humble Christmas.

By the sixth week of my injury, the 30 percent pay drop had really put us behind in the bills. When the doctor finally gave me the okay to go back to work, we were both anxious to get back on track financially. I returned to my job as a carpenter for Fortunoff's department store on Wednesday, December 9. On Friday the eleventh I was laid off due to cutbacks.

Being out of work during a recession with two children and Christmas on the way is not the happiest place to be. We spent a lot of time crying and praying, seeking God, asking why, crying some more, and asking around for employment doors to open. This was one of the most difficult emotional times and also one of the most incredible spiritual times in our marriage. Our situation brought us closer to each other and taught us to depend on the Lord for our every need.

As the days passed, those needs grew greater. Some days we literally weren't sure if we could afford meals. But, somehow, God always managed to provide in unexpected ways. One Sunday our pastor asked us if he could see us after the service. Pastor Tate was a kindhearted, fatherly shepherd who was very hard to refuse.

At the end of the service, he asked us how we were doing and insisted on praying for us. Then he asked if we would mind accompanying him on an errand. We arrived at his office to find bags and packages waiting with our name on them. Large bags filled with gifts and clothing. Several boxes of food and formula, diapers and bottles, and toys. Wonderful toys, quality learning toys for the baby—and for Brittany: the most beautiful, blond-haired doll that she named Rachel Lynn after Pastor Tate's five-year-old granddaughter (whom Brittany loved to shadow).

We were very touched and yet I found it difficult to accept. I had never before been treated with such sincere generosity. I tried to refuse, but P.T. would not take no for an answer.

"Robert," he said to me through those laughing, gentle eyes, "these are from your brothers and sisters in the Lord. When they heard about your situation they all got together and gave from their hearts. Oh, my brother, if you could have seen the joy on their faces as they carried those packages in. That's their reward! Don't deny them the joy of giving!"

He helped us load the car, and we all held each other for a long time and shared more tears of joy. As I went to get in the car, he held my hand tightly and with his other hand offered me a plain white envelope.

"This is an anonymous gift," he said. "Someone dropped it at the church office."

I knew that "someone" was him.

"Pastor," I squeaked, "I just don't feel we deserve all of this."

"It's Christmas," Pastor smiled. "It's a time for giving and remembering the great gift our heavenly Father gave for us. Your family loves you, Robert! Merry Christmas!"

We drove away with tears in our eyes. To think, our heavenly Father cared enough to surround us with a family that could love so completely! When we unloaded our treasures, we could not believe how God had multiplied our prayers.

That Christmas we ate a sumptuous meal and opened some of the most precious gifts anyone has ever received. That "humble" Christmas remains one of our richest memories.

YES, NO, NOT YET

by Theresa Dale Durden, Birmingham, Alabama

My identity was so wrapped up in my profession that my title was usually mentioned within a few moments after an introduction or a brief encounter. "Hey, you're Theresa Durden, the news lady."

That identity changed several months ago when I walked away from the career I had known for ten years. These months of unemployment have been among the hardest of my life. They've also been the most rewarding. I have experienced tears, anger, and frustration to the point of wanting to run away to a new country to start all over, and I've experienced miracles in some of my darkest hours.

One such miracle came in the form of a phone call.

I had been out of work for more than a month after walking away from a three-year contract renewal at a television station in Birmingham, Alabama. I had been the station's main female news anchor for four years, but my relationship with company management had been a roller coaster of emotions. Feeling uneasy about a three-year contract renewal, I asked God to tell me what to do. He gave me sign after sign after sign that I should walk away from the situation. I was a wreck. My inner voice, which I know is God, kept telling me to walk away. Finally, at the end of September, after more than a month of talks, I did just that.

I just knew I'd be okay. I mean, it was God who told me to walk away. And before I left, there were companies outside of television interested in hiring me. I told my family and friends, "Everything's gonna be fine. I won't be out of work for long." My last day was a Friday.

When Monday came, the three companies that had been interested in hiring me suddenly didn't have anything. I went into overdrive, sending out dozens of resumes for news and various other jobs outside the media circle. Every day, I tried to get out at least three resumes.

I surfed the Internet constantly, looking for job opportunities, freelance writing/editing, marketing, desktop publishing—anything. I used the paper. I even went to the employment office and registered my resume with the state.

Days turned into weeks with no phone calls. Weeks turned into a month, then two. Depression set in very hard. Each day, the struggle to get out of bed worsened, until one day I didn't. I couldn't face the day. I couldn't find the courage to face another day of rejections.

Around three o'clock that afternoon, the phone rang. I felt a jolt of hope, only to discover on the caller ID that it was the office at my apartment complex. I answered it anyway.

"Hello?"

"Is this Theresa?"

"Yes."

"This is Joyce at the office."

"What can I do for you?"

"Well, I just wanted to check on you and see how you're doing." I was a little perturbed by this, thinking she must have heard by now that I was out of a job and wanted to be nosy about what happened. I had already gotten plenty of those inquiries.

"I'm doing fine," I hedged.

"Well, someone told me you don't work for the TV station anymore."

Here we go, I thought. *She probably wants some gossip material, and she's afraid I won't be able to pay the rent.*

"That's right, Joyce. I don't work for the television station anymore, but I don't want you to worry. I'll still be able to pay the rent."

"Oh, no, that's not why I was calling," she said convincingly. "I just wanted to make sure you're doing all right. I know sometimes it can be tough."

"Yes, indeed it can." For some reason, I relaxed and opened up to her a little. I began to tell her what happened with the management at the station. I told her that I had good days and some very bad days, and that it had been a very rough few months for me.

"Well," she said, "I know how that is. You know, since the accident we have our good days and our bad."

"What accident?"

"You don't know about my son?"

"No."

Joyce proceeded to tell me about her son, Samuel. "It was back in June. He was working construction. They were working on a house and it had gotten hot, so he and some of the other guys went to a rock quarry, which was right around the corner from where they were working. All the other guys dove in the water, and when it was his turn, he dove in, but he hit a rock. He busted his second, third, and fourth vertebrae. He's paralyzed from the neck down," she said.

I was stunned that all this had happened and she was still functioning. Moreover, I was amazed that I had missed any signs that something was wrong in her life.

"Oh, Joyce, I am so sorry."

"Well, the Lord works in mysterious ways, Theresa."

Joyce told me how her now twenty-four-year-old son was going to a home for quadriplegics after she and her ex-husband tried unsuccessfully to care for him. It was just too much. They couldn't handle it. She said Samuel had been a "wild man" of sorts, and that she was surprised he was taking the situation so well.

"What do you mean he's taking it well? How could anybody take it well? Didn't this just happen in June?"

"Yes, but you know, I went to see him this week, and I was feeding him. . . ." I envisioned a twenty-four-year-old man, good-looking with some muscle tone still left from working in construction before the accident as she spoke. "I held his head and looked him in the eyes, and I asked him, 'Samuel, I know this has been hard. Do you wish that you would have died when you hit that rock instead of having to live the rest of your life like this?' Because, Theresa, he'll never be able to have children, or even be able to take a drink by himself."

"I know."

"But you know what he said?" she asked me rhetorically. "He said, 'Momma, I'm glad I lived. If I had died, I never would have known

God. I didn't know Him before the accident. He gave me a second chance, Momma. He let me live so I could have a chance to know Him. I never knew how wonderful He was."

With that, a tear ran down my face onto my pillow. I was still lying in bed from the depression brought on from self-pity. I thought, *God, what a selfless, beautiful thing to say. To be paralyzed from the neck down, to never be able to scratch your face without the aid of some contraption, to never be able to hug a loved one or even shake hands with an old friend, and he's thankful because he got a second chance to know You.*

Joyce then told me what a woman at her church had said to her. Joyce was telling this woman about her son and what he said. The woman asked Joyce, "Isn't our Lord a gracious God?" Joyce said she was confused. Gracious? Her son is a quadriplegic. How is that gracious?

"Yes," the woman said, "he's going to live his life paralyzed on earth, but he gets to spend an eternity with God."

My conversation with Joyce that afternoon helped to turn things around for me. I got up out of bed and spent the rest of the day thanking God for His graciousness to me. I went back to my computer and back to the business of finding a job.

Someone told me once that the Lord has three answers, "Yes, no, and not yet." I suppose this is the "not yet," so I keep plugging along, getting out of bed to look for the work He wants for me. When my heart breaks because the phone doesn't ring, I try to remember how grateful Samuel is just to have a second chance.

It's all a matter of perspective, and I thank God for changing mine.

THE ANGEL IN THE DUMPSTER

by Ellen DuBois, South Easton, Massachusetts

I was on my way to drop off some clothes at the clothing Dumpster, or "recycling" bin, and I was having one of those "challenging" days that we all have now and then. As I drove, I was thinking about the failing health of my grandmother and the illness of another family member. I was spent from running from rehab to rehab. I didn't want to lose my nana. I was operating on very little sleep, and I was worried about my fiancé's mother as well. I felt so overwhelmed. It was all I could do to control the tears as I drove. As I approached my destination, however, my control began to slip, and the tears came in spite of my efforts to stop them.

It was then that I began to pray.

I asked God for an angel. I didn't know if I deserved one or not. After all, I really had a lot to be thankful for compared to many in the world. But my strength was waning, and in a moment of complete despair, I asked God for an angel to help me get through the long days and nights of worrying and waiting.

I got out of my car, having just finished my prayer, and began to unload the large bag of clothing. As I struggled with the weight of it, I noticed something on top of the lid that you pull down to drop your clothing in the bin. I set the bag down so that I could see what was there.

I found myself staring into the face of the sweetest stuffed angel doll that I'd ever seen. I wondered why someone would leave such a sweet doll. She was obviously lovingly made of patchwork material, yarn hair, flowers attached to her countrylike dress and quilted wings. I couldn't imagine leaving her there. I took her in my arms and smiled.

I didn't just find a doll. God had sent me an angel. At that moment, I knew what it was to be truly overwhelmed, but not with despair— with joy. If I hadn't arrived at that Dumpster at that very moment, I never would have received this beautiful message from God.

Yes. A message from God.

That angel doll, who sits in the chair beside me as I type this, served as a reminder that when things seem their worst and you feel most alone, you are not alone, nor will you ever be.

I went from wallowing in my problems to knowing that all I needed to do was say, "Hey, I need help, please." He didn't let me down. He never does.

And today, I still have my angel, with her cute smile, quilted wings, and patchwork dress, to remind me that I am not—that *none* of us are—ever alone.

Keep your eyes open. Although mine came via a Dumpster, you never know from whence your angel might come!

SPLIT SCREEN

by Gerry Rita Di Gesu, Cape Cod, Massachusetts

Through the porch window I see my neighbors, an elderly couple, sitting in their backyard enjoying the beautiful autumn day. Relaxed in faded, weathered beach chairs, they face each other as they talk. A pink sweater covers her shoulders; the cat snoozes curled in the pocket of her lap. He wears a Yankee baseball cap and takes slow, deliberate puffs on his pipe. As she speaks, she leans forward, bobbing and shaking her finger emphatically to emphasize her point. Her smile and soft laughter brighten the warm afternoon.

Expressive hands punctuate his conversation as he pokes and waves his pipe in the air, punching holes in her arguments. They are in their eighties, truly lovers. It amazes me they have this much to share after more than fifty years of marriage. Although he's been retired for many years, it's wonderful to see them find such joy in each other.

Between our two yards a clothesline crowded with toddlers' bright overalls and play clothes flies in the brisk wind. A young couple and their two children live next door, and I feel a kinship with them as I watch them raise their children and deal with problems I've already faced. The young mother opens her back door and walks across the lawn to visit her neighbors. She is one of a vanishing breed—a mother who enjoys being home with her children and experiencing the joys, surprises, and frustrations of their daily escapades.

Her three-year-old son races across the grass, a lollipop clutched in his fist. He suddenly veers to the left and charges toward the birdbath. Stopping short, he peeks over his shoulder at his mom and then tosses the lollipop into the water. His baby sister bounds forward unsteadily, trying to catch up with him.

Suddenly, I'm aware that I'm midway in life between these two sets of neighbors who are sharing the lovely afternoon. My three children, almost grown, still need the nurturing and loving environment their dad and I try to provide, but they're old enough to allow us more free time to reach and discover new paths to explore together.

I am reminded of Ecclesiastes 3:1: "There is a time for everything, and a season for every activity under heaven."

There is peace and beauty in the picture framed by my window. My friend and her children are a reminder of my past. I'm thankful that shared joys and tears have imbued me with an increased inner strength. In the elderly couple, I see before me the beauty and promise of what my life can be.

What a true blessing to see both sides at once and to understand my season in between.

⌐ You can read more of Gerry Rita Di Gesu's great stories in volume one of God Allows U-Turns: True Stories of Hope and Healing.

CHAPTER ELEVEN

Hope and Healing

If it is possible, as far as it depends on you,
live at peace with everyone.
Romans 12:18

THE BRIDAL BOUQUET

by Charlotte Adelsperger, Overland Park, Kansas

Soap bubbles filled the air around bride and groom Julie and Mark as they emerged from the church on a sunny July afternoon. The guests who blew the bubbles were lining the sidewalk with smiles and cheers as the couple hurried to a gleaming limousine parked on the curb.

The big car headed for the reception, Mark and Julie waving good-byes. Julie turned her eyes to her wedding bouquet of delicate pink and ivory roses. She thought of the printed words on the program: "The bride's bouquet is dedicated in loving memory of her mother, Joan Miller." Julie's throat tightened again. She took a breath of the roses' scent and then smiled at Mark.

"On to the party!" he called to the driver.

After a festive reception featuring a prime rib buffet and dancing, Julie spent private moments with her father, Clay, and gave him a lingering hug.

"Thanks for everything, Dad. It was more than wonderful!"

Again she and her new husband slipped into the white limousine. Mark wrapped his arm around his bride's shoulder and pulled her close. Pastel balloons crowded her side of the seat.

The college-age driver started for their destination, but the groom spoke up about turning another direction.

"Oh, yeah, you two said you wanted to make a stop—almost forgot. Just tell me where to go."

Mark gave him the location.

"It's a cemetery," Julie said softly. The car was quiet. "This is really important to me," she said. "My mom's buried there."

"I bet you don't get many requests like that," Mark said.

"No, sure don't." The chauffeur glanced at the couple through his rearview mirror. "But I understand. . .I lost my mother when I was thirteen." He shared a little about his loss and what a difficult time it had been.

At the cemetery, Julie clutched Mark's hand. What a tender sight—a bride in her long white gown and a groom in a black tuxedo, walking on sun-scorched grass, crossing grave after grave on a July evening. In her free hand Julie gripped her bouquet. Her chin quivered as she neared her mother's grave site. She just *had* to come here—on this special day.

When she and Mark reached the spot, they stood prayerfully in the dusk. Without a word, the bride bent down and gently laid the flowers on the headstone. She touched the raised letters of her mother's name—like she always did when she came. Thoughts of how her mother would have rejoiced in their wedding flooded her. Then she broke into tears, and Mark, moist-eyed, held her to his chest for a long time. When they released, they looked down at Joan Miller's chosen Scripture engraved on the stone: "I know that my Redeemer lives" (Job 19:25).

"I'm ready," Julie said, looking up. The new husband and wife walked hand in hand silently toward the waiting car—and the life before them.

⌐ Make sure to read Charlotte Adelsperger's story, "On a Mountaintop in Norway," in volume one of God Allows U-Turns: True Stories of Hope and Healing.

THE MATCHLESS GIFT

by Stephanie Ray Brown, Henderson, Kentucky

After my second graders completed reciting the Pledge of Allegiance, my students settled back in their seats. But Duane remained standing. Duane was an exceptionally bright and lovable student. However, his home life was far from perfect.

His mother was a single parent who had many problems, such as drinking and an abusive boyfriend. Duane and his three younger sisters were often taken out of the home until social services thought it was safe for them to return. One reason I feared for his safety was because Duane was often burned with cigarettes—as he tried to protect his sisters.

Thinking that maybe he had had a bad night, I walked over to him to see what was the matter. As he looked up at me with dark brown eyes, I could see his hurt and disappointment.

"Mrs. Brown, aren't you going to open my Christmas present?" he asked. "I put it on your desk."

As I looked at my desk, all I could see was an avalanche of papers, stickers, and books. Seeing my puzzled look, Duane went to the front of the room and retrieved his gift from my desk. As he handed it to me, I noticed the wrapping paper was a napkin from the lunchroom.

Carefully removing the napkin, my gift appeared to be a matchbox. Although I had been a teacher for only three months, I had learned the important lesson of asking a child to explain a picture or, in this case, a gift, instead of disappointing him with a wrong guess. So I asked Duane to tell me about his gift.

First of all, Duane instructed that I had to use my imagination before opening my gift. He then began to tell me that this wasn't really a matchbox but a jewelry box. Inside, if I would use my imagination, I would find two precious gems.

As I opened my jewelry box, the sight as well as the smell of two beer caps surprised me. Duane informed me that instead of beer caps they were really two precious silver earrings. He had noticed that I never wore earrings and wanted me to have some pretty ones.

As my eyes began to tear, I was touched by the thoughtfulness of this child's precious gift. Since birth, one of my ears was slightly deformed. Fearing that wearing earrings might draw attention to the ear, I never wore them. But how could I not wear these precious earrings given by this special child? As I placed the earrings on my ears with masking tape, my class clapped, and Duane stood proudly beside me.

Every year after that, the matchbox remained on my desk. It reminded me of this child's kindness and the wonderful lessons he taught me.

Although his situation at home was not the best, Duane continued to see the good in life. The beer caps were an ugly reminder of some problems at home, but Duane had made them into something beautiful—two precious gems. Although my ear was deformed, Duane still wanted me to have pretty earrings. Even though the matchbox once held the matches used to light the cigarettes that had painfully burned his skin, his surprisingly tender heart allowed us all to see it as a treasure box instead of a dangerous weapon.

Although Duane did not have much money, he still wanted to give. Much like the widow and her two mites, Duane gave all he had—his heart.

Whenever I see Duane's gift on my desk, it encourages me. If I am having trouble reaching a student, I try to be like Duane and give that student a piece of my heart. When I am having a trying day, one glance at the matchbox reminds me of the small boy who had a trying day every day as well as every night but still could find the treasures among the trash.

Out of the good heart of a second-grade boy, one teacher will always have a gift to treasure. Many holiday seasons have come and gone, but the memory of my matchbox gift will never will fail to warm my heart or be extinguished from my mind.

May we never fail to let even the littlest souls teach us. They are more than willing to teach. But we must be willing to take the time and truly listen.

SIXTY-SIX POINSETTIAS

by Eva Marie Everson, Casselberry, Florida

"Sixty-six," my neighbor Maryse said. I'd just entered her front door to find her standing, emotionless, staring at the red, pink, and white poinsettias crowding the foyer and lining the hallway. I shivered in the chill that permeated the home—not so much from the December air but from the events of the past week. On December 2, 1987, Maryse's daughter Laura had been killed in an auto accident.

Having been neighbors for nearly a decade, we'd raised our six children together. Mine were as much a part of her home as hers were of mine. We even had special nicknames for the kids. I called twenty-year-old Laura "Laura Sue."

"What?" I asked.

"Sixty-six. Sixty-six poinsettias. Sixty-six reminders that my daughter is dead."

I'd never thought of the traditional flower-giving at funerals in such a way. I also couldn't imagine, nor begin to imagine, the agony my friend was experiencing. I did see that the flowers only seemed to add to her grief, though.

"Do you want me to take them somewhere?" I said softly. "I can do that. I will do that."

"No," she said with a sudden jerk of her head. "I'll think of something."

A few hours later she called. "I know what I want to do. I want to do what Laura would have done. She loved the elderly. Remember how she used to bake cookies and take them to the nursing home?"

I remembered.

"I want to do what Laura would have done," she said again. "Are you and Jessie available Friday night?"

"Sure," I said. Jessica, my six year old, and Maryse's son, Hayes, (Haysie-Bean) were best friends.

Then she filled me in on the plan.

Friday evening, Maryse was armed with the poinsettias. Hayes and Jessica, dressed like Santa's elves, carried candy canes donated by Bob's Candy Company; a friend of Maryse's husband came dressed as Santa, and I toted a camcorder on my shoulder to record the evening. We entered the warm, antiseptic hallway of a nearby nursing home with a "Ho! Ho! Ho!" and a "Merry Christmas!" Tired, age-lined faces broke into childlike amusement and wonder, and their old, watery eyes beamed with excitement.

After acquiring permission, our festive little group made the rounds with Santa's joyful "Ho! Ho! Ho!" proclaiming our presence mirthfully at each room's doorway.

"Oh, little darlings! Little darlings!" the residents extended their arms, welcoming our little elves.

Greeting each resident by name (their names were on the doors), Maryse said, "Merry Christmas," and placed a poinsettia on the nearby bedside tables.

"Merry Christmas," they said. "You're so sweet! So sweet!"

I steadied the camera and peered into the lens through tears. This was the single, most selfless act of love I had ever witnessed. My friend gave out of her grief. She took flowers commemorating her daughter's death and turned them into gifts of the season of hope, joy, and the ultimate gift of love.

I have no doubt that Laura stood next to her Lord and smiled at the five of us. It was exactly what she would have done.

LETTING GO

by Kim Kelly Pullen, Orlando, Florida

In April of 1996, in my fourth month of pregnancy, I found out the child I was carrying had multiple birth defects and would probably not survive. My husband and I chose not to abort the baby but to "let nature take its course." I carried little Aiden for nine more weeks.

Lying on the bed, my husband beside me, I knew the pain that no woman can describe and no man will ever understand—labor.

With a rush, I felt the child pushed out of me and, through drugged consciousness, watched the nurse wrap the tiny, tiny purple form in a bundle before she placed him in my arms. He was bigger than I'd thought he'd be, his little head almost the size of my fist. A little smear of blood that the nurse had missed ran along the side of his nose—my nose, I noticed. He wasn't breathing. His eyes were closed, sealed, never having to look on this world. They viewed another place. My son, my firstborn, was stillborn.

I touched his face, still warm from life. The skin was so smooth, so soft, like a baby's was supposed to be. I stared at him in amazement. He was part of me. This was the little life that had lived and grown and shared space within me. He was mine.

They allowed him to remain with me for a time. As he lay in the bassinet by my bed, I lay my hand on him, feeling his warmth ebbing through the faded baby blanket. His palate was cleft and his hands were twisted, but I couldn't take my eyes off that face. For almost every other woman in the hospital that had a bassinet by her bed that night, her life would be different from that day forth. The other women had a new life in their family, a new addition. They would be different people because of that child and so would every other person that came in contact with them. The world itself would be different because of that child.

But what about me? What about my little Aiden? He would never leave the hospital with me. Nobody else would ever lay eyes on him. Nobody else would ever hold him or touch his face or see his beauty. No one else would ever feel his warmth.

I cried when they rolled him out of my room that night.

The next morning, as we were preparing to leave, I asked the nurse if I could see him one last time. She brought his little bundle in, wrapped up loosely in that same faded blanket, the one that now sits on my dresser at home. He was cold, and in the recesses of my mind I knew they had probably refrigerated him overnight. He looked a little different. In the last ten hours, his detailed features had softened and faded a bit. But he was still mine. My baby.

As I sat there, a thought crossed my mind, entered my heart, and locked there. I knew this was a significant moment, a moment that I had not anticipated and now did not want to face.

It was the moment I had to say good-bye.

Everything in me fought it, screaming, *I can't do this! Not yet! Not now! Not so soon!* I knew I didn't have the strength to do this. I called my husband. He came to my side and quietly he began to pray. I listened to every word he said, begging for strength to let go. Every few moments I'd open my eyes and stare into that little face. Then it was my turn.

I don't recall every word I said or every thought I had. I only remember begging God for strength and courage to do something I felt impossible to do—to let my child go. When I finished, I opened my eyes again and breathed. When the nurse came in to take him, I pulled him to me one last time, kissed his cool brow, and handed him to the nurse.

I am going to be okay, I thought. *I really can do this.*

It was the most difficult moment of my life.

I think about it now and know that I have never been closer to God, never understood Him better, as I did at that moment. I had never felt the mournful struggle to let go of something that I loved as much as I did then.

I realized, too, that I was wrong about something. While my little boy never came home with me, my life would be different. While nobody else may ever have held him or gazed into his little face or touched his softness, he would touch every person that I knew because of how he touched me. Not only would I be different, the world itself would be different because of him.

GOD'S FLYING FLOWERS

by Connie Lounsbury, Monticello, Minnesota

Shortly before her eightieth birthday my mother got pneumonia. She was on a ventilator and kept so heavily sedated that we couldn't communicate with her. My sisters and I spent eight days in the hospital with her, and then she was gone. I knew Mom had gone to a better place and that she had no more pain or sorrow, but my mind was full of regret that we didn't get to say good-bye to each other.

My husband, David, and I had moved her from Bloomington, Minnesota, to our farm an hour away after she suffered a stroke in January of 1998. She recovered completely, and every morning that spring and summer Mom would say, "Well, I better go see what's new in your flower garden today."

Mom loved the huge, vibrant, orange Oriental poppies that waved in the wind. They reminded her of the crepe-paper flowers we kids used to make in grade school and bring home to her. She pointed to my columbine and talked about how she had sucked the honey from wild honeysuckle as a child. It looked just like my columbine. When my peonies blossomed, the fragrance reminded her of my father, who had died years before. He had always loved peonies. My lilacs reminded her of the farm where she grew up, and my hollyhocks were a reminder of her mother's pink hollyhocks that grew against the rough gray siding of her childhood home. My garden was always a trip down memory lane for Mom. It became our best times together.

While we sat and admired the flowers, I told her how much I appreciate the monarchs, butterflies that I call flying flowers. "The monarchs are faithful butterflies," I told Mom. "They migrate all the way to Mexico in the fall and return here to their breeding ground the following spring. Many people believe they represent the miraculous transformation our bodies make when we enter heaven."

Mom tried to get a closer look at the black-and-orange beauties, but they always flew away before she could get close. When I tried taking a close-up photograph, they eluded close inspection by me as well. Now, as my husband and I drove into our farmyard and I saw the September splendor of my garden, my heart ached with grief that Mom would never sit with me in my garden again.

We knew that my brother and his family from Colorado would be arriving at our home any minute. When I walked into the house, even through my tears, I could see that the kitchen floor needed sweeping. I picked up the entry rug and went out on the deck to shake it. David was still outside. As I turned to go back into the house, he called my name. "You have a butterfly on your head," he said.

I turned and looked at my reflection in the glass of the door. A beautiful monarch butterfly was sitting right on top of my head. "Wow!" I said. "In all my years of gardening a butterfly has never landed on me."

I continued to look at our reflection and I felt a warm sensation. I said, "Is that you, Mom?" The butterfly moved her wings up and down slightly. Fresh tears sprung to my eyes. *Yes,* I thought. *Mom has no more pain and no more loneliness. I shouldn't be sad. She is in a far better place, I know.*

I turned my head from side to side. The butterfly stayed in place. I walked across the deck to my husband. "I know this butterfly is a message from God. But I can't believe it is staying there so long."

He looked at me and said, "It's still there, all right." I walked back to the door and looked at it again. The butterfly just sat there looking at me. I stood there for the longest time, watching and listening to the silence. I walked across the deck again. "I don't know why it doesn't fly away," I told David.

"She seems to like being there," David said. I walked back to our reflection. The butterfly looked back at me. "Thank You, God," I said. "Is there anything else You want me to know?" Ecclesiastes 3:1–2 came to mind: "There is a time for everything, and a season for every activity under heaven: a time to be born and a time to die." The butterfly seemed to look straight at me for a few seconds, and then she gently flapped her wings and flew away. As I watched her leave, I knew that Mom was waving a loving good-bye to me.

I eased into a deck chair and felt the warm wonder that replaced the heaviness I had felt earlier. God had sent a monarch butterfly to bring me a final visit and a fond farewell from Mom. And, obviously remembering my frequent prayer to Him, "Lord, please speak to me clearly so I will understand You," He spoke to me in a message He knew I would understand.

CAN JESUS SEE?

by Susan Lynn, Faribault, Minnesota

My daughters and I were on our way home from town in the midst of a Midwestern blizzard. It was slow going and I was already tense when the "whiteout" occurred. Terrified, I didn't dare stop and continued inching the car along, hoping I wouldn't drive into the ditch, or worse yet, another vehicle.

Fighting the panic that was arising in me, I told my daughters, "We are going to pray and talk to Jesus." After praying for help and protection, my nervous three-year-old daughter asked her timely question. "Mommy, can Jesus see?" As I assured her that Jesus could see though we couldn't, a feeling of relief and peace flooded through me.

I've never forgotten that incident even though it occurred many years ago. Later in life, when I was experiencing an emotional storm, I had to remind myself of the truth that Jesus can always see what's up ahead.

As I approached my forties, my children were growing up and leaving home, one by one. My career as a full-time mom was coming to an end, and I had no idea who I was as a person or what direction my life would take. This identity crisis precipitated the return of suppressed memories of childhood sexual abuse at the hands of some male relatives. I tried to push these memories back where I thought they belonged—in the ancient ruins of my past. But they stubbornly refused to go away and I sank into a deep depression.

I was angry with my perpetrators, my parents for not supporting or protecting me, and even God. How could I trust a God who allowed innocent children to be so devastated by abuse?

Realizing I needed help, I finally told my pastor about the memories that were returning with frightful speed. If it had not been for him, I probably would have turned away from the church and God completely, but God had prepared the road for my recovery through this caring pastor. He listened as I poured out my pain and anger time after time. Through this man, God helped me to understand His *unconditional love.* My Bible became a source of comfort as I opened my heart to God. Slowly I began to believe God loved me, in spite of my abusive childhood and my own sinful past.

Many times I was overwhelmed by feelings of guilt, shame, and unbearable sadness. Thoughts of my sin filled me with condemnation, and I struggled to accept His forgiveness. One night as the mental and emotional battle raged within me, God spoke to me with these words, *"Who are you going to believe, Me or Satan?"*

In that moment, I saw that my difficulty in accepting God's love and forgiveness was a lack of trust. God promises forgiveness to those who confess their sins, which I had done many times. Now I had to choose to trust in that forgiveness and love.

Later, while pouring out my pain to God, I heard Jesus say to me, *"I know what you're feeling. I, too, was abused and abandoned by those who should have loved Me."* It was a revelation to me. Of course He understood. He understood better than anyone else. I clasped that truth to myself over and over as my journey toward wholeness progressed.

Although dealing with people from my past can still trigger very strong responses from time to time, I remind myself of the lesson I learned as I drove in that blizzard so many years ago. Jesus can see and He knows the way. I've finally learned to trust His Love.

EYE OF THE STORM

by Eunice Loecher, Woodruff, Wisconsin

Winter comes early in the Great Lakes region. As a recent widow, I was filled with apprehension at the thought of spending my first winter alone. So many things needed to be taken care of before the first snow. Things my husband took care of year after year. Something called Heet needs to be added to the car gas tank occasionally. Another product called Sta-bil needs to be used before storing the lawn mower. The yard becomes a mountain of raking when you do it alone.

I noticed a neighbor cleaning his gutters. The next afternoon, with my ladder in hand, mine were emptied of their accumulation of leaves and debris. New gas containers were filled and ready for the snowblower.

Then the storm came.

The weather forecasters were calling it a hurricane—the worst storm since the early 1970s. I had never heard of a hurricane in northern Wisconsin. The wind and the rain hit about 4 A.M. I lay in bed worrying about losing power or a tree hitting the house. That November storm came in waves, and by suppertime the rain had turned to snow.

After supper I went outside to check my yard for damage. I expected to be buffeted by the same gusts of wind that beat against the house all day. Instead, the winds were calm with a light snow gently falling. A beautiful winter evening.

It took a moment to realize I stood in the eye of the storm. The same storm continued to rage all around me, but I was safe in its center. The calm seemed to surround and fill me.

Pounding winds returned a few hours later and lasted most of the night. The next morning I used the snowblower to clear the snow from my driveway, counting it as one more accomplishment of widowhood.

Life can be like that hurricane, but I've learned that God is in the center. Because of His love and mercy, life can be lived in the eye of the storm.

*⌐ Make sure to read Eunice Loecher's story, "**Winter Bubbles**," in volume one of* God Allows U-Turns: True Stories of Hope and Healing.

FINDING OUR WAY HOME

by Lauren Perotti, San Francisco, California

In the quietest hour of the morning, just before sunrise, in that time between darkness and light, the shrill ring of the phone shattered the silence. My hand instinctively grabbed the phone before it rang again. My heart pounded. A phone call at this time could only bring bad news.

"Laur, it's me." My sister's voice trembled with suppressed hysteria.

"Lis? What's wrong? What is it?" I already knew.

"It's Ronnie," she started. I braced myself. "He's dead," she said, as if she couldn't really believe it herself. "The police found him lying on the floor in some guy's apartment in Chicago. It was a drug overdose. Ronnie is dead."

"Oh, God, *no. No!* Are you sure? He can't be. He can't be. Oh, God, I prayed so hard for him. I was praying so hard," I cried. My mind just screamed, *God, how could You let this happen after everything? Everything our family has suffered, everything Ronnie has tried?*

My twenty-seven-year-old brother had struggled and suffered profoundly with his substance addictions in continuous cycles of recovery and relapse since he was thirteen years old.

Each period of sobriety in a twelve-step or rehab program brought hope for sustained recovery and a happy life. Then, just when his life seemed to be getting in a groove, he would suddenly relapse. Time after time after time. Something was still missing. He wandered through life like a lost soul, searching desperately to fill that hole. No girlfriend could satisfy it; no drug could numb it; no drink quenched it; no job made meaning of it. Each relapse brought him lower. He went from drinking and smoking marijuana to snorting cocaine and crack to sometimes living on the street and eventually to stealing, heroin, speed balls, and prison time.

All those years, while he was slipping down, I was climbing up. Climbing up the corporate ladder, acquiring material things, looking successful. On the outside. I refused to see the turmoil in my marriage and my own problems with alcohol. That is, until my husband declared himself an alcoholic, got sober, and abruptly abandoned me without explanation. I was devastated. I hit bottom.

Since then, I had spent several years in my own spiritual recovery program, faced and overcome my past—and my addictions. I found many others who helped lead me toward a sacred garden. My heart opened. My true self began to emerge. I returned to the Roman Catholic Church, and soon the flickering ember of my long-forgotten faith was fanned into a brilliant blaze by the immense love of God.

I often shared my awakened spirituality with Ronnie, affirmed that by Jesus' wounds he was healed, that God had a plan of good for him. He listened to me and sought my spiritual guidance. It was his last stay in prison when he finally had his own spiritual awakening. I still have the touching letter he wrote to me from there, my tangible evidence that somewhere in the midst of all this turmoil he did finally find a God of his understanding.

"Since I have been here, I have accepted Jesus Christ into my heart. I believe with all my heart that Jesus died so that I could be forgiven. God has always been there for me throughout my life—I just never acknowledged Him. I know that the only way I will get better is through Jesus Christ," he wrote me. Miraculously, he was released from prison and cleared of several felony and misdemeanor charges one more time. Surely this would be the end of his problems, the final solution for him.

It wasn't. And now he had seemingly lost the battle. The ending we had all prayed would never happen had come to pass. Just days earlier he had attempted to get into yet another recovery program called Teen Challenge, a Christian substance abuse residence program for young adults. There was no room for him at this inn. He lost hope.

Four hours after my sister's phone call, I was boarding a plane headed home to Chicago. How were we going to get through this? I would never see my little brother again. I closed my eyes and tried to relax until takeoff. I needed to calm myself.

Standing in the rear of the plane, I closed my eyes for a moment and took some deep breaths. Suddenly, I saw a clear image of my brother. He was wearing a crisp, pure white shirt and a multicolored vest. He stood next to me on my left side and put his right arm around my shoulder, the same way he always did. *I'm all right now, Laur.* I felt his whisper in my heart. Then he was gone.

I was overwhelmed with both sadness and joy. I was sure that my brother's spirit had just come to connect to me, to comfort me. He looked so regal and pure. I wanted him to stay but he was gone.

The next time I saw him, he was in his casket.

Every night while I was in Chicago, I was awakened at four o'clock in the morning, the same time as Ronnie's death, by a bird singing outside the bedroom window. Although I couldn't see the bird, I listened with my heart. The song was both comforting and haunting. I couldn't help wondering, Was it about my brother?

For a few weeks after the funeral, Ronnie came to me unexpectedly at times when I wasn't thinking of him. He was always wearing the same white shirt and multicolored vest. I had nagging doubts about the destiny of his soul. Was he with God now, or eternally lost? What if he didn't make it after all? And why did I keep seeing him in those same clothes?

The answer came one morning over a month later.

I had sold my home. As I packed my belongings, I came across photos and memorabilia. Who can resist the temptation to reminisce while getting ready to move? Noticing a loose photo in the pile, I looked at it closely.

Time stood still for a moment.

I was in a hospital room surrounded by Ronnie, Lis, and Ma. Ronnie was wearing a pure white shirt and a multicolored vest. It had been Easter Sunday, the day I went into remission after undergoing a bone marrow transplant for a sudden onset of leukemia. The day of resurrection and new life. Tears of understanding poured down my cheeks.

Later that same evening I made a quick trip to the neighborhood grocery store for some packing supplies. As I left the store, I noticed a man standing near the door next to a small table bearing a sign that read Teen Challenge.

I walked toward him slowly. "I have to tell you a story," I finally said, my eyes wet with tears. I shared Ronnie's story with him. Then, tentatively, I relayed my experience of seeing Ronnie on the plane and finding the Easter photo earlier that day.

Smiling, the man nodded, reached down, and picked up a Bible. "It's right here in Luke fifteen," he said, thumbing through the pages to find the passage. "The story of the prodigal son. When the son had spent everything he had, he returned home to his father. Overjoyed at his return, his father greeted him with a kiss, called for a feast to be prepared, and put his finest robe on his son. Your brother, the prodigal son, spent everything and had returned home to God his Father. I think I was supposed to be here to tell you that."

I walked home in silent awe.

In the quietest hour of the morning, just before sunrise, in that time between darkness and light, a bird sang outside my bedroom window. Its sweet, holy sound seemed to fill the stillness surrounding it for a moment that I knew was eternal. My heart beat peacefully and I smiled. A bird singing at this time could only bring good news.

IN THE SPIRIT

by Sara Jordan, Canton, Ohio

"Hey, where are your lights?" the neighbor called from her front porch next door when I stepped out of our house to get the mail.

I turned in her direction. "What?"

"Your Christmas lights and decorations. You usually have them up Thanksgiving weekend!"

I glanced down at the mail I was gathering and shrugged before answering. "I guess we're just slow this year," I finally said.

She nodded and smiled, and I stepped back into the house, sighing as I closed the front door. I dropped the mail on the entry table and plopped down in the easy chair near the door, closing my eyes for a minute. It had been a long, frustrating day and I was ready to put my feet up for a few minutes before my husband, Dave, got home from work. Nothing at work had gone right for me, which was par for the course lately. I had been feeling restless and discontented for awhile, and the impending Christmas season had something to do with it.

The neighbor was right—we usually went all out for Christmas starting Thanksgiving weekend. Dave would string the lights around the windows and front porch, I would decorate with window decals and homemade ornaments, and we always got a live tree from the lot down the street. I loved the Christmas spirit, the coziness and softness it lent to everyday living. I could listen to Nat King Cole sing "The Christmas Song" twenty times a day and not tire of it. I liked to pick out gifts for others I knew they would love and then carefully wrap those gifts with specially selected, sometimes even homemade, wrapping paper. Yet, here we were entering the second week of December without the usual fanfare.

"Oh, Lord, forgive me for my lack of enthusiasm," I began to pray. "It's just that this time last year we were sure that we'd have a baby by this Christmas. We've been trying for over five years now. I know You're taking good care of the two babies we lost to miscarriage, but we still miss them. We started the adoption process last year led by Your divine guidance, we're sure. It wasn't supposed to take this long. Why has everything gone wrong? And now the thought of another childless Christmas, a season so devoted to the innocence of childhood, is breaking me. On top of that, I have two relatives and five friends who are either pregnant or have newborns. I try to be happy for them, but it only points out my empty arms. I need Your strength, Jesus. Please restore the joy of my salvation and give me hope again. In Your name, I pray. Amen."

By the time I was done, tears were streaming down my cheeks. *I'm so tired,* I thought. *How can I keep going? How can I face that attic full of boxes of decorations, all filled with dreams of years gone by with no children yet?*

After dinner that evening I approached the subject with Dave, telling him about my prayer.

"Let's just turn up the Christmas music, dig our heels in, and put up the decorations," he suggested.

I reluctantly agreed, knowing it was as good a time as any. We drove down the street to the tree lot and slogged through the mud to choose a tree. My heart wasn't in it, but we finally found one after searching row after row. I had to admit the smell of pine was comforting.

"What's that?" Dave asked when we returned home to see a cardboard box on the porch with a card attached.

We hurried inside and I tore open the card to read it. I saw immediately that it was my mother's handwriting. "It's from Mom," I told Dave as I began to read the note. "She must've dropped it off while we were getting the tree."

I read the note aloud: "To remind you of the true meaning of Christmas so that you will celebrate in your heart. This is for all the future traditions you will have with your children. Love, Mom and Dad."

Dave had opened the box and begun to pull out the protective packing. I dropped to my knees on the floor beside him. Tears flowed again when I realized what was in the box. It was a Nativity scene—a wooden stable, three wise men, a shepherd, Mary, Joseph, and a little baby Jesus. It wasn't just any Nativity scene, however. It was the one my parents had bought the first year they were married and kept for the past thirty years. It had been my job to set up the Nativity every year as I was growing up while my parents told me the story of Jesus' birth. It was a cherished tradition that my parents had passed along to me in the hopes that I would share it with my own children. They still had hope for grandchildren. In fact, they firmly believed that it would happen in God's perfect timing, even if I couldn't understand the plan completely. Through this gift, they had stepped out in faith. How could I do any less?

I picked up the baby Jesus figure, cradling it in the palm of my hand. I wondered how Mary must have felt giving birth to the Savior, the very Son of God. What an awesome motherly responsibility. Aside from that, though, He was still the baby that she had loved and expected for nine months. Jesus had begun His life as a baby, just like everyone else. He faced the hardships and sufferings of life so that He could die as a perfect lamb for me. Christmas is not about my expectations. Christmas is about celebrating the birth of Jesus and in my own distractions I had forgotten. I didn't need external things to "get in the spirit"; the Spirit was already eternally in me.

I smiled through my tears as I told Dave, "God has answered my prayer in a big way today. I've got to call Mom and Dad, then let's put up those decorations!"

That night as we went to bed in a home sparkling with Christmas spirit and homemade decorations, I turned to a favorite Scripture:

"Those who know your name will trust in you, for you, Lord, have never forsaken those who seek you" (Psalm 9:10). I slept peacefully that night for the first time in weeks, the joy of my salvation restored once again.

~ *Make sure to read Sara Jordan's story, "A Sign from God," in volume one of* God Allows U-Turns: True Stories of Hope and Healing.

ALLISON'S CONCLUDING THOUGHTS

Excuse me, please. I can't leave without asking one most important question. Do you have a personal relationship with the eternal God? I'm not talking about "getting a religion." I'm talking about "getting a relationship." You may have read every word of this book and yet never experienced the peace, strength, and hope that our authors have shared with you.

I spent decades of my life looking for fulfillment in all the wrong places. Today I have peace, strength, and hope because there was a time in my life when I accepted Jesus as my personal Savior. That is what I mean by getting a "relationship," not a "religion."

The way is simple. It only takes three steps.
1. Admit that you are a sinner: "For all have sinned, and come short of the glory of God." Romans 3:23 KJV
2. Believe that Jesus is God the Son and He paid the wages of your sin: "For the wages of sin is death [eternal separation from God]; but the gift of God is eternal life through Jesus Christ our Lord." Romans 6:23 KJV
3. Call upon God: "If thou shalt confess with thy mouth the Lord Jesus, and shalt believe in thine heart that God hath raised him from the dead, thou shalt be saved." Romans 10:9 KJV

Our web site has a "Statement of Faith" page that you might find interesting and comforting. On that page you will find helpful (and hopeful) links to other spiritually uplifting web pages. Please visit it at http://www.godallowsuturns.com.

Salvation is a very personal thing. It is between you and God. I cannot have faith for you; no one can. The decision is yours alone. Please know that this wonderful gift of hope and healing is available to you. You need only reach out and ask for it. It is never too late to make a U-turn toward God. . .no matter where you have been or what you have done. Please know that I am praying for you.

God's Peace and Protection Always,
Allison Gappa Bottke

Future Volumes of

GOD ALLOWS U-TURNS

The stories you have read in this volume were submitted by readers just like you. From the very start of this inspiring book series, it has been our goal to encourage people from around the world to submit their slice-of-life true short stories for publication.

God Allows U-Turns stories must touch the emotions and stir the heart. We are asking for well-written, personal, inspirational pieces showing how faith in God can inspire, encourage, heal, and give hope. We are looking for human-interest stories with a spiritual application, affirming ways in which Christian faith is expressed in everyday life.

Because of the huge response to our call for submissions for volumes one and two, we plan to publish additional volumes in the U-Turns series every year. Our web site lists future volume topics.

Your true story can be from 500–2,000 words and must be told with drama, description, and dialogue. Our writers' guidelines are featured on our web site, and we encourage you to read them carefully. Or send us an SASE for a copy of the guidelines.

GOD ALLOWS U-TURNS
P.O. Box 717
Faribault, MN 55021-0717
E-mail: editor@godallowsuturns.com
web site: http://www.godallowsuturns.com

Fees are paid for stories we publish, and we will be sure to credit you for your submission. Please understand that due to the volume of submissions we receive, we will only contact you in the event that your story is selected for use in a future volume. Remember, our web site is filled with up-to-date information about the book project. Additionally, you might want to take advantage of signing up to be on our free "Hotline Update" list for Internet users. Visit us soon at: http://www.godallowsuturns.com.

SHARING THE SUCCESS

The Holy Bible is quite clear in teaching us how we are to live our lives. One of the most profound lessons is that of "giving." Scripture refers to this often, and never has the need to share with others been so great.

"Give, and it will be given to you. A good measure, pressed down, shaken together and running over, will be poured into your lap. For with the measure you use, it will be measured to you" (Luke 6:38).

In keeping with the lessons taught us by the Lord our God, we are pleased to have the opportunity to donate a portion of the net profits of every *God Allows U-Turns* book to a nonprofit Christian charity.

For more information on the beneficiaries of the volume you are now holding, please visit our web site at http://www.godallowsu-turns.com.

VOLUME TWO FOUNDATION
BENEFICIARIES:

The JESUS Film Project

Camp Alandale

ABOUT OUR EDITORS

ALLISON GAPPA BOTTKE lives in southern Minnesota on a twenty-five-acre hobby farm with her entrepreneur husband, Kevin. She is a relatively "new" Christian, coming to the fold in 1990 as a result of a dramatic life "U-turn." The driving force behind the God Allows U-Turns Project, she has a growing passion to share with others the healing and hope offered by the Lord Jesus Christ. Allison has a wonderful ability to inspire and encourage audiences with her down-to-earth speaking style as she relates her personal testimony of how God orchestrated a dramatic U-turn in her life. For further information about Allison, visit her information page on the book's web site: http://www.godallowsuturns.com/aboutauthor.htm or http://www.godallowsuturns.com/modeling.htm.

CHERYLL MARIE HUTCHINGS was born in Ohio where she has lived all her life. She and her family live in a rambling ranch home minutes from "civilization," yet secluded enough to enjoy the area wildlife that ambles through her own backyard in abundance. Cheryll and her husband, Robert, are raising two teenage sons, Aaron, nineteen, and Scott, sixteen. In addition to her work as coeditor of the U-Turns project, Cheryll works for the Brunswick Community Recreation Center.

ELLEN REGAN joined the U-Turns team as a coeditor in the spring of 2000. Although an Easterner by birth, Minnesota has been her home for the last decade. After living in Los Angeles, California, for nearly fifteen years, Minnesota was a welcome respite from traffic, smog, and concrete. At the moment, she and her family live at a college preparatory boarding school where she functions as a dorm parent in the boys' dormitory. Her life is centered around her own two sons, but she also has the privilege of being the surrogate "mom" to other boys on campus. Ellen is active in her church community as a volunteer, singer in the choir, and soloist.

OUR INTERNET WEB SITE

We first announced *God Allows U-Turns* on the World Wide Web in February of 2000. The Lord used this avenue of communication to reach across all borders: geographic as well as racial, political, denominational, and social. Stories began to come to us via our web site, first by the dozens, then hundreds, and now thousands.

While our web site is specific to the *God Allows U-Turns* book series, you will find we also offer important links to other major Christian web sites, links we encourage you to visit. Additionally, we have placed a "Statement of Faith" page on our site to clearly establish our beliefs.

The global opportunities a web site provides are mind-boggling, but we need your help to make the kind of impact we know is possible. Please visit our web site and forward it to your family and friends. Virtually everyone has a story to tell, and future volumes will enable those stories to be told. We are accepting true short stories *now* for future volumes. Visit our "Future Volumes" page on our web site to find out more.

Remember, our web site is filled with up-to-date information about the book project. You will be able to access tour and book-signing calendars on the site, as well as read stories from the current volume. Additionally, you might want to take advantage of signing up for our free "Hotline Update" list for Internet users. Our free yahoogroups.com list can be accessed via our web site. It's easy to join. Don't miss out on current news and reviews.

Visit us soon at http://www.godallowsuturns.com.

AUTHOR/CONTRIBUTORS

All of the stories in this volume of *God Allows U-Turns* were submitted by readers like you. We are blessed to have had this opportunity to glimpse into their lives, if only for a moment, and we thank them for sharing their faith with us. We have included information about each contributor below. In some cases, we have added contact information at their request.

Charlotte Adelsperger is coauthor with Karen Hayse of *Through the Generations: The Unique Call of Motherhood*. She has authored two other books and has written for more than seventy-five publications, including volume one of *God Allows U-Turns* and *A Second Chicken Soup for the Woman's Soul*. She is also a popular speaker and can be contacted at 11629 Riley, Overland Park, Kansas, 66210, or by telephone at 913-345-1678.

Jon Alessandro is a freelance writer who writes frequently on Christianity and Christian living. Visit Jon at his web site, www.writerjon.com, or e-mail him at jon@writerjon.com.

Cindy Appel is an online columnist, a soon-to-be-published novelist, freelance writer, manuscript evaluator, wife, and mother. Her articles, book reviews, and inspirational essays have appeared in over twenty-five publications. Her first novel is scheduled for release in July 2001 from Starlight Writers Publications.

Esther M. Bailey lives in Phoenix, Arizona, with her husband, Ray, where they attend North Hills Church. She is a freelance writer with more than eight hundred published credits and is coauthor of two books: *Designed for Excellence* and *When Roosters Crow*. You can e-mail her at baileywick@juno.com.

Richard Bauman resides in West Covina, California. He is a successful freelance writer, and his articles have appeared in numerous publications. He is the author of the book *Awe-full Moments: Spirituality in the Commonplace*.

Amy Beres enjoys spending time with her husband as well as writing, mural painting, and viewing the wonder of God's creation through the eyes of her three children, ages six, four, and three. They are all active members of a Nazarene church in Pennsylvania.

Mildred Blankenship uses her writing talents to do God's work. She routinely writes letters of encouragement to the sick, those confined to home, and often helps the elderly with their monthly bank statements. Her poems and true-life stories often appear in her church bulletin.

Judi Braddy is a freelance writer and motivational speaker who has published numerous poems, articles, and essays. She writes a regular column for a national women's magazine, serves as the president of Sacramento Christian Writers, enjoys traveling with her minister husband, and spoiling four grandbabies. Her story "The

Vernal Pool" first appeared in the *Sacramento Bee, Elk Grove,* June 4, 2000.

Claudia Breland lives in Maple Valley, Washington, with her husband and two children. Currently a librarian with the King County Library System near Seattle, Claudia has been writing inspirational essays for five years.

Ginger Broslat is director of Community Outreach for Hospice in Marion County. She allows God to use her physical disability to encourage others spiritually. She and her husband live in Ocala, Florida, and have two children.

Stephanie Ray Brown taught first grade for six years. Currently, she is a happy stay-at-home mother to Savannah, who is five years old.

Renie Szilak Burghardt is Hungarian by birth and American by choice. A freelance writer with credits in many books and magazines, she lives in Ozark country and loves nature.

Debbye Butler is a lifelong resident of Indianapolis. A writer/editor for a Fortune 500 company, she has also been published by local magazines, Blue Mountain Arts, and in the Faith and Values section of the *Indianapolis Star* newspaper. She is president and cofounder of Circle City Singles, an ecumenical ministry for Christian singles.

Janice Byrd is a public speaker, "tea-talker," and oral book reviewer. Formerly a mathematics teacher and currently a special librarian, Janice writes about her avocation as a mission volunteer. Married for thirty-two years, with two grown children and one grandchild, Janice and her husband live in McKinney, Texas.

Joan Clayton has written six books and has had over four hundred articles published, including a story in volume one of *God Allows U-Turns.* She is currently the religion columnist for her local newspaper. She and her husband, Emmitt, live in Portales, New Mexico. Her passion is writing. His is ranching.

Leanne Bright Cloudman was born and raised in rural western North Carolina. Leanne presently lives in southeastern North Carolina with husband, Frank, and has somewhere between two and six kids, and various critters. Her book *The Struggle Continues* will be available in December 2001 in which she shares more of her rural life memories.

Jan Coleman, from Auburn, California, is a busy author and speaker. She encourages hurting women to trust in God's promise from Joel 2:25 that *God will restore the years the locust has eaten.* Look for her book on this theme from Broadman & Holman, spring 2002. She can be reached at jwriter@foothill.net. You can also read another story from Jan in volume one of *God Allows U-Turns.*

Denise Davis Courtney is wife to a wonderful husband, Alvin, and mother and stepmother to Casey, Adam, Sarah, Trey, and Katie. A newly published freelance writer, Denise is also a mammographer with twenty years' experience in the health care profession.

Elaine Cunningham has had nine books and many articles published. She lives in Wenatchee, Washington, with her minister husband. Her story "The Pre-Dawn Test" first appeared in *The Christian Reader,* January/February 2001.

Barbara Curtis is mother to twelve children, including three adopted boys with Down's syndrome, and grandmother to seven. She has published over four hundred articles in fifty magazines—including *Guideposts, Christian Parenting Today,* and *Focus on the Family,* as well as two parenting books. Visit her at www.barbaracurtis.com.

Robert Diacheysn Jr. is an actor, director, writer, and puppeteer. He works at Universal Studios in Florida. He and his wife, Sharon, a professional singer, are raising their five children together and aging quickly.

Ron DiCianni has been an illustrator for twenty-five years, working for clients such as ABC, NBC, McDonalds, the Smithsonian, and the United States Olympic Committee. The illustrator of such well-known books as *This Present Darkness* and the best-selling Tell Me series, Ron has also done several of his own books, including *Beyond Words.* A native Chicagoan, Ron lives in Illinois with his wife, Pat, and his two best works of art, Grant and Warren.

Gerry Rita Di Gesu lives on Cape Cod in Massachusetts. She says, "If we look hard enough even on the darkest days, there is always a ray of hope somewhere—life is good. The beauty and order of nature bring balance and perspective to my work. My writing reflects my assurance in the inherent goodness of man."

Cyd A. Donaldson is active in her community and writes creative and inspirational stories in her spare time. A busy wife to Ron and mother to Ashley, Cyd is also a graduate of Blackburn College in Illinois with a B.A. in written communications.

Sharon Doorasamy is an American writer living in South Africa with her husband, Alan, and their three-year-old son, Alan Jr. A stay-at-home mom who freelances on the side, she worked as a reporter for newspapers in California, Rhode Island, and North Carolina prior to settling in South Africa in 1995.

Ellen DuBois is from Massachusetts and has used writing as an outlet since childhood. She has an E-book under contract and was a winner of the Blue Mountain Arts 10-99 Poetry Contest. Her poem "Dare to Dream" has inspired many. She writes to touch others, and you can visit her web site at www.writingsoftheheart.homestead.com/index.html.

Sara A. (Candy) DuBose has articles and stories appearing in numerous publications and anthologies. She is a speaker and Bible teacher and can be reached at 334-284-2010. You can purchase her book *Conquering Anxiety* by calling 1-800-283-1357.

Wendy Dunham is a wife, a mom, a registered therapist, and a writer whose goal is to do all for the "Glory of God." She can be reached at 3148 Lake Road, Brockport, NY, 14420, 716-637-0535.

Theresa Dale Durden is a ten-year veteran of broadcast journalism. She was born and raised in Fayetteville, North Carolina.

Eva Marie Everson is the author of several books, including the new fictional mystery *Shadow of Dreams* (Promise Press), *True Love: Engaging Stories of Real Life Proposals,* and *One True Vow: Love Stories of Faith and Commitment* (Promise Press). She is a wife, mother, and grandmother.

Susan Fahncke of Kaysville, Utah, is a freelance writer and runs her own website.

She has stories published in numerous books and magazines, including volume one of *God Allows U-Turns*. She is the author of "Angel's Legacy." To learn more about Susan and sign up for her free daily inspirational E-mail list, visit www.2theheart.com, or e-mail her at Susan@2theheart.com.

Malinda Fillingim of Roanoke Rapids, North Carolina, is an ordained Baptist minister. She counts it a blessing to have Scott as her brother and finds great joy in being the mother of Hope and Hannah and the wife of David. Malinda's work also appears in volume one of *God Allows U-Turns*. She says, "Life's greatest gifts come in many forms."

Carolyn Fox is an aspiring author.

Karen Garrison is an award-winning writer specializing in stories that encourage faith. A wife and mother of two, she is working on her second inspirational novel when she is not chasing her two small children, Abigail and Simon. You may reach her at innheaven@aol.com or 740-283-3895.

Michael Adair Gibbs has been a police officer for more than thirty years. He has observed, firsthand, uncounted instances of faith in God being the vehicle that carried Christians over the hurdles of adversity and tragedy. Michael is a published author of fiction, nonfiction, and poetry.

Mary Ellen Gudeman was born on a farm in Indiana. She attended Indiana Business College and worked seventeen years as a secretary. She later attended Fort Wayne Bible College and served twenty-six years in Japan with the TEAM organization. She volunteers at a local refugee outreach ministry.

Nelum Himali Haththella lives in Sri Lanka and is currently in her final year at the university studying for a BSC in I.T. and Communications. She is also a mentor at Calvary Church.

Sharon R. Haynes is a freelance writer and photographer living in northeast Ohio. She has written for local newspapers for over twenty years. She enjoys walking on the beach and climbing spiritual mountains. "The Song" has also appeared in *Faith and Friends*, a Salvation Army publication in Toronto, in October 2000.

Elaine Ingalls Hogg is a palliative care volunteer and the author of several inspirational stories, as well as the award-winning book *Remembering Honey*, a story to help parents and children discuss grief. She may be reached at http://www.elainehogg.tripod.com/webpages.

Michele Howe of LaSalle, Michigan, has published over five hundred articles. She reviews for *Publishers Weekly*, *CBA Marketplace*, and *CCM Magazine*. Michele is also the author of *Going It Alone: Meeting the Challenges of Being a Single Mom* and *Bible Stories: Food and Fun*. Her work also appears in volume one of *God Allows U-Turns*.

Dr. Carol Jackson is CEO of Carol Jackson Ministries, Inc. She is a twenty-three-year veteran as a police sergeant and lieutenant colonel in the Army Reserves. Dr. Jackson is an ordained minister and holds a Ph.D. in counseling. She is aspiring to become published in her literary work.

Sally John is a wife and mother. Native Illinoisans, her family lived in California when this story happened. Today the same license plates hang on her grown children's walls. She is the author of three novels including *Surrender of the Heart*, a 2000 Christy Award finalist.

Louise Tucker Jones is an award-winning author and popular speaker. She is the author of the novel *Dance from the Heart* and coauthor of the Gold Medallion award-winning book *Extraordinary Kids*. She has published numerous articles and appeared on radio and TV programs.

Sara Jordan lives in Canton, Ohio. She has been published in Billy Graham's *Decision* magazine, *Lighthouse Digest,* and as a staff writer for *Connection: The Good News Magazine.* Her short stories have appeared in volume one of *God Allows U-Turns, Thema, 3.5 Plus,* and *Nota Bene* literary magazines. She and her husband are in the process of adopting a child.

LaRose Karr lives in Sterling, Colorado, with her husband and their four children. She is a church secretary who enjoys people, travel, and storytelling. She believes her writing is a gift from God and gives Him all the glory. LaRose has a story in volume one of *God Allows U-Turns.* She can be reached at rosiebay@kci.net.

Dr. Muriel Larson, author of seventeen books and thousands of published writings and songs, is a professional writer, counselor, and speaker, and has taught at writers' conferences across the nation. You may contact her at 10 Vanderbilt Circle, Greenville, SC 29609, 864-244-4993 or e-mail at mkljoy@aol.com.

Carmen Leal is the author of *Faces of Huntington's, Portraits of Huntington's,* and *WriterSpeaker.com,* an Internet research and marketing book for writers and speakers. She is also coauthor of *Pinches of Salt, Prisms of Light.* In addition to her writing, Carmen is a professional speaker and singer. She can be reached at Carmen@writerspeaker.com or visit her web site at www.writerspeaker.com.

Pastor Aaron D. Lewis, author and healing apostle, has traveled nationally, conducting Schools of Healing. His anointed messages focus on the kingdom of God, healing, and destiny. Lewis and his wife, Tiwanna, organized The Family of God in East Hartford, Connecticut. They have five beautiful children.

Delores Christian Liesner says, "God's grace, humor, and hope enable me to enjoy many roles: wife, mom, grandma, high school secretary, forensic coach, freelance writer, humorist, and 'health nut'!"

Marita Littauer is a professional speaker with over twenty years' experience. She is the author of ten books including *Personality Puzzle* and *Come as You Are,* and her newest, *Love Extravagantly.* She is president of CLASServices Inc., an organization that provides resources, training, and promotion for speakers and authors. P.O. Box 66810, Albuquerque, NM 87193, 800-433-6633, www.classervices.com.

Eunice Loecher celebrates her life as a full-time grandma and a part-time writer. Living in Woodruff, Wisconsin, she continues to seek God in the eye of life's storms. Eunice had a story published in volume one of *God Allows U-Turns.* Her story "Eye of the Storm" first appeared in *The Phoenix,* October 2000.

Connie Lounsbury is a regular contributor to *Guideposts*. Her work has also appeared in *Stories for the Kindred Heart, Angels on Earth, LifeWise,* and *Evangel.* She self-published her book *Quit Your Job and Make Ends Meet* and has recently completed her first novel. She lives in Monticello, Minnesota.

Susan Lynn has been writing since 1995. Her gift of writing emerged as she journalized throughout her recovery process from childhood abuse issues. What began as therapeutic exercise has become a fulfilling and rewarding accomplishment. This is her first published story.

Merrie Maurer wrote a column for a weekly entertainment paper for ten years. She has been published in several anthologies. www.homestead.com/merriespoetrypage/

Lucinda Secrest McDowell, a graduate of Gordon-Conwell Seminary, is a dynamic national conference speaker and author of four books, including *Quilts from Heaven, A Southern-Style Christmas,* and *Women's Spiritual Passages.* Visit her web site: www.encouragingwords.net, or contact her at cindy@encouragingwords.net.

Meriam (last name withheld) was a Jewish atheist-turned agnostic. Then, as a retired fitness professional, she had an epiphany at the age of fifty-two when she realized that not only did God exist, but that He had become personal and intimate in her life. "Amazing," she says today, at the age of fifty-nine.

Carrie Mikolajczyk-Russell is a twenty-five-year-old mother of two children. She has been married to Steve for five years. She is also a surrogate mother to three children and a business owner dedicated to helping infertile couples.

Kathy Collard Miller is the author of forty-two books, including *Why Do I Put So Much Pressure on Myself?* She is also a popular conference speaker. Her story "I Don't Really Want to Hurt My Child" has been published in seven magazines, the most recent being *Women Alive!* September/October 1992. www.kathycollardmiller.com.

Karen O'Connor is an award-winning author and popular speaker for church and professional events. She was named Writer of the Year for 1997 by the San Diego Christian Writers Guild. Her story "Chicken and Checks" appears in O'Conner's anthology titled *Squeeze the Moment* (Waterbrook Press, 1999), under the title "Following God's Leading."

Linda Parker is the author of *The Sand of the Kalahari,* a book on the Bushmen of the Kalahari Desert. Linda is also the mother of two beautiful daughters.

Dr. Debra D. Peppers is a television and radio talk show host. Also a motivational speaker, university instructor, and author, she shares her faith, a 100-pound weight loss, and her story, "From Troubled Teen to Teacher of the Year," inspiring audiences worldwide. Contact her at www.pepperseed.org.

Bob Perks is president of Creative Motivation, author of *The Flight of a Lifetime,* and a professional member of the National Speakers Association. www.bobperks.com or e-mail bob@bobperks.com.

Lauren Perotti is a consultant and writer currently completing her master of arts degree in psychology (concentration in expressive arts). Her mission is to promote healing and inspire spiritual growth for individuals and communities through multi-arts programs, including combinations of drama, ritual, music, and writing.

Mary Pierce is the humor columnist for Focus on the Family's *LifeWise Magazine,* among other writing and editing projects. She is a motivational speaker for corporate, community, and church audiences, and cohosts a monthly program on Christian radio. She and her husband, Terry, live in Wisconsin. Her story "Mama Schwarzeneggar" first appeared in *LifeWise Magazine,* April/May 2000.

Kim Kelly Pullen was raised in south Florida but now resides in Orlando with her husband, Russ, and her four-year-old son, Tristan. She divides her time between writing, running a small bookstore, and directing productions in local theaters. She is currently at work on her first novel.

Carol McAdoo Rehme is a four-time mother whose life "after kids" includes a career as a professional storyteller/speaker. Her inspirational stories can be found in several *Chicken Soup for the Soul* books, *An Angel by Your Side, Teatime Stories for Mothers,* and many other books. Contact her at carol@rehme.com.

Pastor John Roberts lives in Sterling, Colorado, where he is senior pastor at First Baptist Church in Sterling. He also writes a weekly religious column for the local newspaper and has been previously published in volume one of *God Allows U-Turns.* He and his wife, Debbie, have two talented children: Laura, age nineteen; and David, age seventeen.

Carol Russell is a writer and speaker. She has had several articles and devotions published, as well as many children's stories. Carol speaks at women's retreats, fellowship meetings, and mother/daughter banquets. Her story "Sweet as Strawberries" appears in *Stories of Abudance for a More Joyful Life* by Kathy Collard Miller (Starburst Publishers, 1999).

Suzy Ryan's articles have appeared in *USA Today, CPT, Today's Christian Woman, Decision, Discipleship Journal,* and various newspapers.

Joe Seay is an internationally published writer. Prior to retirement he was a businessman and conducted marriage enrichment seminars. He was also a TV talk show host and a political activist. Happily married, retired, and sixty-seven years old, Joe feels God has blessed him greatly. His story "Don't Hold a Grudge" has appeared in various church periodicals over the past five years.

Brette McWhorter Sember is the author of five self-help books and a contributor to two other books. Her articles and essays have appeared in over seventy publications. Visit her web site at: www.mooseinthebirdbath.com.

Lucy Sennett is a freelance writer and educator who lives in Mississippi.

Margaret Shauers is a Christian writer, mother, grandmother, and teacher.

Sandy Sheppard is a pastor's wife, mother of three, freelance writer, and a substitute teacher. She is the author of one children's book and over one hundred articles.

Dianne Smith lives in Fremont, California, with her husband Marty and their teenagers Janelle and Jordan. She is currently marketing her first novel, *Jessica's Choice,* with the Seymour Agency in New York. She has recently been published in volume one of *God Allows U-Turns.*

Jennifer Smith-Morris has a heart for encouraging women and writes and speaks about family issues. Her current work is a book entitled *Beagles for Breakfast (and Other Hazards of Learning to Love In-Laws)*. She lives in Georgia with her husband and three children.

Brenda Sprayue is a former publicist in the Christian music industry, as well as a former English and typing instructor. She now writes from her home in Arizona, where she resides with her husband and two children.

Gloria Cassity Stargel, freelance writer and assignment writer for *Guideposts* magazine, is author of *The Healing—One Family's Victorious Struggle with Cancer*, a story of faith, hope, and love. The book encourages anyone facing cancer. . .as well as his or her caregivers. Her story "From the Pool to the Pulpit" first appeared in *Decision Magazine*, April 2001, under the title "An Ugly Car, a Pretty Girl, and Mr. Pridgen." Call 1-800-888-9529 or visit www.brightmorning.com.

Karen Strand lives in Lacey, Washington. She has authored one book, *Escape from the Fowlers Snare*. Her articles have appeared in *Moody Magazine, Decision, Today's Christian Woman,* and *Focus on the Family*.

Ronda Sturgill lives in Shalimar, Florida, where she runs R. Sturgill Seminars through which she encourages her audiences to apply biblical principles to their lives. A paraplegic since a horseback riding accident in 1972, Ronda is a Christian speaker who encourages her audiences to look beyond their circumstances to experience God's grace. Married to Tim Sturgill, a USAF chaplain, they have one son, Toby, who attends Liberty University. Ronda's work also appears in volume one of *God Allows U-Turns*. Visit Ronda at www.rsturgillseminars.com.

Tamara Swinson is twenty-seven years old and lives in Tulsa, Oklahoma, with her husband and three children. In addition to the blessing of being a wife and a mother, she is a student and a certified nurse's aid. Her passion has always been writing, and she is grateful to have the opportunity to display this love to the rest of the world. *God is so good!* she exclaims.

Marjee K. Berry-Wellman is a Christian author and very proud mother of four children, one of whom resides in heaven since 1981. She can be contacted at mrjwell@netins.net.

Jill Lauritzen Zimanek, a native of North Huntington, Pennsylvania, lived in Iowa, Tennessee, and Wisconsin before residing in Athens, Georgia, with her sports editor husband, Brad, and two children. She is a homemaker, freelance writer, and Sunday school teacher, daily glorifying God.

Jeanne Zornes of Wenatchee, Washington, is a conference speaker and widely published author of hundreds of articles and seven books, including *Spiritual Spandex for the Outstretched Soul* (Shaw/Waterbrook). Her story "The Giver" first appeared in *Lookout*, March 2001.

WE WANT TO HEAR FROM YOU!

Win FREE copies of

Using this volume of *More God Allows U-Turns,* please select your favorite story for each of the categories below. You may enter your selections on our web site: www.moregodallowsuturns.com or mail them to us (using this page or a photocopy of it) at:

Allison Gappa Bottke
The More God Allows U-Turns Project
My Favorite Story Contest–02
P.O. Box 717
Faribault, MN 55021-0717

From those readers who respond with their comments, we will choose a winner at random every month for one year. Winners will receive five complimentary copies of *More God Allows U-Turns* to give to family and friends. The winner's selections, comments, and photo (if available) will be posted on the *More God Allows U-Turns* web site each month. The deadline for submitting feedback for this volume is November 30, 2002. The first winner will be posted one month after the book's release date December 1, 2001.

CATEGORIES:
1. Most inspiring story
2. Most humorous story
3. The 4-hanky story
4. Most thought-provoking story
5. Most hopeful story
6. Most representative of God working in everyday life